Hope for the Journey

Hope for the Journey

HELPING CHILDREN THROUGH GOOD TIMES AND BAD

C. R. Snyder,
Diane McDermott,
William Cook,
and Michael A. Rapoff

WestviewPress
A Division of HarperCollins*Publishers*

Copyright © 1997 by Westview Press, A Division of HarperCollins Publishers, Inc.

Published in 1997 in the United States of America by Westview Press, 5500 Central Avenue, Boulder, Colorado, 80301-2877, and in the United Kingdom by Westview Press, 12 Hid's Copse Road, Cumnor Hill, Oxford OX2 9JJ

Library of Congress Cataloging-in-Publication Data
Hope for the journey : helping children through good times and bad /
C.R. Snyder ... [et al.].
    p.   cm.
Includes bibliographical references.
ISBN 0-8133-3156-0 (hardcover)
1. Child psychology.   2. Children—Conduct of life.   3. Hope.
4. Self-talk.   I. Snyder, C.R.
HQ772.H62   1997
305.231—dc21   97-15327
                                                            CIP

The paper used in this publication meets the requirements of the American National Standard for Permanence of Paper for Printed Library Materials Z39.48-1984.

10   9   8   7   6   5   4   3   2   1

To the children—
may the story of hope
go with you

Contents

Foreword

*H*OPE LIES AT THE HEART OF HUMAN WELL-BEING. Although this insight can be traced through many cultures and thousands of years of human storytelling, its personal and planetary significance has only recently been systematically studied. The authors of this book are among the most respected contemporary students and teachers of hope. In these pages they have captured and conveyed the preciousness of hope in human development throughout one's life span. Here you will encounter numerous stories that illustrate the formidable power of positive possibilities in helping people to cope with and grow from the challenges of everyday life.

Even though it is intended to be read by parents, teachers, and other caregivers, this book is fundamentally for and about children. In very clear and engaging language, the authors present an overview of children's development from birth through their adolescent years. Central to their presentation is the well-documented role of narratives—stories—that offer personal meaning, historical perspective, and future possibilities for positive engagements with life. Stories for children of different ages and for children facing different personal challenges are generously presented along with helpful suggestions for storytelling. Moreover, these stories are woven into a fabric that reflects a theory of hope appropriate for people of all ages. Just as children need "hope for the journey," so, too, do parents and teachers, counselors and elders. Simple and straightforward ways of measuring hope are offered, and a valuable appendix lists numerous children's books that offer hopeful stories for a wide range of personal life circumstances.

Throughout their collection of stories, recommendations, and observations, the authors speak with a tone of warmth, engagement, and exploration. They have chosen to tell stories from their hearts—stories that are bound to touch the hearts and lives of our children. It is most appropriate that they share these stories as valuable companions to the *journey* of life. Movement is their key metaphor. Although the historical origins of the English word "hope" are lost in antiquity, many language scholars now believe that it was once related to the word "hop" (a short jump). How fitting, then, that *Hope for the Journey* conveys so many personal examples of everyday "leaps of faith" into the next small steps on life journeys.

In his philosophical *Essay on Man* in the early part of the eighteenth century, poet Alexander Pope wrote that "Hope springs eternal in the human breast." In the present century we have come to question that assertion. The rising incidence of both childhood and adult depression makes painfully clear that hope must be nurtured, encouraged, and cultivated throughout our life journeys and across generations. This book is a valuable act of that encouragement, and I hope that it reaches the hands of many grown-ups and the hearts of many children.

Michael J. Mahoney

Preface and Acknowledgments

SOMEWHERE ON THE ROAD TO BECOMING ADULTS, we forgot how important stories were in our childhoods. Not only the stories about the wondrous heroes and heroines who slew dragons and conquered other scary circumstances, but the stories we carry around in our heads about the kind of people we were or wanted to be. This book brings those "self stories" back to life and shows how they can help children become more productive and, in turn, happy adults. Life is a journey, and children need good stories for the trip.

As psychologists and parents, the authors have long used hope as a guiding principle. However, until recently we did not fully realize the degree to which stories are a means of building hope in children. As our research has progressed, and as we have thought back about our clinical experiences with children over the years, it has become evident that stories are the very stuff for constructing and maintaining a sense of hope in children. With this insight, the present book has almost written itself. Our purpose, therefore, is to show how stories can be used to infuse hope in the children with whom you interact. In this book, we will help you to understand how your stories about yourself serve as guides for daily living. Once you have an idea of how hope works in your own stories, we will then teach you how to use stories to foster hope in children.

Who should read this book? If you are a parent, teacher, or someone who works with and cares about the welfare of children, this book offers a means for understanding what hope is, as well as how to increase it in children of various ages. The suggestions we make are based on research we have conducted as well as our clinical experiences over the past two decades. Although this book is based on theory and research, it also should come to life for you in the sense that we have described many case histories in which you can vividly experience how hope was kindled in children. We also have included many illustrations to pictorially show what we are saying; likewise, there are simple line drawings for many of the principal characters in the stories throughout the book. If you are using these stories with your children, we suggest that you make copies of these pictures and allow the younger children to color them. In short, this book is a lively read, filled with real-life examples and motivation for both you and your children. Hope is essential, and we invite you to learn more about it in the following pages.

You should rightfully ask what our qualifications may be to write this book. The first author, C. R. (Rick) Snyder, is a Ph.D. clinical psychologist who has been the Director of the Clinical Psychology Program at the University of Kansas for the last 23 years; moreover, he has been a Professor of Psychology since 1980, and the Editor of the *Journal of Social and Clinical Psychology* since 1988. He has published widely on adults and children, and is an expert on the topic of measuring and instilling hope, having been recognized with Fellow status in the American Psychological Society, the Society for Personality Assessment, the American Association of Applied and Preventive Psychology, and in four divisions of the American Psychological Association. He also has seen children and adults in his clinical practice for more than two decades. The second author, Diane McDermott, holds a Ph.D. in counselor education and is an associate professor in the Counseling Psychology Department at the University of Kansas. She has seen clients for over three decades and is recognized as having provided psychotherapy education to scores of professionals who are presently in the field. Her passion for instilling positive thinking has influenced waves of students, clients, and children over the years. The third author, William Cook, is a Ph.D. clinical psychologist widely known in Missoula, Montana, and the surrounding region for his inventive and inspiring clinical work with children and families. For approximately two decades, Dr. Cook has brought stories to life for his clients (large and small), and he has written widely about the therapeutic use of stories. He is presently working on the development of a television program based on his use of therapeutic stories. The fourth author, Michael Rapoff, is a Ph.D. developmental and child psychologist known for his scholarly and clinical work in rehabilitation and pediatrics. Dr. Rapoff presently is a professor and section chief of behavioral pediatrics in the Department of Pediatrics at the University of Kansas Medical Center. His research, which is supported by ongoing national grants, is concerned with helping children and adolescents cope with pain and the demands associated with having a chronic illness.

In writing this book, we have many people to thank. To our many clients, including the children themselves as well as their caregivers, we owe a debt of gratitude for sharing their lives with us. These remarkable little and big people have taught us profound lessons about hope. Indeed, their stories fill this book. Of course, we have changed the names and the circumstances, but the underlying stories reflect the lives of real children and adults and how they learned to hope through the stories that they told about themselves.

To our first high-hope editor at Westview, Michelle Baxter, goes a full dose of praise for nurturing this book at every step. More recently, our new editor, Cathy Pusateri, has admirably continued the editorial process. High-hope people help others to get things done. The same goes for editors.

To our family members who asked, "What are you doing?" we now can show them that the hours spent away from them did have a tangible result—the book you have in your hands. That our families gave us hope should be obvious in the following pages. In fact, in the subsequent pages you will read about some of their hope-filled adventures.

Bill Cook would like to thank Patrick Friman for generously keeping the circle of giving spinning round and round.

Rick Snyder would like to thank two Kansans—Fritz Heider and Karl Menninger—whose ideas and thinking were pivotal in the development of hope theory. Also, Ruth Leibowitz deserves a full dose of appreciation for her detailed feedback about the writing in the following pages. Her guiding editorial hand has made this book a better read, and the reader can only trust us when we assert that the earlier drafts truly were "rough." Likewise, Lynne Cobler and Martha Dickinson provided superb assistance in typing various portions of this book. Their help in this and other projects deserves special thanks.

Our gratitude is extended to two doctoral students, Deborah Abraham Lind and Debi L. Lastinger, who wrote the stories of Sarah, Maggie, Jeremiah, and Caitlyn.

We acknowledge the permission granted by the Free Press Division of Simon and Schuster to use a portion of the previously published "Appendix B: Books on Children's Hope-Related Issues" from C. R. Snyder's 1984 volume entitled *The Psychology of Hope: You Can Get There from Here*. This information represents part of an expanded source guide appearing in the present volume (see Appendix B: Children's Books on Hope-Related Issues). Thanks are extended to our assistants Adam Albin, Anne Rosel, and Dixie Williford, who helped to update Appendix B.

Our heartfelt thanks go to Elizabeth Kelley, the artist who brought the stories of hope to life throughout this book. If hope is a story, Elizabeth also shows us that it can be a picture.

In writing this book, we were reminded of a small five-year-old child who looked at us in wide-eyed wonder upon realizing that she wouldn't always have to think that bad things were going to happen. Her rhetorical question was, "You mean, I could think that things will be OK?" The resounding answer when children ask this question must be "Yes, you can have hope!" Children not only can, but they *deserve* to have hope. The following pages tell this tale.

C. R. Snyder
Diane McDermott
William Cook
Michael A. Rapoff

1

Hoping:
Journeys of the Mind

Good and Bad Trips

It is September, and all the fourth graders are required to give a short talk about their summer vacations. Jeannie stands in front of the class, filled with excitement about her tale. "You are not going to believe this!" she exclaims. "We went white-water rafting on the Colorado River. We had these brochures about the various trips, and my mom and I looked them over last winter. They seemed kind of scary, but real fun too. Anyway, we decided to take some one-day float trips. We packed the station wagon and took everything we needed—like camping gear, cooking stuff, and most important, bug spray (class chuckles) and toilet paper (more laughter). It took us a day to drive there, and I could hardly sleep the night before we went rafting. The next morning, about 20 of us piled into this big old bus, with the rubber rafts on the roof, and we bounced along back roads until we got about 20 miles upriver. And so we got off the bus and got in these big orange rafts, with the guide in the back, and mom and me and two other people up front. Oh yeah, we had life preservers and helmets on. Each of us also had an oar, and we paddled like the guide told us. Well, it was really quiet and smooth at first, but then it got bouncy, and we were *all* over the place. Hollerin' and havin' fun. The ride was a blast, and the river was so noisy that I could scream as loud as I wanted. So, I'd holler out, 'Ride em Jeannie!' We were gone for a week, and we went on four raft trips. Mom and I got better at it, though it was a real challenge. I can't wait till we go back next year. Oh, I forgot, I'm wearing a 'White Water' tee shirt I got there." (Class applauds loudly.)

Sarah stood up next, looking frozen. "Go ahead," said the teacher. "Well, well, . . . " stammered Sarah, "there really isn't much to tell." By now Sarah was fidgeting, looking at her shoes. Again, the teacher prodded her, and Sarah said, "You know, we just got in our car and drove around." "Where?" asked one of her classmates. "Don't really know," replied Sarah, "but my dad said he wanted to make at least 500 miles a day. I sat in the back seat, read comic books, and was sort of 'out of it.'" An awkward silence followed, whereafter Sarah, still looking at the floor, said, "That's about it," and scampered back to her seat. (The teacher applauded, and a few classmates followed.)

Jeannie and Sarah, with their respective stories, are displaying differing perspectives. Jeannie is literally brimming with energy as she describes what happened on her vacation, and what will happen in the future. She knows what she wants and how to get there, and she is highly motivated. In short, she is full of hope. Sarah's tale, in contrast, reflects a vagueness and uncertainty. There are no goals or plans, and no sense of enthusiasm. In brief, Sarah seems hopeless.

In this book, we will explore how children like Jeannie develop hope-filled story lines in order to travel the sometimes smooth and sometimes bumpy roads of life. But even more important, we will suggest how children like Sarah can bring hope alive in their minds and in their lives. Because we envision that readers will want to learn how to instill hope in children through narratives, we will focus on this in the following pages. These suggestions flow directly from our research and treatment work with children's hope over the past two decades.[1] Our ideas are for parents, teachers, and others who are responsible for instilling hope in the next generation. Before turning to the implementation of hope-filled personal stories, however, in this first chapter we will describe what we mean by hoping, as well as how hope develops in children.

Mental Preparations for the Journey

Imagine that you are about to embark upon a trip. The destination for your "travel" involves some coveted place, event, person, or object. You may have wanted to take this journey for years, or the idea may have just popped into your head moments ago. Whatever your goal may be, however, it is sufficiently important that you definitely want to reach it. Attached to your thoughts about this goal are two other necessary components. One is *waypower thinking,* which pertains to your perceived capacity to generate pathways to reach your goals. A second, called *willpower thinking,* taps your perceived ability to initiate and sustain

Goal

movement toward your goal along the selected pathways. The journey of hope involves the targeted goal, and the associated thoughts about pathways to that goal (waypower thinking) and one's energy for employing those routes (willpower thinking). Accordingly, it should be highlighted that *the journey of hope lives first and foremost in our minds.* When we move into action, it is precisely because we have previously hoped; furthermore, hope continues to fuel us as we journey to our goals.

Does this process sound familiar? It should, because in one version or another, we each make such a mental journey in our minds many times a day. In fact, we humans are prepared mentally to make journey after journey in search of the things that we want. To think about our desires and how we will reach them is to hope. On this point, it may be useful to examine the components of hopeful thinking—goals, waypower, and willpower—in some greater detail.

Destinations: Goal Thinking

The objects in hopeful thinking are *goals.* Goals are all the wonderful targets that are the subject of human desires. In this regard, take a few minutes to watch carefully the people around you. You will notice that they are not moving around randomly. Instead, they are trying to get somewhere, or to get something accomplished. Although you obviously cannot look into the minds of these people, if you could, you would see that they are envisioning all sorts of goals. A goal may relate to a physical location, for example: "I want to get to Chicago." In another sense, a goal may be to acquire any of the inanimate objects that fuel our desires. For example, we may say to ourselves, "I want a candy bar," or we may seek a grander object such as a car or house. Goals also may reflect intangible objectives such as getting a college degree, overcoming a serious illness, or learning to play the piano. Anything that serves as the target of human desires can be a goal. As may be apparent, these goals may be short-term ("I'm going to get

a cup of coffee") or more long-term ("I'm going to lose 25 pounds"). Whatever the goal, the person's thoughts clearly have focused upon it.

Even if you grant that goals are important, you may not know just how much of a role they play in our daily existence. Close your eyes and let your mind wander for a minute or so. How long did it take before you thought of something that you wanted to happen? If you are like others whom we have asked to perform this activity, it was a matter of seconds before you conjured something that you desired (i.e., a goal). Perhaps you wanted to get this exercise over with, or you began to think about an impending deadline on a project. It is virtually impossible to keep yourself from thinking about some outcome or object.

Now that you know the purpose of this exercise, try it once again. This time, however, try *not* to think about a goal of any sort. You probably won't be successful—some form of a goal eventually will pop into your mind. For example, if you decide not to try this exercise again, this becomes your goal. Or, if you start and then opt out of it, the termination of the exercise becomes your goal. Even if it were possible not to think about a goal, by trying not to think about one, you paradoxically will have adopted this as your goal!

If you would like a quick assay of your goals right now, try another exercise. Say the initial phrase "I want . . ." and write down (or speak into a tape recorder) all the objects that come to mind. You may be surprised at how many goals fill your mind. Likewise, the diversity of your goals may be noteworthy. This exercise may hearken back to stereotypes about egocentric children who whine, "I want _____ (fill in the blank)." We adults don't often express our goal as obviously and plaintively as a child might, but our goals are nonetheless there. Although we could spend many pages describing why people are goal oriented, our conclusion is that such thinking is essential for survival.[2]

Road Maps: Waypower Thinking

You can have the clearest goals imaginable, but you will be stymied if you lack a sense of how to reach them. What you need are clear mental pathways. The protagonist in the previous illustration has envisioned one major route to a goal.

As shown by the arrow connecting our protagonist to the desired goal, typically one route is perceived to be the best and most easily traveled one. This main route may have worked previously for the person, or it has worked for others the person has observed. Generally, the more planning we have done concerning a given goal, the more likely we will have a main route for achieving it. Likewise, for the more important and recurring goals, we are likely to have planned through what may be the most serviceable routes. Planning obviously is all about figuring out how to reach our goals.

How is such planning done? When we imagine a goal, we might search our memory for how we have behaved in similar circumstances. On this point, research suggests that memory is organized according to goals *and* their related pathways.[3] In fact, these frequently used waypower thoughts to our recurring life goals may become so automatic that they may not be in our awareness.

Fortunately, the usual paths work most of the time. But suppose that the tried and true route to your goal is blocked? Life throws roadblocks in our paths, and during such instances we must do some on-the-spot rerouting to reach our goals. Here, waypower thinking turns to the production of additional routes to the desired goal. As shown by the indirect arrows in the above schematic, the protagonist must chart alternative ways to reach the coveted goal.

Sometimes people plan for possible impediments even before setting out to reach a goal. With such waypower forethought, the person can readily turn to the preplanned alternative when the main route is closed. Such anticipatory building of alternative pathways characterizes hopeful thinking. Whether alternative routes are planned before or after encountering an impediment, however, *flexibility is essential to waypower thinking.*

Higher-hope children and adults are facile at finding new passages when barriers to their goals are encountered. Indeed, we have found that high-hope people have not lived lives of ease where they always have readily attained goals via preferred routes. On the contrary, they have encountered many instances where they were blocked, and they have learned how to develop new routes to successfully achieve their goals. In fact, it is when people run into barriers that hopeful thinking may prove to be especially helpful. That is to say, finding workable routes to goals is advantageous under normal unimpeded circumstances, *but it becomes pivotal when encountering barriers to one's goals.*

Engines: Willpower Thinking

Willpower is the psychological reservoir of mental energy, determination, and commitment that helps us move toward our goals.[4] Accordingly, we sometimes speak to ourselves in terms of our potential for movement. Perhaps the best example of such willful self-talk is the phrase "I can . . . ." This phrase captures the determination and energy that the person can call upon when it is necessary to put plans into action. Among people today, this willpower component is described as "Getting psyched to . . . ." Such phrases suggest images of springing into action toward a desired goal. In the mind's eye of our cartoon character on page 6, we can see the action potential that characterizes willful thought.

Willpower is manifested more strongly when the goal is clearly conceived and when the person has envisioned a well-specified pathway (or pathways) to that goal. We have worked, for example, with adults and children who have vaguely defined goals, and such people tend to be lethargic. Similarly, if one does not have well-articulated pathways to goals, it is difficult to sustain much willful thinking. There is a synergy between one's thoughts about targeted goals, routes to these goals, and energy to successfully navigate these routes to attain these goals.

Putting Together the Hope Machine

Hope is a way of thinking in which a person has the perceived waypower and willpower to achieve goals. High hope necessitates three mental components—goals, pathways to these goals, and the willpower to employ the pathways. If there are difficulties with one or more of these components, then the hopeful thinking will be undermined. In contrast, improvements in any of the three components will increase the likelihood that the other components may improve. Our point is that goals, the pathways to these goals, and the sense of willpower to transverse these pathways form a natural mental trilogy that we learn in infancy and use throughout our adult lives. How such hope develops in childhood is our next topic.

You may be surprised to learn about the pervasiveness of storytelling when a mother is at home with a toddler. In an average hour of this setting, over eight stories are told.[5] Along with taking in many stories from the outside, the child is creating a storehouse of special tales from within—tales in which the child forges new territory and overcomes obstacles. It takes time, however, for these hope-laden story lines to take shape. In the second part of this chapter, we will examine the development of hopeful personal narratives. Initially we will focus on the infant to toddler years; thereafter we will continue through the various stages of childhood.

Infant to Toddler Years

So that you can understand the development of hope-filled self-narratives, we will begin by retracing the earliest months of a child's life. Although the newborn does not yet have language capabilities—much less a sense of his or her personal story—the essential ingredients for forming a personal narrative are being acquired systematically during the child's first two years.

Waypower Thinking

A child learns three critical processes to the waypower thinking in the first six months of life. These are sensations/perceptions, linkages, and goals. Let's explore each of these thinking processes more fully, and then consider how they come together to produce waypower thought.

Sensations/Perceptions: "What Is Out There?"   If you could step back in time and experience things as you did when you were a newborn child, you would find the world utterly fascinating. To the newborn, the world enters consciousness via sensation. Everything is being experienced for the first time. Our physical equipment is set up for taking in a host of sensations—eyes for seeing things, ears for hearing noises, skin for tactile contact, noses for odors, and tongues for registering flavors. We are alive with seeing, hearing, touching, smelling, and tasting. As adults, we have been doing this for years, but the senses are assaulting the newborn with novel input. Newborns cannot be content with mere input, however, because the human mind is built not only to receive sensations but to organize and recognize them. For example, a particular arrangement of facial features is not just any face; the infant must learn to perceive this one face as Mom's.[6] When raw sensations have been organized and comprehended in the infant's mind, perception has occurred. Perception reflects the mind's sophisticated storing, organizing, and acting upon raw sensation-based input.

Linkages: "This Goes with That."   From the moment of birth, the newborn is a scientist of sorts who searches constantly for organization in the surrounding environment. A sense of order and predictability is built, in part, by the process of forming perceptions that we discussed in the previous section.[7] By learning to recognize those things and people in her environment, the newborn has some sense of "understanding" about her world. As important as the perceptual recognition process is, however, the newborn must learn to discern even more complicated patterns—what events tend to co-occur. Recognition of co-occurring events is the precursor to later causal thinking in which the older child learns what antecedent events elicit subsequent events.

The infant's knowledge that certain things seem to be followed by other events reduces the perceived random or chaotic nature of her environment. There is some order to be found, and one major task of the newborn is to identify any recurring patterns.[8]

The newborn's growing abilities do not end here. Such "this goes with that" thinking also enables the child to predict what will transpire. It is likely that from the moment of birth, infants are capable of learning to anticipate events, and as such they are attaining a rudimentary sense of planning. For example, if you have ever been around a baby when he is hungry,

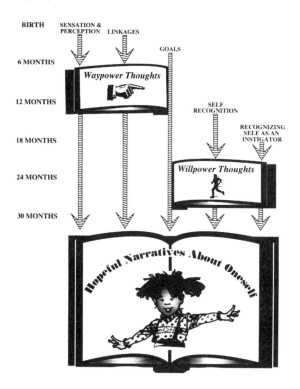

it is obvious that the infant recognizes what events lead to getting fed. A crying infant may quiet down when Mom picks him up or when he is taken into the kitchen where the food is normally served.

Goals. Lessons involving perceptions and linkages proceed rapidly in the first few months, and they are solidified as the ability to form simple goals is acquired. For example, very young infants can point out objects, a behavior suggesting that the baby not only recognizes an object but also desires that particular object among the many possible ones.[9] The desired goal object may be a toy, something to eat, or an older sibling. Accompanying this pointing process, the infant may wiggle around and make noises aimed at procuring some help in order to get the desired goal object. Within the first six months, the baby perceives a variety of objects and can predict what events seem to go together. Such perception and linkage thinking often is focused upon particular goals. As can be seen in the above illustration, the thinking related to perceptions, linkages, and goals coalesce to form the essence of waypower thought. Perception provides the basis for learning how one event follows another, and such perception also yields objects selected for particular attention. Linkages enable children to discern what given perceptions warrant their attention so as to have greater predictability in their lives. Finally, goals are the coveted perceived objects that often are the target of linkage thoughts.

Willpower Thinking

Waypower thinking, as we have discussed, taps those processes related to finding routes to our goals. Willpower thinking, in comparison, reflects thoughts about one's motivation to use such road maps. More specifically, willpower thoughts are anchored by goals and the accompanying recognition of oneself as a person who can and will move toward attaining those goals.

Self-Recognition. It is obvious to adults that we are separate people with different identities from others, but we did not know this at the time of our physical birth. Although there is debate about the time when we acquire knowledge about our own selfhood, research suggests that such self-recognition begins in the early months of our life and is in place for most children by their first birthdays. A simple experiment can illustrate this insight. If one smears a small dot of red rouge on the nose of a very young child and puts a mirror in front of that child, different reactions can be expected depending on the child's age. For children under one, no special attention will be paid to the nose as seen in the mirror. Children at least one year old, however, will consistently touch their noses in the mirror and, as such, are demonstrating self-recognition skills.[10]

Another marker event occurs at around 18 months of age, when children begin to employ the pronouns *I* and *me*. Such personal pronouns signal a psychological birth in which the toddler realizes his or her distinctiveness relative to other children and adults. Parents also can play a game with their toddlers to illustrate the awareness of selfhood. For example, ask your toddler to name a particular body part ("Where are Chuckie's ears?"). Or, the larger variant of this same game would be, "Where is Chuckie?" (Little kids love this one and will point to themselves with great glee).

The Self Recognized as an Instigator. For willpower thinking to take hold, the toddler also must believe that he or she is the source for causing things to happen. It is instructive to explore the content of toddlers' speech beginning around 21 to 24 months of age, when words full of volitions, empowerment, and action emerge from their mouths. Consider the following examples:

"I can . . . ," "No, I can do it myself." (girl, age 2 years, 8 months)
"I *can* do it!" (girl, age 2 years, 7 months)

"Me too," "(I) want . . . ," (I) won't . . . " "Me do it." (boy, age 2 years, 11 months)[11]

Such examples show that toddlers are thinking in terms of future-oriented action sequences, and they are clearly the authors of the actions. It also should be noted that such self-instigative thoughts are focused upon some goal or goals that the child envisions herself pursuing.

Binding Together the Story of Hope

As is shown in the previous diagram, goals, self-recognition, and the insight of oneself as being the initiator of actions form the trilogy of thoughts related to willpower. Likewise, the figure on page 9 shows that the basis of waypower thinking appears to be in place by approximately six months of age, whereas willpower thinking is solidified later, at approximately 21 to 24 months of age. As such, waypower thinking precedes willpower thought, but it should be emphasized that the two share a common and pivotal component: goal-directed thought.

The language of hopeful toddlers is filled with story lines about how they are successful in pursuing their goals. They place themselves as the central, heroic protagonist in short stories depicting their past and projected exploits. In developing such brief stories, they are weaving tales laced with general waypower and willpower thoughts about goals. It should be emphasized that goals are the linchpins by which waypower and willpower thoughts are tied together in the theater of the toddler's mind. Hopeful personal narratives reflect combined waypower and willpower thoughts *about goals*. The goals in the visualization at the bottom of the illustration on page 9 are aptly located at the book-binding center of hopeful narratives.

Over or Around: The Protagonist Meets a Barrier

Our saga of the developing child in the infant to toddler years shows how hopeful thoughts are built over time, but we have left out an important set of lessons—those dealing with how children learn to handle the road blocks that appear in their lives.[12] As any adult can attest, the paths to our goals often are impeded. Children must learn to cope with such barriers, and this is where waypower thinking becomes especially important. We are never too young to learn that we must try an alternative route to our goals when the usual path is blocked.

Waypower thinking is adaptive under normal circumstances, but becomes especially important when children are facing obstacles. High-hope children and adults have not lived lives of ease with their goals always within reach. On the contrary, they have encountered difficult situations and have been taught or discovered how to solve problems, often through circuitous routes. Relatedly, the plots of many children's books concern the adversities that are met and conquered by the child protagonist. In our experience, the stories that high-hope children have about themselves mirror this same theme—the hero faces a difficult situation and finds a way to get what he or she wants. Parents and caregivers do young children a service by allowing them to undergo difficult goal pursuit situations, *as long as we also help them to learn how to come up with different ways to overcome their obstacles.* The child who successfully handles adversity is better prepared to think in a hopeful manner in future situations.

Connecting to a Caregiver

The processes related to goal-directed thought do not occur in a vacuum. Hope flourishes when the child establishes a strong bond to one or more caregivers during this infant to toddler stage.[13] In American society, this bond typically is to a mother who provides the bulk of the interactive care. Instilling hope in children is based, in part, on their perceived security. Secure early attachments relate to a sense of empowerment and goal-directed thought. The caregiver is a wonderful coach for learning the lessons we discussed earlier (e.g., forming goals, learning what goes with what, and so on). Because an attentive caregiver responds to the infant's needs, the child is more likely to perceive him- or herself as having some sense of control in a big and otherwise confusing world.

High-hope children are social creatures, and their ability to connect appears to come from early strong attachments to primary caregivers. High-hope adults report having established a close bond to at least one caregiver, and they describe this caregiver as spending large amounts of time with them. In turn, these high-hope adults have positive views about relationships in general. They seek out and enjoy the company of other people. High-hope children and adults are able to form strong attachments to other people, and their personal stories reflect their involvement with such people. These stories may reflect fond memories of interactions with a primary caregiver as well as tales about successful relationships that they have formed as adults. When the child (or adult) encounters a barrier of some sort, the ability to relate to other people and enlist them as part of solving the problem becomes especially important.

The Plot Thickens: The Remaining Childhood Years

Having described how hopeful thoughts are established in the first two years, it is time to explore how the personal narrative grows over the preschool, middle, and adolescent years. As we will see, during each of these periods children develop increasingly more elaborate hopeful thoughts about themselves. As such, the older child no longer weaves the simple tales of goal pursuit that typified the first two years of life.

Preschool Years (Ages 3–6)

Words, Words, Words. From ages three through six, the repository of hopeful narratives—the brain—grows from 50 percent to 90 percent of adult size and weight. This growth spurt is accompanied by growing language skills. In fact, the increase of sheer word power during this period is remarkable, going from an average vocabulary of only 50 to almost 10,000 words. Likewise, the short phrases of words put together by a two-year-old increase to multiple-word sentences for the preschooler.[14] This explosion of language skills is important because it helps children to express their goal-directed thoughts in the form of hope-filled narratives.

Language is a shared system of labels for conceptualizing the multitude of events, objects, people, and ideas in our world. All of the components to hopeful thinking, including goals and the accompanying waypower and willpower, are identified by language. We literally could not hope if we did not have language as a shared system of identifying the elements in our world. Language also serves to help us in interacting with our environment. Sometimes it takes the form of an internal mental dialogue with ourselves, and at other times it aids us in interacting with other people. In both cases, language is the very stuff of which high-hope personal narratives are constructed.

Scripts. Beyond the building of the language repertoire, the preschooler also is learning scripts from caregivers. These scripts are mental guides about the sequence of events that are appropriate for given situations.[15] Scripts are similar to brief stories about how events are to unfold for a particular situation. One such script might be "What you do in the morning to get ready for school." Here, the child is given a time line of activities that are to take place in order to reach a goal—leaving for school. Such a script could involve going to the toilet, washing hands and face, brushing teeth, and so on. Children are attracted to the order and predictability of such scripts. The caregiver becomes much like an acting coach, coaxing from the child the next behavior in the particular script sequence. Scripts are brief story lines that children can call upon throughout their lives.

Can you recall some of these scripts that you had in your childhood? Related research, where adults are asked to recall important childhood memories, shows that the mental scripts of children in the preschool period form crucial autobiographical memories. If life is like a theatrical stage, our early scripted lines appear to stay with us.

During their preschool years, children especially love to hear and tell stories. The stories are especially fascinating when they relate to the child's own circumstances. The hero of most children's stories implicitly or explicitly embodies hopeful thinking, and often this hero must face obstacles as a part of his or her quest. Later in the book we will show such hero stories as well as how the story line can be used to augment the child's hope. For present purposes, however, we would emphasize that preschool children are primed to learn from hopeful stories as they are building and elaborating their own self narratives.

Perspective Taking. As preschoolers augment their abilities to process and create scripts, they also begin to see things from the perspective of other people.[16] Unlike toddlers, who are quite egocentric, preschoolers can imagine the thoughts of other people and can envision the world as it is visually perceived by others. Furthermore, preschoolers learn to understand the expectations that others have of them, and they adjust their behaviors accordingly. With the advent of understanding the perspectives that others may have, the preschooler's personal narratives accommodate the reactions of important others. Thus, the contents of personal stories are modified so that other people will believe them; moreover, the content of the personal story must fit into the desires of the important others. On this latter point, the preschooler is sensitive to the fact that the pursuit of one's goals must occur in a social context where other people also want to reach their goals. Thus, the child becomes more careful about offending others, making them feel bad, and selecting goals that threaten their peers or caregivers.

Middle Years (Ages 7–12)

From Learning to Read to Reading to Learn. During the preschool years the child is focused upon acquiring the skills to read. Once the mechanics of readings have been partially mastered, the child is now able to read for pleasure and to increase his or her information base.[17] Children are highly impressionable, and what they read teaches them—for better or worse—life values. It is therefore important that children in their middle years be exposed to stories about goal-pursuit activities. Most obvious are biographies of people who have set difficult goals and overcome obstacles in attaining these goals. The history of advancement in any discipline has stories about prime movers who had visions about their world and who worked to fulfill these visions.

Our point is that with the tremendous increase in factual information that is built through reading in the middle years, the child is also learning about the people and processes that produced the facts. In our experiences, children in this age range are particularly interested in the people and stories underlying those facts. Stories about previous historical figures are intriguing to children in part because they are busy constructing their own personal tales and are desirous of models.

Memory Up, Speed Down. The capacity of the child's mind to hold information increases from the preschool to the middle years. Additionally, during the middle years children can retrieve and process information more quickly than before and with greater capacity to understand layers of meaning.[18] These two changes have implications for goal-pursuit thinking in general as well as for the generation and use of personal narratives. In regard to goal-related thought, the child in the middle years can imagine goals clearly, as well as the related pathways to achieve those goals. Turning to personal narratives, increased storage capacity means that children can construct more elaborate and complex personal stories. Also, the child can access personal stories very quickly from memory. Lastly, children begin to recall and discuss previous stories about themselves during the middle years, and these stories serve as guides for their interactions with other people. Specific scripts that have been effective in the past may very well aid the child in subsequent goal-pursuit activities. Just as we would find advantages in a computer with a very large memory and a fast processing capability, so too do we find hope-related advantages in the mind of the child in the middle years.

Mine/Thine Friendships. Some large strides are made in taking the perspective of other people during the preschool period, but it is particularly during the middle years that the child must master the balancing of personal desires with those of other people.[19] Neither peers nor adults will allow a child in the middle years to maintain an egocentric view; admonitions such as "Act your age!" or "Grow up!" will be reigned down upon the 12-year-old who does not consider the views of others. During this period, the child pays more attention to social conventions and must think about his or her goals as being sought with the implicit (and sometimes explicit) support of other people.

During the middle years children also often settle upon one best friend. The mine/thine perspective is critical for strong friendships because friends must agree on a shared goal or learn to alternate between goals such that both children take turns in pursuing their goals with the support of a friend. We have found that high-hope adults usually can recall strong friendships during their middle childhood years that continue to play a central role in their stories about themselves. High-hope people describe their friendships as being mutually satisfying. Indeed, they describe themselves as being social creatures who enjoy the company of other people.

Adolescent Years (Ages 13–18)

Relationships and Sexuality.   During the adolescent years, boys and girls mature sexually. Simultaneous with this maturation, the typical pattern of relationships also changes to girl-boy pairing.[20] These exclusive relationships provide an arena for the exploration of sexual matters. Society generally provides scripts about the nature of such relationships, and these scripts are transmitted by parents and peers as well as the media. Teenagers often spend considerable amounts of time thinking about their relationships and accompanying sexual activities. The goals of having a relationship and expressing oneself sexually become intertwined in the thoughts of teenagers. In our experience, teenage boys accentuate their sexual activities as they talk about themselves, whereas teenage girls emphasize the romantic aspects of the relationship.

Personal Identity.   Early adolescent children often have several identities that vary depending on the situation. Because they need peer group approval, teenagers may find themselves pulled in different directions.[21] By late adolescence, however, the teenager behaves more consistently across situations and begins to focus on career goals. Typical high-school seniors, for example, have reasonably good ideas of their talents and have begun pointing toward particular lines of adult work. In late adolescence, teenagers also are aware of their interests and preferences in regard to leisure activities, as well as their political beliefs.

Increasingly during the teenage years, teenagers are asked to tell stories about different aspects of their lives. As friendships and dating relationships develop, the participants are asked to describe themselves. This "getting to know you" ritual dictates a personal rendition of one's self story. Also, in high-school class assignments, students are asked to tell their stories in a more public, less personal arena. Furthermore, when teenagers apply for jobs or fill out applications for trade school or college, they are asked to describe themselves. Here, the self-story must be edited to achieve a practical end. Everywhere teenagers turn, it seems as if they are asked to convey their personal stories. The personal story is requested so routinely that it appears to be a key for the passage into young adulthood. For this reason, many teenagers create a collection of stories that describe different aspects of themselves. There may be a "main" story, but there also are stories that relate to the teenager in varying situations. *Indeed, in adolescence,*

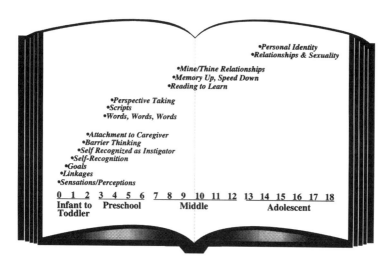

it becomes abundantly clear that one simple story does not suffice. The successful teenagers resolve this by settling on a core story that reflects who and what they are, as well as satellite stories that can be flexibly applied to differing life arenas.

The Hopeful Tale in Review. Throughout childhood, developmental tasks influence how children think about themselves in regard to goal pursuits. Their thoughts form the stories that children hold to be true about themselves. These stories are learned early and are modified and strengthened as the child matures. As can be seen in the above illustration, tales of hope are influenced by developmental processes that begin at various stages in the child's life. We have discussed these processes previously, but we would emphasize that once these lessons are initiated, they continue across the years. For example, although linkage lessons begin almost at birth, they continue throughout childhood and beyond. Hopeful stories are being reviewed and revised constantly over the childhood years. A high-hope child often may have several personal stories that all turn on themes of successful goal pursuits. In turn, these stories provide a template for what may transpire in the future.

"Once Upon a Time" Isn't Just About the Past

In the latter part of this chapter we have presented the case for the development of hope and have simultaneously argued that such goal-directed thoughts naturally contribute to how we describe ourselves. That is to say, our personal stories are inextricably tied to hope-related thinking. As individuals, we have undergone a multitude of experiences; moreover, we have been raised by particular caregivers and have journeyed through varying childhoods to reach adulthood. Unarguably, we have been shaped by the people and events of these "wonder years." Each of us has come through this process with a set of stories about ourselves, and these stories serve to tie us to our version of the past. More importantly, however, these stories have hope-filled themes that make them more than just retrospective tales. Indeed, these stories provide a means of navigating the future—*they are prospective*. We are on a pilgrimage from the past to the future, and our hope-laden personal tales help us to chart this journey.[22]

2

A Good Story Goes a Long Way

Jeremiah, the Story Boy

Jeremiah was an eight-year-old boy who loved to listen to stories and to tell them. Sometimes when he was bored, he would make up his own stories. So when he saw an advertisement for a story-writing contest, he decided to enter.

Jeremiah wrote a story about a grasshopper named Goober. He got his mom to type it on the computer and help him spell some of the hard words. He thought it was very good story and was disappointed when a ten-year-old won first place. Jeremiah got honorable mention as the youngest contestant, but nobody said anything about what a good story he had written. He decided to talk with his teacher, Ms. Markham.

"Ms. Markham, what can I do to write better stories?" he asked.

"Jeremiah, I like the stories you write," said Ms. Markham. "I think you do a fine job."

"Yes, but I lost the story-writing contest and I want to be able to win the prize next year. I think I can if I try really hard."

"You must remember that the boy who won was two years older than you, Jeremiah. You will get better as you get older."

"But I want to be better now. Isn't there something I can do to get better right now?" asked Jeremiah.

Ms. Markham thought for a while. "You know, there are two parts to writing a good story. One is the idea for the story itself, and the other is the words you choose to tell a good story. If I wanted to improve my story

JEREMIAH

ideas, I would simply practice writing a lot of stories. But if I wanted to improve the words I use to tell stories, I would read a lot, because then I could see how other good writers put words together." She smiled at Jeremiah. "If I were you, I would try to write one story idea every day and read at least one book a week. I bet that would improve your story writing."

Jeremiah decided to follow her advice. At first, finding new story ideas was hard. The things he knew the most about were people and animals, so he came up with ideas about a boy and his dog, a girl and her cat, a frog named Mr. Hop, and a bird named Chippy. Then he got the idea to tell about some of the things that had happened to him. So he wrote about a boy learning to ride his bike, and a girl who won a spelling contest, and a mom who put salt instead of sugar into a cake. Then he began to use his imagination more, wondering things like, "If a fish could talk, what would she say?"; "What if I went to the moon, what would it be like?" and, "What if it were day all the time?" He wrote answers to each of these questions. Some days he had very good story ideas, and other days his stories were just okay, but he always kept writing.

Locating books to read was hard for Jeremiah. At first, he just read some of the old favorites he had at home, but when he wanted to read some new things, he couldn't believe how many books were available. He decided to ask the librarian, Mr. Wilkes, for advice. Mr. Wilkes had the perfect answer. "Every year, a group of people read all the children's books that are published and select the best one. I have a list of all the Newberry Award winners for the past 50 years. I suggest you start reading some of those."

Jeremiah took the list and began his reading program. The books were really good, and soon he began to see what Ms. Markham was talking about. Some of the authors used words and groups of words that were just so beautiful they couldn't be any better. He began experimenting with different ways of saying things in his own stories. His reading was so interesting that he soon was getting through two books a week, and then three. He loved the way the words made the stories come alive.

When school got out for the summer, he had even more time to read and write. And in early August, he got a call from Ms. Markham. "I see the story-writing contest is about to start. I was wondering if you were planning to enter again this year?"

"Yes, I am, but I'm not sure what to write. I have so many ideas from this past year," said Jeremiah.

"I think the best thing is to pick out your five best story ideas, and write those. Then you can read the stories and see which one you think is the best," said Ms. Markham.

Jeremiah did just that. He wrote about learning to ride a bicycle, which was kind of funny, and about the death of his turtle, Rocky, which was very sad. He wrote about giant bugs taking over the world, which was scary, and about a fish named Goldie, which was kind of sweet. And he wrote about his dad almost falling off the roof, which was very, very funny. When he finished his stories, he still couldn't decide which was the best. He asked other people to read them, but they, too, couldn't pick the best. So when the day came to enter the contest, he decided to submit three—the stories about the turtle, the fish, and his dad.

The days passed until it was time for the award ceremony, and Jeremiah was nervous. He knew he had won something because the committee had called to be sure that he and his parents would be there. But when he looked at all the older children at the ceremony, he was afraid that he would win only an honorable mention.

Jeremiah was wrong. He won the first prize. In fact, one of the judges read out loud the story about Jeremiah's dad fixing the roof, and the whole crowd laughed and laughed. Then he was presented with a $50 savings bond. He saw Ms. Markham and Mr. Wilkes in the audience and winked at them. And he decided right there that he would be a writer when he grew up.

The story of Jeremiah represents a defining series of events that set a young boy in the direction of becoming a professional writer. He told this story to himself and others throughout his childhood, and it created a script of hope thinking. His tale was one of hope, involving a clearly de-fined goal or goals (i.e., becoming a better writer and winning the writing contest), waypower thinking (i.e., asking for advice from Ms. Markham and Mr. Wilkes), and willpower thinking (i.e., following through in the reading and writing assignments).

As evidenced by Jeremiah, benefits accrue to the child who experiences a hope-engendering event and then repeats a self-descriptive high-hope story of that event. Thus, the hopeful story flows from an initial set of experi-ences, and the story of those events not only chronicles the past but guides the future. Indeed, this story served Jeremiah throughout his subsequent childhood and young adult years as he continued in his quest to become a writer. The power inherent in high-hope stories resides in their proscriptive advantages. That is to say, children's hopeful narratives about themselves as being effective in the pursuit of life goals set the stage for the subsequent successful attainment of those goals. Conversely, if children craft hopeless tales about themselves, these become self-fulfilling prophecies of subsequent doom. In this chapter, we will explore important factors related to the telling of personal tales, as well as how these tales are carried from childhood into adulthood as scripts for successes and failures.[1]

Every Story Finds an Audience

A child's story is for people. But which people form the audience to whom the story is directed? In the field of psychology over the past three decades, an increasingly popular viewpoint is that what children and adults say and do is aimed largely at external audiences. This modern view is called impression management.

In reality, however, the idea that we are like performers acting parts in a real-life drama can be traced back centuries. For example, the term *personality* is derived from the age-old notion that people put on a mask (the persona) for the external audience; in the early forms of theater the actors wore masks to exemplify their roles. For our purposes, personal stories provide scripts that children and adults can use to "act out" their lives. Through the telling of these stories about themselves, children are making a place in their social context. As such, these stories serve as a means whereby children can make claims about their public identities. If children are successful in "selling" their stories to external audiences, they are said to have maintained social "face." Further, if children are consistent in their self stories, people near them can know what to expect from them. Thus, children's stories are expected to provide a social marker of who and what children are, and they help others to understand what it is they are after at any given point in time. That is to say, through their stories children tell the external audience what they want.

Undoubtedly, children's personal stories are in part aimed at the important people around them—for example, parents, caregivers, teachers, coaches, clergy, and other "authorities." But to stop with this conclusion would mean that another absolutely critical audience has been missed—the children themselves. In Chapter 1 we explored how children go through various developmental stages in building and elaborating thoughts about themselves in the pursuit of goals. Often, such thoughts do not have any obvious external audiences. In other words, one of the primary consumers of a personal story is the very child who lived and created it.

Which is the most important intended audience? Is it the external audience of important others, or the internal audience of the child storyteller? Our answer to this external vs. internal audience question is, "It's both." Much like the revolving face shown in the following illustration, children attend to both internal and external audiences as they construct and employ their personal tales.[2] How can this be? Children's goal-related think-

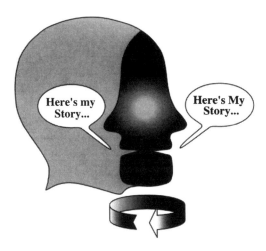

ing reflects an inculcation of caregivers' thinking. Through personal stories, children inform themselves and other people about who they are, where they have gone and, most importantly, where they are going. Accordingly, children's personal tales are never lacking an audience.

The Never-Ending Story

At this point, you still may be skeptical about the sheer prevalence of stories in your daily adult life. Surely these stories are merely child's play, you say, and they do not invade our adult lives. We disagree. There is no doubt that personal stories are being built and augmented over the course of childhood, but you may be surprised at the amount of time you spend each day in telling your adult stories.

As a revealing experiment, we would ask you to pick a two-hour period on any day. During that interval, merely place a check on a 3 x 5 inch note card for each instance in which you thought about a story that pertained to you. If you verbally recount this story to one or more people, this would qualify for a check on your note card. If you think about a personal story and do not speak of it to another person, this also qualifies as a check on your note card. The stories may be about a sequence of events that transpired in the past, or they may be anticipated events in which you are the protagonist of a future-oriented tale. All that is required to count as a storytelling example is that you think about yourself as being the central character in pursuit of some desired goal.

The typical results of this exercise are shocking to people in that they previously had no idea about the sheer prevalence of personal stories in their lives. The average person will tell (or think about) at least three stories per hour. That is right—*three stories per hour*. Further, if a person is in a setting where she or he is interacting with other people, the number of stories may be even higher.

Based on this exercise as well as the sampling research of other psychologists, we suggest that adulthood is laced with never-ending personal stories. These personal stories fill our hours, days, and adult years. In the library of one's mind, therefore, there is an ever-expanding novel about a fascinating protagonist who is struggling to reach his or her goals. If you were to stop reading this book at this point, your mind probably would drift off to the story line that is dominating your life right now.

Our point is that we spend an enormous amount of time in building, revising, and telling our personal stories—sometimes mostly to ourselves, sometimes mostly to other people, and often to both audiences. If this is the case for adults, *it is because we learned during childhood to think about ourselves in terms of stories.*

Then and Now Time Travelers

Hope-filled thoughts are time travelers. In our therapy and research experiences, we have found that children and their parents are fascinated by the time differences between "then" and "now." Indeed, we would suggest that "then and now" analyses are central to the manner in which children and adults live their lives. "Then" in the "then and now" focus may refer to either the past or the future. In American society, we typically have focused on the "then" that pertains to the future and the "now" that pertains to the present. Most children are future-oriented, and their stories serve to guide us into the future "then." Some children, in contrast, become focused on the temporal difference between a "then" that represents the way that things used to be and the way they are now.

Reminiscing obviously reflects stories about previous events. Conversely, predicting taps stories aimed at future events. In this regard, children's stories take children both where they have been and, more importantly, where they are going. Stories are a means to travel through time: Their themes traverse the past and stretch into the future. Each child carries a unique personal history that is catalogued in terms of stories about goal-related activities. On this point, existential philosopher Gabriel Marcel described hope as a means of remembering how we have been successful in the past so that we can use this as a source of hope for the future. In Marcel's words, hope is "a piercing through time . . . a kind of memory for the future."[3]

A nine-year-old girl sits near her grandmother and recounts her troubles in school and elsewhere. The girl is beginning to think that nothing is going to turn out well in her life. Hearing about her granddaughter's struggles, the 75-year-old woman asks, "Have I told you about the time your grandfather went to the hospital for the last time?"

"Well, no, Nana, you haven't, but . . . ," the girl trails off, looking bewildered at what this has to do with her own problems.

"He was frail, and it was hard for him to breathe. Tubes were running in and out of him. He looked different on the outside, all old and shriveled up. But on the inside he was the same young man I fell in love with. Slipping away from me, his breathing was shallow. . . . And he squeezed my hand and I knelt down near his head. He whispered, 'One thing I don't want you to forget—there are more good memories ahead for you,' and then he was gone."

"There are more good memories ahead for you," repeated the girl, softly.

"And that is what we have to remember, you and me," said Nana.

This interchange was an intergenerational gift of hope. It helped the girl, and it helped the older woman. The story stretched from the past, to the future, to the room in which they sat together at that moment. What worked previously still provided hope for today and tomorrow.

Storytelling and Hoping

Perhaps it may be useful at this point to describe how a child's storytelling and hoping are intertwined. A story is built upon a time line of events. These events may have happened in the past, they may be going on right now, or they may be tied to the future. Likewise, there is some description of the event so that the listener has an idea about where it is taking place, the people involved, and what they are doing. Finally, personal stories have a protagonist who is trying to accomplish something.

Consider the following story:

"I jus wanna be left alone, but Bobby keep followin' me . . . so I says to him, 'Go away.' Does no good, cause all mornin' I have him hangin' around. Then he comes in here cryin' and stuff, and I get blamed. He's not my job, he's your job. I mean, let me alone. . . . He just a little kid. Pleeeeeaaaassssse, do something! I can't stand this!"

These are the words of an exasperated six-year-old boy who wants his younger brother to go and play somewhere else. The time frame is recent, and the protagonist in the story is the six-year-old, who evidently has just endured an entire morning with his younger brother. The point of the story is that the six-year-old wants the parent to take care of Bobby so that the older boy can play more freely. Additionally, by not having his brother around so much, the older boy perceives that he can avoid getting blamed for any scrapes that the younger brother encounters.

This example also shows how the components of hopeful thinking can emerge in a personal story. In this case, the protagonist clearly states that his goal is to have his younger brother cease hanging around him. His waypower thinking is evident in that he has come to his parent for aid with this problem. Moreover, he is displaying waypower thought when he suggests that it is the parent's job to take care of Bobby. The willpower is inherent in his words imploring his parents to "Pleeeeeaaaassssse, do something! I can't stand this!" Finally, he is showing willpower by making his wishes known to all.

An elevated level of hope is inherent in the six-year-old's story. As a counterpoint, consider the next example. Sniffling and crying, 11-year-old Rhonda says, "Nobody likes me. I mean nobody. My braces make me look goofy, and I'm too fat. Today at school lunch, I just sat by myself. There's my supposed friend Alice sitting at another table with Mandy. I could have died. I'm no good. . . . Look at me. Nobody sat with me on the school bus either. I ran home as fast as I could. Tomorrow looks rotten. I don't feel good."

This event was reported by Rhonda to her mother. The time appears to center around the events of the previous school day. Although there is no explicit goal in her story, Rhonda implicitly may be suggesting that she wants to change her appearance and to have a friend upon whom she can count. Rhonda's personal story is rather low on the components of hopeful thinking in that she does not have any thoughts about how to get what she wants (waypower), and she is demoralized and finding it hard to go on (willpower).

Sometimes the story reveals one component of hopeful thought but not the other. Consider an interchange between 16-year-old Shandra and her dad that took place over the dinner table.

SHANDRA: You know how you always tell me to "stick with it" and all that? Well, I did today, and it didn't work.
DAD: I don't understand. What happened?
SHANDRA: OK, Jackie and I took the pickup over to the farm, and I was driving. . . .
DAD: Hey, where is the truck?
SHANDRA: I'll get to that. You see, the back road looked pretty dry, but I guess it wasn't. Well, I know it wasn't, 'cause we got stuck in the mud, and you wouldn't believe how long I tried to get the truck out. I kept racin' the tires, and after two and a half hours, we're only deeper in the mud. And Jackie is just sitting there in the cab laughing her fool head off.
DAD: (Looking incredulous) So, it's still stuck there?
SHANDRA: Yeah, but that's not all. You know me, I kept at it until, well . . . I think it ran out of gas.

As evidenced by this example, we know a good deal about Shandra's hopeful thinking. There is little doubt about her willpower thoughts as manifested by her repeated attempts to get the truck out of the mud. Unfortunately, she did not have an equal dose of waypower thought because she tried only one solution to get the truck out of the mud. This pattern of high willpower but lower waypower gives us an important clue about where we would want to make changes if we were working with Shandra: She needs to think more in terms of waypower. Indeed, she has bought into the theme of perseverance as taught by her parents, but she does not consider other ways to get the truck out of the muddy road.

The stories we tell about ourselves reveal our hope, whether implicitly or explicitly. A personal story is inherently laden with thoughts about how we go about pursuing the goals in our life.

Return Engagements:
Déjà Vu and Hopeless Too

Of course, not all personal stories are filled with hope. Stories often can give us a ticket to an unwanted destination. Consider the case of Janet, a 17-year-old girl who came to one of the authors for treatment. Her parents described Janet as sullen and morose. Furthermore, she had a pattern of getting into relationships with boys who would mistreat and abuse her.

"Guys are no damn good," says Janet, glaring at the therapist.

"Tell me about it, would you?" asks the therapist.

"OK, it's like it never fails. I mean, I see some guy who looks real hot . . . you know, and I know beforehand exactly what's gonna happen. . . . (pause) I'll start hangin' around him, and the first thing I know, well, we're doin' it and I hardly feel anything. Its like I'm just sitting in a chair by the side of the bed watching the same old sex scene time after time."

"What happens?" asks the therapist.

"Well, he gets tired of me. Oh yeah, did I tell you that he starts to knock me around too? You know, the whole macho thing. And there I am, just takin' it, right? So after a while, he leaves, and I feel rotten because it's happened again. So what do I do? I go out and get another jerk who is just as bad as the last one, maybe even worse."

"You don't seem very emotional about this. What do you make of that?" inquires the therapist.

"No way am I gonna show any emotion to these guys. I'm the tough little bitch, that's my part. Yeah, I'm the tough little bitch," repeats Janet.

This case reveals how a young woman has adopted a personal story line that is hopeless and has become a self-perpetuating script that she follows from one lover to the next. This places her as a passive recipient of sexual escapades as well as violent behavior. The story does not provide a means for her to get out of such relationships, but the "tough little bitch" role reflects her attempt to maintain some semblance of control. Unfortunately, her story provides a carousel for continued reenactments of sexual exploitation and abusive relationships with men.

We will return to the topic of hopeless personal stories later in this book, but for our present purposes we would like to emphasize the repetitive and self-defeating nature of such stories. Children sometimes come to think of themselves as the passive lead characters in tragic tales. In their minds and in their real-time lives, they constantly find themselves in similar negative circumstances.[4] Additionally, they sometimes have a detached and distanced view of themselves, as if they are watching the same bad story unfolding time after time. There may be a cynical, hardened quality to their personal tales that suggests abandonment of any hope for their futures. To turn a negative twist on the subtitle of the present chapter, a bad story also goes a long way.

The Boy Who Learned That "Hope Is Like a Rope"

Throughout this chapter we have been suggesting that stories can provide the child with a means for handling the good times and, especially, the bad. A personal story can be used as a guide for dealing with some of life's difficulties. Several years ago, one of the authors was seeing a 15-year-old boy in psychotherapy. The boy reported that he became overwhelmed when something he wanted did not go as he planned. He felt that these situations kept cropping up in his life, and he increasingly felt stymied when he encountered problems. In the process of describing his sense of futility, he likened it to climbing a rope, only to have the rope fall to the ground. In fact, he could so easily imagine this recurring rope event that the therapist asked him to describe this imagined event as a story about himself.

Seizing upon the vividness of the boy's story (the "falling rope"), the therapist asked the boy if he would be willing to make some changes to it. The boy said he would try, but he didn't know how to change it. Because the rope seemed to be the key to the story, the therapist asked the boy to think of the rope as a giant lasso that he could throw around something he wanted to attain. If he wasn't able to successfully throw it around his desired goal on the first try, he was to continue until he could rope his goal. If it really was the case that no amount of expert roping would succeed in lassoing the first goal, the boy in the story was to look around for another goal that he could successfully capture. When the boy in the story had roped his goal, he was supposed to use the rope to pull himself toward whatever he wanted. As you can see, the props of the boy's story were shaped into a more hopeful script.

The next phase in treatment was to ask the boy to practice the new story both during the actual therapy sessions and outside of the treatment settings. Instead of being haunted by a story that was not conducive to hopeful actions when facing adversity (the "falling rope" script), the boy now had a script that offered a framework for thinking more in terms of having the waypower and willpower to achieve his goals. This new hopeful story was available when he encountered future difficulties, and he found it to be a very useful script as he navigated through his subsequent teenage years.

It is interesting to note that almost two decades after this case was reported, psychologist James Averill and his colleagues performed a search of the metaphors about hope that appear in literature, and one of their findings was the notion that "Hope is a rope."[5]

Our clinical case shows how an older child can rewrite a story and begin to use the new script as a model for more adaptive and hopeful goal-directed thinking. Throughout much of this book, we will focus on the means to implant such positive stories in the lives of children to help them tell tales that will pull them toward desired futures.

Sarah and the Rest of the Story

You may recall Sarah from Chapter 1. She was the seemingly hopeless girl who could not give her summer vacation speech. Here is the rest of the story.

"Bam!" The door to the fourth-grade classroom slammed shut as the teacher, Ms. Campbell, began to take attendance. Sarah was a new student, and she was very nervous about being in a new school. Now that the door was shut, it would be difficult to make a quick escape if she needed to. She did not know if Ms. Campbell would be as nice as Mr. Denny, her fourth-grade teacher where she had lived in Texas.

As Ms. Campbell read down the list of names, Sarah heard, "Bill Nugent" "Here!" "Claire Parsons" "Here!" and then, "Sarah Prentiss." Sarah kept her eyes glued to the floor and whispered "Here." Ms. Campbell then did what Sarah was dreading—she told the whole class about her.

"Sarah is a new student in our class. She just moved here from Texas and will be with us for the rest of the year. When you have a chance today, I would like you to say hello to her." When Sarah looked up from the floor, everyone was staring at her. No one looked like the friends whom she had known before! They looked strange and not very friendly. She could feel her face getting red. She saw those same girls that had giggled before look at each other and giggle again.

The worst part of that first day was when they had to get up in front of class and talk about their summer vacations. Sarah could barely talk. She thought the day would never end. When she got off the bus, she ran into her new house, bolted up the stairs to her room, and began to cry. She cried harder when she realized that she wasn't in her old, familiar room with its shaggy carpet and walls exactly the light blue color of a robin's egg. Sarah stayed in her room until her mother got home from work. When her mother came upstairs to see her, Sarah began to cry again.

"No one likes me there and I HATE the new school! I wish I we were back in Texas where people are nicer," she sobbed. Sarah's mother did not say anything for a while and just held her until she stopped crying.

"Sarah," she said. "I know it is going to be hard on you now that we are living in a new place. I do want you to give it a try and be patient. Sometimes it takes a while before a new place begins to feel like home."

Sarah thought about what her mother had said and decided that she could figure out some way to become part of this new school and make friends with some of the girls. After all, she had moved to the school in Texas when she was in the second grade, and she had been able to make new friends then.

The next week in school, Sarah tried hard to make this new school feel like her old one. She had not made any new friends yet and decided that she would try to fit in more so that the girls would like her. Sarah noticed that they all wore bows in their hair, so Sarah asked her mother to buy her some bows just like everyone else's. The day she wore her new bows to school, she waited and hoped all day long that one of the girls would come over and make friends with her. No one did.

Sarah began to watch very carefully to see what the children brought in their lunches. She noticed that the girls who giggled at her before all brought in juice drinks that were a mouth-watering ruby red color. Sarah begged her mother to buy her these drinks because she really wanted to be liked and noticed. The next day, Sarah proudly opened her lunch and pulled out a beautiful red drink. No one said a word to her, and when she looked over at the giggling girls, they had purple ones instead of the red!

That night, when Sarah was at home, she cried as she told her mother what had been happening. "No one will even notice me," cried Sarah. "I try as hard as I can to be like them and they just stick with themselves."

Sarah's mother looked at her with love and said, "Maybe you need to stop trying to be like everyone else. If you try to be the same as everyone, they won't know that you are special and important and different." Sarah thought a lot about what her mother said to her and decided that she really did need to show the class that she was special. As she lay in bed, she came up with an idea that would let people know something about her that might be different and exciting.

The next day in school, Sarah could hardly wait for "show and tell." When Ms. Campbell asked if anyone had something special to share, Sarah raised her hand straight up so that she would be noticed. "Well, it looks like Sarah has something for us today," said Ms. Campbell. Although her stomach was doing flip-flops because she was nervous, Sarah stood up tall and pulled a photograph out of her pocket.

"Today I wanted to tell the class about my fish tank," she said. "Some people also call it an aquarium. If you treat it very gently, I will pass around the picture and you can see all of the beautiful and colorful fish that live in the tank." Sarah then explained how she had special plants and other creatures besides fish that make the tank seem like a real home for her fish. Even the giggly girls seemed interested and did not giggle once. Sarah noticed that one of them, named Lisa, looked at the picture a long, long time.

Sarah

That afternoon at recess, Sarah caught up to Lisa and said, "I was wondering if you would like to come over tomorrow afternoon and see my aquarium." Lisa looked at her and smiled and said, "That would be great. Let me ask my mom if I can go to your house after school."

Lisa came over the next day and loved Sarah's aquarium, and Sarah explained everything about the fish and plants that she knew. Because she was being herself and wasn't trying to be like all the other girls, Sarah was relaxed and fun to be around. Lisa had a good time, even when they weren't looking at the fish tank. Sarah had found a friend.

This story shows that parents can patiently and lovingly help their children get past horrible, seemingly hopeless events so that they do not become indelibly ingrained in the minds of children. Perhaps even more importantly, the child is left with a story that is even more useful and powerful *because it shows the child that he or she can confront difficult situations and find the means and the energy to get what they want.* Stories that involve the overcoming of obstacles, therefore, especially show how "A Good Story Goes a Long Way."

The Power in the Tale

Consider the following story. Rabbi Israel Baal Shem-Tov went to a particular place in the forest to meditate when the Jews were threatened. There, he made a fire and said a special prayer, and a miracle that prevented the disaster occurred. Years passed, and the rabbi's first disciple, Magid of Mezritch, went to the forest when Israel was in crisis. Magid told God that he wasn't certain about how to light the fire, but he could say the prayer. As before, the miracle was granted. More years passed, and the Rabbi

Moshe-Leib of Sasov made the same journey to save his people; unfortunately, he had to tell God that he didn't know how to light the fire or say the prayer, but he did know the proper place in the forest. It worked again. Finally, Rabbi Israel of Rishyn needed to save his people from misfortune. Sitting in his armchair, Rabbi Rishyn recounted his shortcomings to God: he couldn't light the fire, he didn't know the prayer, and he was at a total loss about finding the special place in the woods. God listened and again performed the rescuing miracle. When asked why He did this, God replied that He had made humankind *because He loves to hear all of our stories.*[6]

This parable suggests that divine intervention comes from the mere telling of the tale. We agree that stories can have potent effects. Indeed, our approach focuses on the benefits that accrue to the child who crafts a particular kind of self-descriptive story—one that is hopeful in content. Such content, we suggest, makes for a particularly powerful tale.

3

Measuring Hope in Children

Hope Yardsticks

If we are to help our children improve their levels of hope by the use of positive personal stories, it is critical that we have ways to *measure* their hope. In this chapter, we will describe several approaches to the measurement of hope in children of different age groups. So that parents and teachers can have one or more means of quickly measuring hope in young children, we have developed both story-based and self-report instruments as well as observer versions. Feel free to select the techniques that fit your specific needs.

Children Ages Five Through Nine

Young Children's Hope Scale, Story Form

The Young Children's Hope Scale (YCHS), Story Form, was developed for use with children ages five through eight. It is based on the premises that a young child can listen to short stories about other children and can identify which child in a given story is most similar to him or her. In the YCHS–Story Form, the child is presented with a series of vignettes. Each vignette features two main child characters—one who displays hopeful thoughts and actions, and another who does not. Both children are dealing with a particular situation (such as a problem with a playmate). By identifying with one protagonist over another, the listening child reveals his or her own level of hope.

The YCHS–Story Form was developed with two sets of 18 vignettes, with parallel versions for boys and girls. The actual content of the 18 items is the same in the male and female versions, thereby avoiding gender stereotypes, but the names of the protagonists are female for the female form and male for the male form. Nine vignettes center on waypower thoughts, and nine focus on willpower thoughts. Accordingly, a child who identifies with the hopeful protagonist in each of the 18 stories would obtain the highest possible score of 18, with 9 points each for willpower and waypower. Conversely, the child who identifies with the non-hopeful protagonists in all of the stories would obtain the lowest possible total hope score of zero, with zero each for the waypower and willpower subscale scores. An average score on the YCHS–Story Form is approximately a 12.5, with scores of 16 or higher being in the top 15 percent, and scores of 9 or less being in the bottom 15 percent.

Perhaps it will be helpful to describe two of the vignettes. In one, which concerns waypower thinking, the child is instructed to answer the question, "Which child is more like you?" For the female version, the first item reads, "Rachel and Julie have a problem. When they are at school, another child calls them names. Rachel and Julie want this child to stop calling them names. It is hard for Rachel to think of ways to stop the child from making fun of her. It is easy for Julie to think of ways to stop the child from making fun of her." The child is asked, "Which child is more like you?" If she says it is Julie, she receives one point for waypower thinking; if she says she is more similar to Rachel, she receives zero points for waypower thinking. Eight additional female vignettes tap waypower thinking, such that the total number of vignettes for waypower is nine.

A second vignette concerns willpower thinking. The female version reads: "Marilyn and Sharon are at the park. They want to play 'tag' with the other children. Marilyn tries very hard to get the other children to let her play 'tag.' Sharon tries just a little to get the other children to let her play 'tag.'" The listening child is asked, "Which child is more like you?" If she says it is Marilyn, she receives one point for willpower thinking; if she says she is more similar to Sharon, she receives zero points for willpower. Eight additional vignettes concern willpower thinking, such that the total number of vignettes for willpower is nine. The complete information about the Young Children's Hope Scale, Story Form, is shown in Appendix A.[1]

The Young Children's Hope Scale, Self-Report Form

The Young Children's Hope Scale (YCHS), Self-Report Form, (see Box 3.1) was devised as an orally delivered self-report instrument that can be given to children ages five through nine. Children ages five through seven often need an adult to read the items aloud once or twice so that the children can

---

BOX 3.1   Young Children's Hope Scale, Self-Report Form

Directions: The six sentences below describe how children think about themselves and how they do things in general. Read each sentence carefully. For each sentence, please think about how you are in most situations. Place a check inside the circle that describes YOU the best. For example, place a check (✔) in the smallest circle (o) beside "Never" if you don't ever think this way. If you think this way "Sometimes," check the middle-sized circle. If you "Always" think this way, place a check in the biggest circle. Please answer every question. There are no right or wrong answers.

1. *I think I am doing pretty well.*

   o Never   ○ Sometimes   ◯ Always

2. *I can think of many ways to get the things I want.*

   o Never   ○ Sometimes   ◯ Always

3. *I am doing just as well as other kids in my class.*

   o Never   ○ Sometimes   ◯ Always

4. *When I have a problem, I can come up with lots of ways to solve it.*

   o Never   ○ Sometimes   ◯ Always

5. *Things I have done before will help me when I do new things.*

   o Never   ○ Sometimes   ◯ Always

6. *I can find ways to solve a problem even when other kids give up.*

   o Never   ○ Sometimes   ◯ Always

---

understand them. We have found, however, that children are capable of understanding and using the response continuum differences between "never," "sometimes," and "always." Furthermore, children with good reading skills can complete this instrument with little or no adult supervision. It is permissible, however, to provide supervision if you have concerns that a child may have difficulty understanding the directions, reading the items, or keeping focused.

When working with groups of children, we have used one adult to monitor the administration of the scale to three or four children. If the child is randomly marking items, looks confused, or is peering at a neighbor's work, the adult can ask if the child has any questions and can gently bring the child's attention back to the task at hand.

To derive the child's overall score on the YCHS–Self-Report Form, add the responses to the six items (i.e., "Never" = 1; "Sometimes" = 2; "Always" = 3); as such, the lowest possible score is a 6, and the highest score is an 18. The waypower subscale score is the sum of the three even-numbered items, and the willpower subscale score is the sum of the three odd-numbered items. Each subscale score can range from a low of 3 to a high of 9. The average score for children completing the YCHS–Self-Report Form is 14, with scores at or above 17 signifying those children in the top 15 percent, and scores at or below 11 signifying children in the bottom 15 percent.[2]

The Young Children's Hope Scale (YCHS), Observer Rating Form

With slightly modified wordings on the aforementioned items of the YCHS–Self-Report Form, adults can use the instrument to derive hope scores based on observations of the child. To make this change in the YCHS–Self-Report Form, substitute "she" or "he" where the personal pronoun "I" appears in the six questions; correspondingly, the verbs also will need to be modified. For example, item 2 would become, "She can think of many ways to get the things she wants."

This revised observer form can be used to rate a child on the six items (using the same three-point continuum, going from "Never" = 1, to "Sometimes" = 2, to "Always" = 3). Think about those instances in which you have observed the child in action (or inaction), and rate him or her based on these observations. This rater's version of the Young Children's Hope Scale can produce 12-point variations in scores (a low of 6 to a high of 18); additionally, the willpower and waypower subscale scores each can range for a low of 3 to a high of 9. In our experience, teachers' ratings of a child's hope have generally been in agreement with those produced via the child's self-report.

Children Ages Nine Through Sixteen

The Children's Hope Scale, Self-Report Form

We have developed the Children's Hope Scale (shown in Box 3.2) as a self-report instrument that can be given to children ages eight through sixteen.[3] Assuming the child has reasonably good reading skills (in our experience, this only has been a problem with a few eight-year-olds), the child can complete the Children's Hope Scale with little or no adult supervision. Children appear to understand and correctly use the six-point response

BOX 3.2   Children's Hope Scale

Directions: The six sentences below describe how children think about themselves and how they do things in general. Read each sentence carefully. For each sentence, please think about how you are in most situations. Place a check inside the circle that describes YOU the best. For example, place a check (✔) in the circle (○) above "None of the time" if this describes you. Or, if you are this way "All of the time," check this circle. Please answer every question. There are no right or wrong answers.

1. *I think I am doing pretty well.*

○	○	○	○	○	○
None of the time	A little of the time	Some of the time	A lot of the time	Most of the time	All of the time

2. *I can think of many ways to get the things in life that are most important to me.*

○	○	○	○	○	○
None of the time	A little of the time	Some of the time	A lot of the time	Most of the time	All of the time

3. *I am doing just as well as other kids my age.*

○	○	○	○	○	○
None of the time	A little of the time	Some of the time	A lot of the time	Most of the time	All of the time

4. *When I have a problem, I can come up with lots of ways to solve it.*

○	○	○	○	○	○
None of the time	A little of the time	Some of the time	A lot of the time	Most of the time	All of the time

5. *I think the things I have done in the past will help me in the future.*

○	○	○	○	○	○
None of the time	A little of the time	Some of the time	A lot of the time	Most of the time	All of the time

6. *Even when others want to quit, I know that I can find ways to solve the problem.*

○	○	○	○	○	○
None of the time	A little of the time	Some of the time	A lot of the time	Most of the time	All of the time

continuum going from "None of the time" to "All of the time." If you suspect that the child has difficulty with reading, however, you can read the items aloud and record the child's answers in the appropriate boxes.

Add the scores (i.e., "None of the time" = 1; "A little of the time" = 2; "Some of the time" = 3; "A lot of the time" = 4; "Most of the time" = 5; "All of the time" = 6) on all six items in order to compute the overall Children's Hope Scale. Possible scores can range from a low of 6 to a high of 36. In samples of over two thousand children completing Children's Hope Scale to date, an average level of hope is a score of approximately 25. Using the markers for each item, this suggests that the normal child thinks hopefully "A lot of the time." The good news here is that most children, from middle childhood to adolescence, are on the hopeful end of the continuum.

Children scoring 29 or higher are in the top 15 percent. Such children are reporting that they have the willpower and the waypower to achieve their goals "Most of the time." Children scoring at or below 21 are in the lower 15 percent, and such children are reporting that they have the willpower and waypower for their goals "Some of the time." Even these low-hope children, however, are reporting some degree of will- and way-related thinking (i.e., they typically are not using the "None of the time" option).

As a parent or teacher, you also may be interested in the willpower and waypower subscale scores that can be derived from the Children's Hope Scale. To obtain the waypower subscale score, merely sum the three even-numbered items; to obtain the willpower subscale score, sum the three odd-numbered items. The waypower and willpower subscales scores each extend from a low score of 3 to a high of 18. Average waypower or willpower scores are each approximately 12.5; translating this score to the option markers, children are reporting waypower or willpower "A lot of the time." Scores at or above 15 reflect waypower or willpower that is in the highest 15 percent; conversely, scores at or below 10 reflect waypower or willpower in the lowest 15 percent.

The Children's Hope Scale, Observer Rating Form

In addition to having the child complete the Children's Hope Scale, it is possible to use this scale in a slightly modified version so that an adult observer can rate the child's hope. To make this modification, take the Children's Hope Scale (see previous section), substitute "he" or "she" where the personal pronoun "I" appears in the six questions, and modify the verbs accordingly. Then, use this revised form to rate a target child on the six items. This rater's version of the Children's Hope Scale, like the self-report version, can produce 30-point variations in scores (a low of 6 to a high of 36); moreover, the waypower and willpower subscale scores can have 15-point variations in magnitude (a low of 3 to a high of 18). We have employed the Children's Hope Scale Observer Rating Form with a variety of raters. Generally, the more the observer knows about the child, the more likely it is that the observer-rated hope will approximate the hope revealed through the child's actual self-report. We have found that a variety of adult observers, including parents, camp counselors, and teachers, can effectively use the Children's Hope Scale Observer Rating Form to rate hope in children.

Doing both methods of rating simultaneously can lead to results that can have interesting implications. For example, to what degree were you able to predict your child's hopeful thoughts as self-reported on the Children's Hope Scale? Were there particular items, or perhaps the waypower and willpower subscales, where you differed in the rated hope relative to that reported by the child? It may be helpful to discuss your discrepant view with the child, if for no other reason than to increase your understanding of how that child sees his or her goal pursuits.

Children and Young Adults

The Trait Hope Scale

The most valid index of trait adolescent and young adult hope can be obtained by giving the Trait Hope Scale (see Box 3.3).[4] This scale is designed as a trait measure, which means that it taps enduring patterns of goal-directed thinking that should not vary greatly over time intervals. That is to say, the adolescent may retake the test after several weeks or months, and his or her score should remain similar. This instrument can be used for adolescents age 16 and older as well as young and older adults. Take a few minutes and answer the subsequent items as they apply to you.

To derive your overall hope score, add the numbers you wrote in the blanks. Hope Scale scores can range from a high of 32 to a low of 8. Scores around 24 are typical for adults in the United States. In an absolute sense this means that for each of the eight items, the average person evidences hopeful thoughts as being "Mostly true." If you scored above 24, your level of hopeful thinking is elevated relative to most people, just as scores below 24 reflect relatively lower hopeful thought. If you would like to know your willpower score, sum the four odd-numbered items. Similarly, your waypower score is the sum of the four even-numbered items.

This eight-item Trait Hope Scale has been used extensively with adolescent children and young adults, ages 16 though 20. This self-report scale is written in simple language and can be self-administered by the older child

---

BOX 3.3   Trait Hope Scale

Directions: Read each item carefully. Using the scale shown below, please select the number that best describes you and put that number in the blank provided.

1=Definitely False   2=Mostly False   3=Mostly True   4=Definitely True

___ 1. *I energetically pursue my goals.*

___ 2. *I can think of many ways to get out of a jam.*

___ 3. *My past experiences have prepared me well for my future.*

___ 4. *There are lots of ways around any problem.*

___ 5. *I've been pretty successful in life.*

___ 6. *I can think of many ways to get the things in life that are most important to me.*

___ 7. *I meet the goals that I set for myself.*

___ 8. *Even when others get discouraged, I know I can find a way to solve the problem.*

---

with the reading skills expected of junior high and older students. If there is a question about the reading skill of a child, however, the scale can be read aloud by an adult, or the Young Children Hope Scale described previously in this chapter can be employed.

As is the case with adults who complete the scale, an average score for older adolescents is 24, with scores at or above 28 signifying children in the top 15 percent, and scores of 20 or less signifying children in the lowest 15 percent.

The State Hope Scale

The best index of state adolescent and young adult hope (ages 16 and up) is obtained from the State Hope Scale (see Box 3.4).[5] This scale is designed as a measure that applies to any given point in time, and accordingly it should vary over time intervals. That is to say, depending on when the adolescent takes the State Hope Scale, his or her score will vary in response to the circumstance.

An Agency subscale score is derived by summing the three even-numbered items; a Pathways subscale score is derived by adding the three odd-numbered items. The total State Hope Scale score is derived by summing

---

BOX 3.4   State Hope Scale

Directions: Read each item carefully. Using the scale shown below, please select the number that best describes *how you think about yourself right now* and put that number in the blank before each sentence. Please take a few moments to focus on yourself and what is going on in *your life at this moment.* Once you have this "here and now" set, go ahead and answer each item according to the following scale:

> 1=Definitely False
> 2=Mostly False
> 3=Somewhat False
> 4=Slightly False
> 5=Slightly True
> 6=Somewhat True
> 7=Mostly True
> 8=Definitely True

___ 1. *If I should find myself in a jam, I could think of many ways to get out of it.*

___ 2. *At the present time, I am energetically pursuing my goals.*

___ 3. *There are lots of ways around any problem that I am facing now.*

___ 4. *Right now, I see myself as being pretty successful.*

___ 5. *I can think of many ways to reach my current goals.*

___ 6. *At this time, I am meeting the goals that I have set for myself.*

---

the Agency and Pathways items. Scores can range from a low of 6 to a high of 48.

The Trait and State Hope Scales, Observer Forms

As has been the case with the other self-report scales described in this chapter, the Trait and State Hope Scales can be adapted to become an observer rating instrument. Similar to the modifications described for the other instruments, substitute "she" or "he" where the personal pronoun "I" appears, and modify the verbs as necessary. Then use the appropriate response continuum (a four-point one for the Trait Hope Scale: 1 = "Definitely False"; 2 = "Mostly False"; 3 = "Mostly True", and; 4 = "Definitely True"; and an eight-point one for the State Hope Scale: 1 = "Definitely False", to 8 = "Definitely True") to rate the degree to which each item applies to the target child. Rated hope on these instruments relates positively with those hope scores as actually reported by adolescents.

Sizing Hope and a Case in Point

Small's, Half's, and Large's

Most children are relatively equal in the magnitudes of their reported way-power and willpower thoughts.[6] This undoubtedly reflects the fact that these two subcomponents of hopeful thinking are positively related to each other. Occasionally, however, there are children who have markedly different scores on the waypower and willpower subscales; adults can use this information to tailor their interventions so as to enhance the component of hope-related thought that is lower. A child who is low in waypower thinking represents a somewhat different challenge than the child who is low in willpower thinking.

With all the self-report measures and observer counterparts we have discussed, four basic combinations of waypower and willpower thoughts can emerge. There is *small hope,* which reflects the thinking of a child with low waypower and low willpower; *half hope,* where a child has elevated waypower thinking and lowered willpower thought; another type of *half hope,* this time for a child with lowered waypower thinking and elevated willpower thought; and lastly, *high hope* (or *large* hope), as shown by a child with elevated waypower and willpower thinking.

We will close this section by recounting a true story of a size "large" hope—a child named Robin who is brimming with waypower and willpower thought. Whether Robin took one of the self-report instruments or was rated by those who knew her, all measures would lead to the same high-hope conclusion. This story of Robin is one that we have read to children so that they can get a good example of high hope in action. As you read this story, pay attention to how Robin clarifies her goal and then employs waypower and willpower thinking to get what she wants.

Robin: Waypower Up, Willpower Up

Robin is a bright-eyed nine-year-old girl with long black hair who lives with her mother, father, and three brothers in a small town in Oklahoma. She a member of the Creek Indian Nation—her mother is a Creek Indian and her father is Creek and Cherokee. Many of Robin's cousins, aunts, and uncles also live in town. There are a lot of children for her to play with, but she has a problem that stops her from playing many of the games the others play. Robin was born with one leg shorter than the other, which causes her to limp and keeps her from running fast enough to keep up with the other children.

When Robin joins her brothers and cousins in their games,
they try to include her, but after
a while they forget and go running off. She often feels left out
and alone. She feels that no one
except her dog really notices
her. Even though Robin loves
her family and being part of her
small community, she wants
something that would make her
special in a good way, not just
because of her leg.

ROBIN

One evening Robin was trying to play hide and seek with
her cousins down by the stream.
She decided to hide in a small
hole she found in the bank near
the water. As soon as she started to crawl inside, she heard a hissing sound.
She moved back, afraid it was a rattlesnake. Then she realized it wasn't a
rattle, but a hiss. She crept closer, using a long stick to brush aside some
bushes, and looked into the hole. Inside Robin saw a raccoon—at least, she
thought it looked like a raccoon. She was used to small wild animals, so
she went quietly away, leaving the raccoon alone.

She had forgotten the raccoon until the next week on the way to school.
From her school bus window, she saw a raccoon lying dead beside the
road. She said a little prayer for the animal's spirit, as she always did when
she saw an animal that had died. Later that day, Robin got to wondering if
it had been the raccoon in the hole who she had almost bumped into.

In the evening when Robin got home, she went to the hole by the stream
and cautiously ventured to the entrance. This time, instead of a hissing
sound she heard a high mewing noise. The mewing sounded like a baby
something, but what? She crept up closer and closer until she could put the
stick clear inside the hole. Because nothing happened to the stick, Robin
cleared the brush away so that she could see inside the hole. She found two
baby raccoons, very small, and now, very quiet with fear. She quickly
backed away from the hole—what if the raccoon mother or father returned
and found her there? Yet, where were the parents? Robin realized she
didn't know much about raccoons, but she did know someone who did.

That night after dinner, Robin went to her grandfather's house and
asked him what to do about those baby raccoons. Did he think their
mother had been hit by a car? Where did he think the father was? Robin's
grandfather said that it might be that the parents were gone, but that the

raccoons were meant to be wild and should be left alone. He said she would not know how to take care of raccoon babies, and even if she could keep them alive, what would happen to them later? Besides, he said, raccoons are pesky and get into everything.

That night Robin tossed about in her bed with thoughts of lonely baby raccoons. Before the school bus came the next day, she went to the creek and looked in the hole. Sure enough, they were still there and were mewing even louder.

During that day, Robin could hardly pay attention to the teacher because she was so worried about those raccoon babies. As soon as she got home, she went to the hole to look, and found them there and still alone. By this time, Robin was certain they were orphans and so she did a daring thing. She got a cardboard box, put a towel in it, and carried the raccoon babies up to her house. Her mother was in the kitchen beginning to fix dinner, and Robin was able to slip past her up the stairs to her room. Because she had only brothers, she had a very small room all to herself, which, for a while, would be a good hiding place for her little raccoons.

Now that she actually had rescued the raccoons, she had to figure out what to do to keep them alive. She did another daring thing next. Robin asked her oldest cousin, Jim, who lived next door and had a car, to drive her into town to talk to the veterinarian, Dr. Smith. She confided to Jim what she was doing because she was so excited she could hardly keep still. Jim said he would help her if he could, but she would have to tell her family because they would hear the raccoons' noise and probably begin to smell them before too long.

Dr. Smith was nice and very helpful. He told Robin and Jim to buy some cat chow and fresh fruit and corn to feed to the raccoons. He also said that raccoons could eat worms and bugs. Dr. Smith cautioned Robin that it isn't a good idea to try to keep wild animals and that, if they lived, she could not keep them as pets. He said she would have to feed them often and that they probably wouldn't live without their mother. But Robin was determined to do everything she could to help her little raccoons grow.

At home, with the food she had gotten and the bugs she had found, Robin told her family. Surprisingly, her parents were very encouraging and said they would help her buy more food. Her mother said she would do the feeding while Robin was at school. Robin's brothers said they wished they had found those babies, but thought it was going to take a whole lot of work to keep them alive.

Robin did set to work, feeding each raccoon every three hours except at night. She petted each one and made sure they had lots of love. She often had to change the paper in their box because, like all babies, they were messy.

Word spread though the small town that Robin was trying to raise the baby raccoons. Children in her school wanted to come and see them or have her bring them to school. But she didn't want too many people around them yet because they were still young. Many people asked her how the raccoons were doing. Jim and Robin took them back to the veterinarian for a checkup, and Dr. Smith gave them some free shots because he was so pleased that Robin was not only keeping them alive but helping them grow big and healthy.

As the raccoons grew in size, they also grew in mischief. While Robin was at school one day, the raccoons climbed out of their box and took a lot of her clothes out of her drawers and generally messed up her room. After that, Robin's parents borrowed a cage from an uncle who raised rabbits. It was certain now that the babies were growing into healthy raccoons.

Robin had a new problem: What should she do with the raccoons now that they were growing up? A lot of people wanted them for pets, but her grandfather and Dr. Smith said that grown raccoons get into too much trouble and that it isn't a good idea to try to make pets out of wild animals. Robin had an idea that she discussed with Dr. Smith. Tulsa had a children's zoo that she loved to visit, and she wondered if the raccoons could live there. Dr. Smith said he had a friend who worked as the zoo veterinarian and that he would ask. Soon they had an answer. Yes, the children's zoo would love to have the raccoons, and when they were all grown up, they could live with the other raccoons.

Robin took the raccoons to school finally, just before they went to Tulsa, and all the children saw how big they had grown. Robin was very sad to part with her little fellows, but the day her parents and Jim drove her to Tulsa a lot of the townspeople came out to wave good-bye to them.

Robin cried on the way home from the zoo, but she knew, in her heart, that the raccoons might not live in the wild now that they were so tame. She also knew that they would not have lived had it not been for her. And best of all, everyone knew she had saved their lives, and she was now known to everyone as the girl who rescued the raccoons.

Measuring Up

In this final section on the measurement of hope, we touch upon conclusions we have reached based on our use of the different instruments to measure hope in children. In many instances, our attempts to measure hope in children have resulted in surprises.

Hope Can Be Measured

Perhaps it is useful to again state the obvious: Hope can be measured in children. Against the historical backdrop of skepticism about the whimsical and vague nature of hope, the present instruments suggest a more "hopeful" conclusion about our ability to measure hope.[7] Indeed, with each of the scales described, children appear to understand the underlying willpower and waypower thoughts related to goal pursuits. Further, children are able to give consistent and seemingly reliable input about their goal-related thoughts. There usually is a concern when testing children, especially younger ones, that they are incapable of reporting accurately about themselves. When it comes to hope, however, it appears that children are able to reveal their goal-related thoughts in a coherent fashion.

Hope Is Stable over Time

As implied in the previous paragraph, one of the criticisms leveled at hope is that it is extremely malleable, almost to the point of being impossible to measure. Contrary to this conclusion, we have found that children retaking the hope instruments tend to score at similar levels. (The only exceptions here are for children taking the State Hope Scale, which is designed to be sensitive to change, and children who have undergone hope-related interventions or educational programs.) Whether the interval is a week or a month, both very young and older children respond consistently over the time intervals. This does not mean that a child's level of hope cannot change; rather, it means that the circumstances for most children probably are conducive to their maintaining their level of hope once it is established. In later chapters we will explore the various means for using narratives to increase hope in those children in whom hope measures relatively low.

For Most Children, Hope Is High

Prior to developing our various instruments for measuring hope, we were uncertain what the average level of hope would be for American children. Certainly the media tend to portray a society where citizens experience great difficulty in reaching their goals. Moreover, the troubling effects of violence, unemployment, hunger, and disease, to name but a few, are visiting our children's lives. With such negative forces in action, one might conclude that our children are the heirs to hopelessness. On the contrary, the children in our samples reveal that this is not the case. On average, children from varying geographic and socioeconomic backgrounds manifest high levels of hope. This does not imply, of course, that there are no children with low hope. Indeed, there are, and as adults we especially need to attend to such low-hope children. Based on our research, however, the story of hope is alive and well in the minds of most of our children.[8]

Hope Has No Gender

Psychological literature has suggested that men are primarily interested in instrumental matters related to getting what they want, and women are drawn to matters that are more expressive and communal in nature. This view has fed into stereotypes about men and women that appear in popular news outlets and introductory psychology textbooks. Accordingly, one would expect boys to have more hope than girls. *Our findings provide no support for this stereotype.* Just as has been the case when we have measured hope in adults, we generally have found no gender differences in the hope of girls and boys. In fact, in those rare instances in which a gender difference does emerge, it is the girls who score somewhat higher in hope. These findings appear to mirror more recent research on gender differences, which suggests that *both* sexes are primarily oriented toward instrumental activities. Our findings, taken together with those of other researchers, provide an antidote to this particular gender-based stereotype. If you are hunting for hope in children, therefore, it can be found in both girls and boys.

Hope Is Biased Positively

One of the characteristics revealed in our measurement studies is that higher-hope children are somewhat biased toward imagining and expecting positive outcomes.[9] It is not that high-hope children exhibit extreme positive personal illusions. Rather, they bend reality in their favor. More specifically, higher-hope children engage in socially and self-desirable responding so as to put themselves in a positive light. They also believe that they are going to be more invulnerable to sources of harm than are their low-hope counterparts, and they are less likely to distort upcoming events in a negative way. In general, then, high-hope children think well of themselves. It should be emphasized, however, that they are not extreme (i.e., delusional) in their biases.

Our findings are consistent with many other recent ones regarding the role of illusions.[10] Such research suggests that it is strongly adaptive to have positive personal illusions, as long *as these biases are in the slight to moderate range.* Further, high-hope children actually do fare better in attaining their life goals than do low-hope children. When the present findings about the positive biases of high-hope children are placed in the context of storytelling, therefore, we adults should realize that some stretching of the facts actually may serve to benefit the child.

Even the Lows Have Some Hope

Children who score low in hope are not necessarily without any hope.[11] We base this conclusion on two factors. First, children rarely use the "None of the time" or "Never" options to describe their low waypower and willpower thoughts in the self-report measures of hope. Second, a little detective work on the part of an adult uncovers one or more arenas where the low-hope child reports having higher hope. Contexts in which the low-hope child does experience hope provide something upon which to build. Rarely is hope totally dead; to find it alive somewhere in the thoughts of a child is a discovery of considerable importance.[12]

You Can Do It

Don't be turned off by the many means of measuring hope that we have presented in this chapter. You probably will use only one or two of these approaches. With a little practice, you should be able to obtain a reliable and valid measure of hope. Further, it takes a very short time to measure a child using one of these techniques. Lastly in regard to measurement, as we have suggested throughout this book, it is important to remember the high-hope mantra: You can do it!

4

A Parent Needs Hope

Hope Begets Hope

Of the many influences that children will encounter, parents and other primary caregivers unquestionably are the most powerful. It is true that other individuals such as teachers, peers, and community people may also have important effects on youth, but parents typically have the closest connection, and thus the greatest impact. If parents want their children to become hopeful, they must act as hope-inducing models from whom their children can develop goals as well as the associated willpower and waypower thinking. To beget hope in your children, therefore, you need to have it in your own life. In this chapter, we explore parental hope, including the means to increase it.

Start by taking a careful look at your own hope. Parents are invited to assess their own levels of hope by completing the Trait Hope Scale for adults (provided in Chapter 3). Hope may be high or low for one or both of the willpower and waypower components. A quick perusal of your scores will tell you where you currently stand.

If your scores indicate the need to develop higher hope, the subsequent pages in this chapter should prove helpful. Even if you are relatively high in hope, however, this chapter may offer some useful tips.

Your Family Tree

This book is about increasing hope through the use of stories. Adults, as well as children, can use stories to foster and increase their own hope. Some families appear to have a theme of high hope that permeates family tales, whereas other families seem to languish in low hope generation after generation. For example, many families who live in poverty see no way out of their situation, and thus their marginal existence appears to be handed down from parents to children. Other families have a history of difficult immigration, or of living through horrible conditions in another land. Examples that come to mind are Dust Bowl survivors who traveled across the country to begin new lives, immigrants from war-torn countries such as Viet Nam who braved tragedy and loss to begin again in a new country, and Irish immigrants who crossed the sea to give their families new dreams after the poverty of the potato famine. As a parent, it is important to remember that you are a relatively recent branch on the family tree and, for your sake, as well as for your children, it is crucial to make your story a high-hope one.

Here is a story drawn from our clinical experience. It serves to illustrate an intergenerational low-hope pattern and the potential for change.

Toby

Toby was a 35-year-old man who worked as a hod carrier (someone who carries bricks for the bricklayer). This occupation pays minimum wage, and the main qualification is having a strong back. Toby quit high school when he was 16 and married his pregnant girlfriend. They eventually had five children; Toby was barely able to feed them from his hod carrier's wages. Toby's wife worked nights in a fast-food restaurant, but her meager income contributed little to meeting their needs. The family was barely getting along, when Toby fell while carrying a load of bricks and injured his back. The doctor said he would have to quit hard labor and find some type of sedentary work.

Toby was devastated. He did not want to be on welfare for long, although it helped the family to have some support. He was not eligible for any long-term disability, but he was entitled to six months of unemployment insurance. During this time, Toby went to the employment counselor, who told him of a new retraining program. The counselor mentioned a number of training possibilities and said Toby would need to take some interest and ability tests to find which ones best suited him. Toby was reluctant to try the tests, emphasizing that he had been out of school for a long time. But on the appointed testing day, he showed up and took a long battery of tests that measured a variety of aptitudes, abilities, and interests.

When Toby discussed the results with the employment worker, he was surprised to learn he had scored very highly on the aptitudes that were required of a computer programmer. It happened that this was one of the training programs offered. He was advised that if he would get his high school equivalency, he would qualify for this computer training program. Toby was cautious and skeptical about this news. He had never known anyone who did that kind of work. Furthermore, no one in his family had *ever* had any type of specialized training. The thought of wearing a suit and tie to work was intimidating, as were the months of hard work needed to complete the training.

When Toby discussed this idea with his wife and parents, they too were doubtful but not totally discouraging. They pointed out that there seemed to be no other choice, and it wouldn't hurt to try. When Toby returned to the employment office, he was still hesitant but agreed to take the high school equivalency test. Evidently he had picked up a fair amount of knowledge in the years since high school because he passed all the sections of the test, giving him a high school equivalency diploma. With that step behind him, Toby had a little more courage. His hope was beginning to rise. He then spent the next four months in the computer programming course, when he otherwise would have been sitting at home collecting unemployment insurance.

Toby's hope grew with each passing week. He found that he was able to learn the necessary skills, and he thought the work was interesting. Because the program was designed for individuals who needed retraining, the other students in the course were in situations similar to his, and he began to make friends with people from other walks of life. He also learned things about himself that he had not known before. His wife began to look forward to obtaining her high school equivalency, with an eye toward working as a secretary rather than settling for fast-food employment. In turn, Toby's children began to see new vistas through their parents' eyes, and they even began to consider preparing for college.

When Toby completed his training, he was very employable as a programmer. He had done well in his computer course and received solid letters of recommendation. Indeed, he obtained a job with a communications firm at a salary that was far higher than he had ever dreamed. As an added bonus, he didn't have to wear a suit and tie.

There are stories like Toby's, of course, where the ending is not so happy. Many people when faced with difficult choices retreat into the safety of the familiar. Their life situations may not be good—in fact, they may be very uncomfortable—but at least the circumstances are known and are not as scary because of this familiarity. As Toby looked back at everything he had known in his life, including all the models he had, he saw no one who had ventured very far. *There were no family stories of struggle and success, only struggle and low achievement.* Yet, when he was backed into a corner, he was willing to take a chance and embrace a goal he had once thought impossible. Each success produced an increase in hope, a desire to continue trying, and a willingness to work hard. His final achievement produced a high-hope story that he can share with his children and grandchildren. Now let's look at how a high-hope story can inspire several generations of a family.

Harry

Nearly one hundred years ago, Harry was born in a small ranching town in Montana. His father was the only doctor in the county, and from the time he was a small boy Harry often made calls with his father on horseback or buggy. The people of the small community and the nearby ranches held Harry's father in high regard, and Harry vowed that when he grew up, he too would be well respected. Harry wanted to do great things and to make his father proud.

As Harry grew into his teens, he realized that it would be difficult to do the things he dreamed of in that small Montana town. He began thinking about where he would go to college, and he looked forward to a more exciting and sophisticated life. He finally selected a large and prestigious university in the east because that was where his father had gone to medical school. The school, located in a large city, was indeed fun, and life became more exciting with each passing day. Harry joined a fraternity during his first year and soon discovered the pleasures of wine, women, and song. In fact, he imbibed and cavorted far more than he studied. As a result, he was soon sent back to Montana for failing his courses.

Harry was disgraced, but his father was a patient and wise man. He knew that Harry would soon long to be in college again and that he had not given up his dream of doing something meaningful with his life. Harry's father also knew there was a difficult lesson to be learned from the failures of this first college year. When Harry asked to be sent to college again, his father told him he would have to pay for it himself this time. In order for him to save enough money, he would have to work for at least a year. Harry had no idea where he could find a job in that small Montana town. He had no skills, and certainly he had learned nothing of use in his one year of college.

There was, however, one thing Harry could do extremely well. He could ride a horse better than most people in the county. The mail in those days was always delivered by horseback, and Harry was able to secure a job riding many miles covering the entire postal district each day. Mail carriers are noted for being reliable, whether the weather was fair or foul. Harry spent many months that year trudging through deep snow, slipping on icy paths, or wading through muddy creeks in an effort to uphold the reputation of the United States Postal Service. During one especially bad blizzard, he lost part of two fingers to frostbite. In another storm, his favorite horse died. Harry almost quit after these events, but the desire to work his way back to a good college and do something meaningful and important was too strong. It was a grueling year, but Harry was determined to prove to both his father and himself that he could be a responsible and reliable person.

At the end of the year, Harry had saved enough money to return to college. He chose to go to the University of Montana instead of returning to the large eastern city so that he could afford to complete the entire four years with the money he had earned. Upon his return to college, Harry worked very hard on his studies, eventually graduating with honors. After he completed college, Harry was admitted to a fine Ivy League university to study law. His father gratefully paid. Later, Harry did go on to do great things, gaining the respect he desired. He became a well-known judge and a member of the Montana legislature. His year spent delivering mail stood him in good stead for the rest of his life, and it provided a high-hope story for his family to repeat for generations.

Whenever a family member commented on Harry's two missing fingers, he often was prompted to tell his tale. Harry was, despite the missing digits, an excellent pianist, and when he played, his hands were a curiosity to his children and grandchildren. It seemed that no matter how many times they had heard the mail delivery story, they were eager to hear it again. The story became a family legend that was repeated to his descendants with many exciting elaborations.

A high-hope family tale essentially says, "This family has determination to reach its goals and will work hard to overcome obstacles." The implication is that hope runs in families. If it has been in your family, as a parent you can realize and embrace this theme for yourself. Although there is no reason to suppose a genetic link, *there is every reason to suppose that one generation learns its stance with respect to hope from the previous generation.* Hope cannot be learned, however, without communication and modeling. That is why it is so important for parents to understand and develop their own hope. After parents learn to hope for themselves, they are in a better position to convey this hope more effectively to their children.[1]

Both of the previous stories have been about men, and the story of Harry happened a long time ago, even though the repercussions continue into the present generation. Let's look at the life of a modern-day high-hope woman who was able to cope with obstacles that have devastated many women and men.

Tomika

When Tomika graduated from high school she married T. J., the young man she had dated for three years. Things looked wonderful for this young couple, though they knew it would be a struggle to achieve the kind of life of which they both dreamed. T. J. worked as an auto mechanic during the day and as a clerk in a convenience store four evenings a week. Tomika worked as a motel maid but quit to give birth to their first child. Soon after their son was born, she became pregnant again, and they had a little girl. Between his two jobs, T. J. earned enough money to meet the most basic family needs so that Tomika could stay at home and look after the children. Although it was a struggle to pay bills, they were a happy family who believed that with hard work they would make a better life than either had known as children.

Disaster struck one evening when T. J. was working at the convenience store. A group of young men carrying weapons robbed the store, and in the process T. J. was shot and killed. Although the robbers were caught, their conviction was little comfort to Tomika and her children. T. J.'s employment carried no death benefits, and the family had not been able to afford life insurance. Life ahead looked grim and lonely for Tomika, who with no marketable skills and virtually no experience had no idea how she would support her two young children. Furthermore, neither Tomika's nor T. J.'s families could lend financial support, although Tomika's aunt volunteered to baby-sit if Tomika could find a job.

Tomika did look for employment. She tried state and private agencies but was always told the same thing: "Get training or experience and then come back." Tomika thought about being a motel maid again, but the pay was far too low to support her children on her own. She also considered working for one of the popular housecleaning services, but again the pay was too low. While Tomika was interviewing with the manager of one of the cleaning services, however, she got an idea. Why couldn't she set up a cleaning service and employ other women who also needed work? The more she thought about it, the more excited she became. She also began to realize that there was much to learn about management and that she would need some way to develop credentials to start a small business.

Although Tomika had never wanted to accept welfare, it seemed the only way she might be able to go to school and learn about business management. She spoke with a social worker and submitted her welfare application, but she didn't say anything about her plans, fearing the social worker would think she was unrealistic and attempt to discourage her. Instead, she asked for permission to take some courses at the local junior college. The social worker agreed, and Tomika soon enrolled in business

courses at the college. With the help of her
aunt's child care and by moving to a very
low-cost apartment, Tomika survived the
two years it took her to obtain an associate's
degree. During that time she learned much
about management and business practices. It
seemed as if the more she learned, however,
the more difficult her dream became. There
were so many problems to overcome, the
first and foremost of which was obtaining
enough money to begin her business. What
was she to do? Tomika decided just to tackle
one problem at a time and not let herself become overwhelmed by future difficulties.

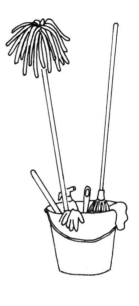

Finally, credentials in hand, Tomika applied for a small business loan. Because she
had a good idea about providing a useful service and would be able to employ a number
of currently unemployed women, she was
granted enough money to get started. Her

TOMIKA

training had served her well. She knew how
and where to advertise, what to look for in future employees, how to talk
to the many women who began to request services, and how to manage the
business end of the service. Tomika also did some things a little differently
than the other cleaning services, and this made her employees happier and
more dependable. She paid them a higher salary, which enabled single parents to work for her, and with the help of her aunt, organized a baby-sit-
ting cooperative so that her employees would not have to pay large
amounts of money for child care. Tomika's employees highly valued their
employment, and consequently they provided excellent service, making her
cleaning service the most sought after in the city.

In time Tomika paid back her small-business loan and was able to buy a
home of her own in a comfortable neighborhood. She watched her children
grow up safe and happy, secure in the knowledge that T. J. would have
been very pleased by what she had done. Tomika's energy, her willingness
to work in pursuit of her goal, and her ability to cope with the many problems she encountered were an inspiration not only to her family but also to
the many women who worked for her over the years.

Perhaps you have encountered many difficulties in your life. It is important to remember here that stories of struggle against terrible odds, even
when the outcome is sad, can be developed into high-hope messages. Let's
look at the story of David. Although his struggles are truly extreme, perhaps there is some aspect that bears a resemblance to your story.

David

David was born in 1935 during Hitler's rise to power in Germany. Being Jewish in Germany at that time was very dangerous, and David's family tried unsuccessfully to immigrate to England. In due course the entire family was sent to Dachau, a prison camp. At three years of age, David lived in the women's barracks and was given as many scraps of food as the women could find to keep him alive. After David's mother was killed, the other women hid him until the camp officials apparently forgot about him. As David got older, he learned to hide when the barracks were searched. Women came and were killed, and more women came to take their places. But each group passed along the care and teaching of this young boy. They taught him to read and write Hebrew as well as German. They taught him mathematics and other subjects that the various women knew. In 1945 when Dachau was closed and the survivors were released, David was among them. He found, sadly, that he was the only surviving member of his family. His father, mother, brother and sisters, and grandparents all had been killed.

Surviving Dachau was a miracle, but surviving what came after was nearly as difficult. In the camp there had been dozens of "mothers" to care for him. There his main challenge was to hide himself successfully. In the free world at last, he had to figure out how to survive with no family and no caring "mothers." He was on his own. He and many other survivors walked hundreds of miles over hostile terrain searching for a place to stay. Farmers and villagers turned them away. They slept in the open and ate anything they could find, including roots and rotting field corn. David was often discouraged and frequently frightened, but he was determined to stay alive and to carry on his family name.

Reaching the new country of Israel became his goal. The camp survivors had heard that it was to be a refuge for people such as they, and it sounded like the promised land. Eventually, David boarded a boat to Israel. As a child alone, he was placed in a kibbutz, a place for him to learn and be cared for by the new families settling Israel. David felt safe at last. He thrived and was like a sponge taking in all the new information. With time, he became a doctor and immigrated to the United States. He forever carries with him the reminder of his sad childhood, but also of his high-hope life. The numbers tattooed on his left forearm attest to the hope he needed to be a survivor.

There is no question that David's story is a sad one; every member of his family was killed by the Nazis. But David's story shows an individual of high hope who overcame incredible odds to live and achieve his goal. The focus of this story, as retold to his children and grandchildren, could be on the deaths and horrors of the Holocaust, and indeed it is important to keep this aspect in mind. But if in retelling the story, David and his family focus on the courage and determination of a little boy who survived, his children and grandchildren will learn the lessons of hope.

A large part of discovering hope is the ability to reframe our life stories so that the individual, rather than being thought of as, for example, "*poor* Grandfather David," becomes "*brave* Grandfather David." If the formula of "willpower + waypower for goals = hope" is applied to any specific story, it is possible to see how the story can then become a lesson in hope. The more determination that is shown and the more struggles that are overcome, the higher in hope the story will be. Let's take a look at a brief family history through both a high-hope and a low-hope lens to illustrate how reframing can be done.

Alice and Len

The story of this family begins in Oklahoma during the 1930s when that state was racked by drought and high winds. The Dust Bowl brought poverty, disease, and frequently death to every family who lived in the region. The disaster hit Alice Morgan's family harder than many because they had a small crop to begin with and ten children to feed. In order to survive the drought years they borrowed money from relatives in other states, mortgaged their small farm, and went hungry and poorly clothed most of the time. Life was extremely difficult, and many times they wondered if they would make it through. Eventually, the rains fell and the land became fertile again, but the family was left nearly destitute. As each of the Morgan children reached early adolescence, he or she was forced to quit school and help on the farm or get a job in the nearby town in order to bring money into the family.

Alice Morgan was the oldest of the five girls in the family and, as such, had the most responsibility to help her younger siblings. She quit school after the eighth grade and went to work in a grocery store in town. When she was 18, she married Len, a boy she had known all her life. Her husband was from circumstances very similar to her own. They decided to leave western Oklahoma and move to another farming community where they could be tenant farmers for a landowner who lived in the city. This went well for some time until Len severely injured his shoulders in an accident. Unable to properly work the fields, Len was forced to quit. Alice, in the meantime, had begun working again so that her young family, which now included a son and daughter, was able to survive.

Len's former landowner boss felt sorry for him and agreed to loan him enough money to begin a small business. The business never grew to large proportions, but it did well enough for Alice and Len to build a modest home and put both children through the state college. When their children were grown and married with children of their own, Alice and Len settled down to a life of frugal retirement. They had enough to live on, as well as the enjoyment of their grandchildren and the warmth and comfort of old friends.

The history of this family is a common one. Many families came through the Dust Bowl or similar situations and settled into very average lives, much like Alice and Len. In this particular family, however, the effects of the Dust Bowl were far-reaching, permeating their lives for generations. Stories were told of the hardships, of the dust and wind, and of the crops withering long before harvest. Individual family members added their own scenarios of hard work, quitting school, little food, and hand-me-down clothes and toys. Len and Alice were afraid to spend money for desired things that would have made life easier because they always had the sense that disaster was just around the corner. They usually chose the safe road whenever choices had to be made. They encouraged their children to go to small local colleges and to choose what they believed would be steady, if not exciting, occupations. They lived life as if everything could fall apart tomorrow. Their children, in turn, did not pursue the interests they might have wished, simply because the risk of failure was present. The offspring's views of life, similar to that of their parents, were always shadowed by memories of the Dust Bowl disaster.

How might we reframe the story of Alice and Len? Surely it contains a wealth of high-hope material. Taken as a whole, the story is one of survival. The things the Morgan family did to survive can be seen as creative innovations, and the individuals undergoing the hardships can be seen as brave and strong. Later, when Alice and Len created their own family and a new life, their struggles can be reframed in much the same way. They never gave up. They knew they could have a comfortable life if they kept on trying. Starting a small business was, in fact, a risk for Len, but he was determined to make a go of it. Both Len and Alice worked very hard and succeeded in building a secure and comfortable life. Their children attended college, the first in the family to go beyond high school, and both have established families of their own. Len and Alice have a great deal of which to be proud, and their story can be presented as one of high hope.

We parents have interesting stories to tell our children, and sharing these stories helps us recognize our own high hope. It is important that children be aware that their parents have experienced problems and yet have had the determination to strive for success. Even though parents and children live in different generations, their dreams, goals, and even the problems they encounter may be very similar. Children should be made to see that they are not alone, that others have experienced similar obstacles. The stories parents can tell children about their own lives are discussed further in Chapters 5 and 6, and examples and guidelines are given there.[2]

Writing Your Story

What we are suggesting is that you probably do have some high-hope stories about yourself. How can you bring these into your awareness so that you can gather strength from them? To begin, do the same thing we ask the children in our school research to do. Think of a goal you set for yourself at some earlier time in your life, think of the energy you put toward achieving the goal, and then think of the difficulties that arose and how you were able to find ways around them. Write all of this out as a story you might tell to someone else—your children, for example. Don't worry about writing style. Try to remember when you had high-hope thoughts and associated feelings as you write your narratives. After you have written several of these narratives you will begin to realize that you have, in fact, demonstrated high hope in several instances in your life. This exercise will take you back to those times when you successfully pursued a goal, perhaps a goal that you attained yesterday, or one that you achieved years ago in your adolescence, and so on.[3]

Rethinking Old Thoughts and Rewriting Your Story

Another method that parents can use to increase their hope is based on the idea that the messages we tell ourselves about reaching goals and surmounting obstacles is a large part of determining how hopeful we will be. It is very difficult to stir up enthusiasm for a goal if, the moment the goal is decided upon, negative "I can't" messages intrude. These messages, especially common to low-hope people, may be based on the individual's past experiences as well as on negative family history messages. Many people give themselves equivocal messages such as, "I'll try," with doubt in their voices all the while. Or, they may begin with the attitude that the project may just be too hard; thus, when difficulties arise, they are ready to quit. Everyone may adopt these attitudes at times. For the low-hope person, however, these messages have become habitual each time new and difficult opportunities are presented. The low-hope person will frequently marshal "rational proof" in support of the negative position, so it takes personal insight and a willingness to be very honest in order to choose to raise one's level of hope.

Once the decision has been made to examine one's messages, the next step involves keeping a brief record of what those messages are and when they are used. Don't worry about how daunting this process appears; it is not a complicated procedure and need not be done for long. A few days, a week at most, should be enough time to discover when and where negative messages are used.

One type of message might look like this: John has just been given a work assignment that involves organizing several people to complete a job. His immediate thoughts are, "This job is unattractive," "No one will want to work on this," and "I may not be able to get anyone to help." Such messages typify low hope in that they presume John has no power to attract coworkers to the assignment and that he cannot find ways to induce them to help. Indeed, if he approaches his fellow workers with such a low-hope mindset, he will probably prove himself correct. No one will want to enlist in an effort so tinged with negativity. However, John can change his self talk to higher hope messages such as, "This could be an interesting assignment," "There are probably a number of people who would like the chance to work on it," and "These people will learn a lot through working together." With these positive beliefs, he then would stand a much better chance of getting volunteers. Such messages would convey high hope and, because hope is infectious, his coworkers would be more eager to join the project.

Here are some simple steps to change your negative self-talk. For a few days, or perhaps at most a week, carry a small notebook in which you write down three things:

1. Note what you tell yourself about the things you have to do, especially the goals you may have set.
2. See how you feel when you have said that particular message.
3. Note what the goal is.

At the end of the week, examine what kinds of messages you have told yourself. For any negative messages, reframe them into more positive statements, such as we have done for John. For the positive messages, actively try to say them more often. For example, in John's case it would not be sufficient for long-term hope increases to simply change the few messages he identified. He will need to examine other instances of negative self-talk and change each message to a positive statement. This work is a little more difficult, but start small and it can be accomplished. Take one or two situations where you usually have negative self-talk. When those situations occur, make a concerted effort to use the reframed positive talk instead. After a while, the positive self-talk will become a habit in those situations, and then you can move on to other situations. As you succeed with each instance, the subsequent ones will become easier. You might even discuss this process with your family. They can help you be aware of the messages you send to them as well as yourself, and in the process you will be providing an excellent role model.[4]

Let's examine in greater detail how messages can be changed by looking at Tandy, who has been struggling for years with a common but difficult problem, that of being overweight.

Tandy

A homemaker and mother of four children, Tandy became increasingly overweight after the birth of her first child. Having tried and failed at every new diet, she had almost given up on looking or feeling good again. She told herself that no matter what she tried she would stay fat, that she had no willpower, and therefore she was not a worthwhile person. She began to doubt her husband's affection, even though he repeatedly said his love was not based on her appearance. He was concerned about her emotional and physical health, however, and encouraged her to change with respect to eating, exercise and, most importantly, her prevailing attitude about being unable to succeed.

Tandy received an invitation to her 15-year high school reunion and very much wanted to attend—but not looking fat. She decided to attempt one more time to change her eating and exercise patterns. But this time she knew she must also change the messages she had been telling herself about achieving her goal. Although she knew all the correct things to do to lose weight, having read and tried so many suggestions, she had never tried to change her self-talk and thereby increase her hope about becoming a thinner, healthier person.

Tandy decided to begin her program by keeping a journal in which she would record not only what she ate each day but her exercise, her weekly weight, and her thoughts and feelings as she changed her behavior. The first two days went very smoothly, and her personal messages were positive. The third day, however, was different. By mid-morning she was famished despite having eaten a good breakfast. Immediately her thoughts focused on a desire to snack, followed by "I can't do this" messages. She wrote these in her journal and thought about what else she could say to herself, as well as what else she could do. She wrote 25 times, "I can improve my eating and I can lose weight." After doing that, Tandy took the dog for a long walk, removing herself physically from any snacks. By the time Tandy got back, it was time for lunch. She felt good not only about eating a healthy lunch but about overcoming a tough bout of low-hope thinking. This scenario repeated itself many times over the next few weeks.

There were many rough periods ahead for Tandy, such as holiday meals, coffee klatches with friends who loved rich pastry, baking cookies for her children's events, and parties with huge buffets. Tandy decided to take one day at a time and not pressure herself to be perfect. One previous hope-destroying message was to tell herself she was a failure if she ate too much on occasion (or ate the wrong things). She changed this self-talk to the more hopeful message that one occasion neither spells total failure nor means she is a worthless person.

As Tandy made a conscious effort to reframe her self-talk, there were times when she felt she was just going through the motions, that she was fooling herself. As the weeks progressed, however, the higher-hope messages became more routine. She found that she was developing the habit of correcting her low-hope thoughts and no longer felt as if it were a game. Tandy found, as research supports, that changing a behavior also helps to change the accompanying feelings.

As the weeks unfolded, Tandy began to lose weight and felt more energy than she had in years. Exercise became a pleasure rather than a chore, and her cooking took on new dimensions as she explored low-fat meals. Her family was totally supportive of her efforts but did not criticize her if she ate a little more or a dessert. She still continued to keep her journal and found many new situations in which her low-hope thoughts could be reframed. She did this in the same way she had done with her weight self-talk: She recorded the negative thought, found a way to frame it in a more positive way, and then consciously corrected herself.

Creating high hope, just as losing weight, is not a speedy process. It takes time, effort, attention to detail, and a willingness to examine one's approach to life. Some people find it useful to discuss the process with a counselor, but many people can identify and change their messages alone or with the help of supportive friends and family. Once the decision to create higher hope has been made and the process begun, the positive effects will begin to snowball. We say that hope is infectious, and indeed it is. One can continue to reinfect oneself as well as others. One very compelling reason to examine self-talk, and change it if it is negative, transcends the benefits that will accrue to you. *Namely, the types of messages we give to ourselves are also the ones we give to our children.* For example, parents who face new challenges with low hope are more inclined to pass their low-hope messages on to their children when these youngsters want to try new and difficult things. Conversely, high-hope parents will give encouraging "You *can* do it" messages.

Changing messages, as we have pointed out, involves first recognizing what is being said, and then consciously changing the messages into more positive ones. It is not necessary to know the underlying reasons why one has negative messages, *but what is important is to change them.* Clinical research has shown that once the behavior, in this case the self-talk, has changed, the feelings and attitudes will follow. This process takes some time and attention to personal thoughts. It also takes the willingness to make a change in one's approach to life. It is clear, however, that once the shift in a more hopeful direction has been made, the benefits are immense. Not only will you see a difference in your own life, but you will begin to see positive changes in your children.[5]

5

Parents Instilling Stories of Hope: An Introduction

You Can

By building tales of hope for our children, we enhance and promote their well-being. Since ancient times, stories have been one of the most effective approaches for helping children understand their lives. Although reading published stories is good, telling oral stories created especially for a particular child is probably an even better way to hold a child's attention and at the same time teach important lessons of willpower and waypower. As psychologists who have worked with children, we have seen firsthand how children love stories that give them hope. Stories are not just a frill. They teach children how to live and how to cope with challenging situations. In our "high tech" age, it would be easy to lose the ancient art of storytelling. This chapter provides a model for how to reclaim this tradition.

If you have never created a children's story before, you might wonder how to make up a story, much less several stories. You may prefer to rely on a book you can read, rather than create your own narrative. Our belief, however, is that telling stories is about as difficult as learning to cook. In the beginning, you may be somewhat unsure of your skills. You may make a few mistakes, but gradually you are able to gather recipes and build a base of experience that allows you to enjoy and succeed at cooking. In this regard, parents with whom we have worked consistently report increasing their success in learning to tell stories to their children. It might be helpful for you to repeat the following litany that we use in storytelling workshops:

"I can tell a story about almost anything."
"It's not that hard."
"I think I can learn to do it."

The simple truth is that you *can* "tell a story about almost anything." For example, right now we are looking around the room and into the front yard. Everything that we see suggests a story. Here are a few examples:

- The front porch light is on—it strikes us that this would be a wonderful symbol that something new or different is going to happen. Thus, when the porch light is on, it could become a symbol that an elf is waiting outside for the child to go on some type of special adventure.
- A tree—the maple tree out front is 80 years old. A tree this old could talk to children and share stories about what it has learned looking down at the world for all those years.
- A rug—the old rug in the room might be turned into a magic carpet, which would immediately lead to a number of exciting adventure stories.
- Water—it's about to rain, which makes us think of water and the powerful symbol it has been in children's literature. We might want to tell a story about a well and how a child could gain special powers if he or she drinks from the well.
- Stormy weather—when your children are bored because of bad weather outside, you might tell them a story about a major storm. Faced with the power and destruction of a storm such as a hurricane, everyone needs to do their part to provide protection and security for themselves, each other, and their town. The metaphor of working together and being responsible for common goals comes through in this type of story.[1]

These examples only scratch the surface. The interested reader also may want to consult "how to do it" books on storytelling methods for parents in your local public library.[2]

Children are not harsh critics. They do not expect us to create a masterpiece, a Grimm's fairy tale that will stand the test of time. Rather, they want the comfort of your voice sharing with them what only you can share, and your time, attention, and involvement. Stories are nonthreatening to children. They can decide whether they want to "own" the story and incorporate the story protagonist's approach into their personal narratives.

Who's the Leader of the Band?

Let us tell you a personal story. One of the authors set out to fulfill a dream of having a family band. We'll let him continue:

Every band needs a solid guitar player, and my oldest son, who was seven at the time, seemed like the perfect candidate. Having taught guitar lessons to children in the community for a couple of years, I thought I knew how to proceed. I purchased a small guitar for a young child, and we started home lessons. I was a highly motivated teacher. This process lasted two weeks, until my once-dutiful son made it clear that he had very little interest in playing the guitar, at least at that time.

At this point, I decided that a female guitarist would be wonderful. I waited patiently until my only daughter turned seven so that she would be old enough to assume her role as the guitar player in the family band. Here again, history repeated itself—my daughter saw herself as a flutist rather than a guitar player. After playing only a few notes on the guitar, she threw herself into flute lessons.

Having learned a lesson of my own, I concluded that trying to impose my vision of things onto the children clearly did not work, and so I decided not to mention anything about musical instruments or lessons to my youngest son. For some unknown reason, however, music was the only thing that seemed to interest this boy. He simply loved music. When he was only two years old, he took a music stand apart and put a lid from a pan on top to make a cymbal. He turned the pan over to make a drum, and this was the beginning of his own home-made drum set. The next year, Santa Claus brought this budding musician a small antique mandolin banjo. He loved the banjo, but more time was spent tuning the strings than making music.

Undaunted, when this youngest son was four years old, he announced that he wanted to play "the thiddle." I assumed that the boy was far too young and would have to wait until he was older. Not wanting to wait, the youngest son said, "I want a family meeting so we can talk and talk and talk until we decide when I can get the thiddle." Family meetings were used to solve problems, so one was set. Mom and I explained that he could get a violin when he was about ten years old and could join the school orchestra. The four-year-old did not like this idea at all. He wanted to get the thiddle "right now!" We parents did not see how this was possible.

Christmas was approaching, and my son decided that he would ask Santa Claus for a violin. He explained that "Santa is a very musical person." He was sure that Santa would get him a thiddle. We were still unsure about what to do.

One day, he woke up from a nap, came down the stairs rubbing his eyes, and said to his mother, "You know, I played the thiddle long before I met you." Mom was speechless. She did not know what to say. When I heard

THIDDLE

this latest story, I knew that something had to be done. Eventually, a very small violin was located, and lessons were arranged. The rest, as they say, is history. My son loved the violin, and he learned to play it so well that we wondered if he might have actually played it "a long time ago." He now has been playing the "thiddle" for 14 years. The biggest irony of this story, however, is that he also became a guitar player. In fact, playing jazz guitar is his major passion in life.

With hindsight, the lesson of this story seems rather clear. To have a family band was dad's goal, not the children's. Thus, the story of the ill-fated family band is a good example of how not to do things. Or is it? Most stories have a silver lining. Over the years, the "thiddle" was woven into a story that the youngest son heard many times. It contributed to his sense of who he was, both as a person and a musician. This was an empowering story of hope. It helped this child to see himself as a determined and persistent music student, full of both willpower and waypower thoughts to achieve *his* goal of being a musician.

We cannot impose hope from without; rather, we need to help facilitate the hopeful goals that our children establish for themselves. The relationship between parents and children is always a dynamic one in which there must be mutual respect. Thus, the parent needs to listen to the child as well as the child being able to listen to the parent.

In this chapter we will next discuss three general categories of stories that help facilitate this process of mutual learning: stories of family roots, stories created specifically for your child, and stories where the adult and the child take turns telling the narrative.

Family Roots

As we saw in the "thiddle" story, one of the first ways to build hope in children is to tell them about events that occurred when they were too young to remember. This helps them to see their strengths and to discover their identity. Essentially, we can help our children discover how the story of their life has unfolded. As children discern their unique gifts and talents, their sense of hope about the world is being built. They become empowered to develop these gifts.

Children love to hear about the first, second, and third years of their lives. By telling them short, anecdotal stories, we help them to integrate the past into the present. For example, one of the authors often told his oldest boy, "When you decided you were ready to walk, no one could stop you. You were so proud of yourself. You walked back and forth across the living room between the two couches with the biggest smile on your face. You were only ten months old, and I was afraid you would crash into the coffee table, but you had no fear. You were strong and confident; you knew what you were doing."

By telling children stories about their own history, we help them to see how they have solved a wide variety of previous problems. This past success greatly expands their sense of hope about the future. For example, it can be very helpful for children to remember how they solved the problem of being afraid of the dark or going to kindergarten on the first day of class. Other examples include being able to cope with swimming lessons, going to the dentist, and learning to ride a tricycle or two-wheel bike. In telling these kinds of stories, we communicate themes to our children. We help them see that they were capable of focusing their goals, finding ways to achieve these goals even when there was a problem (waypower), and remaining energetic and persistent when in pursuit of their goals (willpower). Here is a story of a little girl who was determined to conquer a Halloween fear. This child, as she grew older, loved to have this story told and retold. For her, it became an example of her high hope and her courage.

Lizzie the Little Witch

When Lizzie was four years old, she announced that she was old enough to go trick or treating at the scariest house in town. The Hinckle house was indeed a frightening one, with gothic turrets on the third floor, arched windows, and a high wrought iron fence surrounding its big yard. Mr. Hinckle took great delight in decorating the house at Halloween so it looked like the site of a ghost story. All the children were just a little afraid of Mr. Hinckle because he dressed up like Dracula and made scary noises as he handed out his candy. But his candy was the best in town. He gave children full-sized candy bars, and several at a time. Lizzie had always been too frightened to go to Mr. Hinckle's door, even though she really wanted the candy. This Halloween, however, she was big and brave enough to do it.

Lizzie's mother made her a witch costume with a wig made of green yarn for hair, a tall peaked hat, and a small broomstick. On Halloween, after dark, Lizzie set out to collect candy and treats, with her mother a few steps behind. When they approached the Hinckle house Lizzie almost turned

LIZZIE THE LITTLE WITCH

away, but her courage overcame her fear and she walked right up to the big front door. The door was covered with cobwebs, and an eerie light shone from inside. Lizzie knocked on the door, which creaked open at her touch. There stood Mr. Hinckle, but he was dressed like an ordinary man.

When Lizzie said "Trick or treat," Mr. Hinckle said he would have to get the candy out of a big steamer trunk he had sitting in the entry hall. He bent over the trunk with his back to Lizzie, apparently rummaging around in its contents. When he stood up and turned around, he had an entirely different face. He had become a werewolf! Lizzie took one look at the frightening mask and gave him a sound swat on the top of his head with her broom. She turned to run out the door, but not before grabbing the two candy bars he still held in his hand.

Later, the "wicked witch's" revenge was the talk of the neighborhood. Many parents felt Mr. Hinckle had deserved the swat for being so frightening to the children. Lizzie felt extremely brave and very proud of doing what she had been so afraid to do in the past. She had set out to conquer a fear and had succeeded in doing so.

Telling Your Own Story

Another way to help children understand their history is to tell stories about yourself. Avoid the "walking through five feet of drifted snow to get to school" stories, unless you are prepared to make them humorous and allow your children to laugh and poke fun at you. A better approach is to talk about "the worst day of my life." Children love these "worst day" stories. Consider the following example: "It all started when my teacher asked me to pick up a scrap of paper. Because there was a mound of trash on top of the can, I first attempted to delicately drop the paper scrap into the can from shoulder height. When the teacher said, 'Squash the papers into the can,' the most amazing opportunity for comedy emerged. I thought that by jumping into the can, all the trash could be 'squashed' into the bottom, so that is what I did—jump into the can! Somehow, I sensed the other children would find this very funny—and they did. As soon as it happened, however, I felt sick. And numb. The teacher put me on detention for three days."

If you tell your child a similar story, you will find that she or he will be delighted to know that you actually made mistakes and survived. It is helpful for your children to hear about these times when you were foolish, impulsive, or silly. With these kinds of stories, we free our children to be themselves and to be human, rather than striving for some type of unattainable perfection. As parents, we also become more approachable when our children have problems or make mistakes.

Many people think that intimacy results only from positive, entertaining activities such as going to the movies or swimming at the beach. In our experience, intimacy often reflects a sharing of deeper and more troubling experiences. Much of the meaning of life comes from learning to cope with its many challenges. If you tell some of your "worst day" stories, you provide another piece in the puzzle that helps children to develop a model for how to be hopeful in meeting life's difficulties.

A Tale of the Little League

Besides our "worst days stories," we also might talk about challenges that must be dealt with over a period of months or even years. One of the authors likes to tell about the years when he played organized baseball. Growing up, sports were the measure of a boy; those who played were cool. Unfortunately, he was the worst player on his Little League team. The coach would yell: "Watch the ball! Hit the ball!" Unfortunately, he could hardly do this, and a foul ball was often the best that he could muster.

He could have given up, but instead he put a great deal of energy, enthusiasm, and practice into improving his baseball skills. He was hopeful because he had both a plan and the associated persistence to reach his goal. The kids in his neighborhood would throw the ball to him underhanded, as slowly as possible, so that he could hit it. His brother threw him balls, his father threw him balls, and he kept striving to improve. By the end of the year, however, he was still the worst player on the team. During his second year, he had improved some. And after three years, he could do most of the things required of Little League baseball players—but from his subjective 12-year-old perspective, he gave himself a C–. As he entered puberty, this slow improvement continued. By the time he was 15, his batting average was over .300 and it was almost impossible to strike him out! He knew how to walk like a jock and to talk like "one of the guys." At the end of the season, an informal all-star team was organized, and he was chosen as the starting second baseman. It had taken him six years to move from humiliation to relative stardom. Nothing about the process had been easy, but eventually his hard work paid off. This type of story can be helpful for children who are coping with any problem that we know will require years of effort rather than a simple, quick solution.

Gramma B

Another related way to help children understand their unique history, as we discussed in Chapter 4, is to tell them stories about relatives so that they can discover their "roots." Children take delight in hearing about their ancestors. Alex Haley's television mini-series "Roots" was phenomenally successful, in part, because people are starving for this kind of information. A child gains a very important perspective by hearing stories of the family's past. For example, consider the following intergenerational story about Gramma B:

In 1976, my 91-year-old grandmother was in a nursing home. Due to her illness, she stated this was the first presidential election in which she would not vote since women had won the right to vote in 1919. My sister, who was visiting her, marveled at the very idea that her grandmother had been present when women could not vote. "Gramma B" had lived 34 years without this right, but once the law had been changed she had then voted in 14 consecutive presidential elections. Gramma B described the intimidation suffered by women who spoke openly about their right to vote prior to the 1919 election. Indeed, she had advocated women's suffrage and had been chastised for her beliefs. Therefore, it was unthinkable to her that she would not use her right when it finally became a reality. In every subsequent election, my sister recalled this story, and it always spurred her to vote. Later, when my sister's daughter turned 18 and showed little interest in voting in the 1992 election, she was told the story of her great-grandmother. The story prompted her to see the importance of voting in a totally new light, and the vote was cast.

A story of hope keeps giving as it is passed from one generation to the next. This story helped a young woman see that she came from a family of responsible citizens who believe in democracy and participate in it. Such an experience is much more compelling than reading a school history book. Every family has its own transgenerational stories—its own themes of struggle, honoring positive values and participating in history. These stories of real people in children's families help to shape their sense of who they will eventually become. If you do not know many family stories, it will undoubtedly be a fascinating experience to talk to relatives to learn some. Stories of family roots are appropriate for children of all ages. Sometimes the very act of sharing stories from "the old days" can help an extended family come closer together. Thus, you and your child are not the only beneficiaries of this hope-inducing process.

Creating Individualized Stories

A second way to build tales of hope is to tell stories created for a specific child. Warning: If you begin to make up stories, your children may be so interested in these tales that they will begin to ask for them virtually every day. Our advice, however, is to relax, believe in yourself, and see that you are capable of rising to this challenge. Most importantly, remember that children love to hear these stories. For example, one of our workshop participants began to tell stories to his four-year-old son. One year later, the child's smile lights up the room when he knows he is going to hear a "told story." This youngster always has enjoyed stories from books, but now he much prefers the oral stories made up by his father.

The major reason for learning to tell stories is that your child is unique. You know which problem or developmental issue your child is facing at any point in time, and you are in the best position to know how to help; no book can adequately meet the diverse needs we see in specific children. One child is afraid to play in the backyard alone; another child of the same age needs to learn self control to keep from running wildly in the street. One child is a fussy eater; the next literally eats you out of house and home. Parents can search for books on these topics, or they can learn to trust their intuitions to create stories that are individualized to meet their children's special needs. We have seen more success with the second approach.

Try to create fun and entertaining tales for your children about 90 percent of the time. This leaves about 10 percent of your storytelling to be more problem focused. One point here is that parents should not spend all of their time trying to help their children. There is absolutely nothing wrong, however, with telling entertaining stories on a regular basis. These stories help to keep the child's interest and to make them more attentive to the stories dealing with challenging personal issues.

Five Simple Steps

At this point we introduce a simple five-step process for creating stories to tell your children. In looking back at the hundreds of stories that we have told over the years, they typically employ the five following steps:[3]

1. Introduce the main character(s).
2. Tell about the problem.
3. Talk to a wise person.
4. Try out a new approach.
5. Summarize the lesson.

Imagine that you are ready to begin your first story. This is how you might think about developing the plot using the five steps listed above.

Step 1: Introduce the Main Character(s).   This is an easy way to get started. Explain where the character lives and briefly describe the setting. It helps if you choose a name that is very similar to the name of your own child. Examples would include "Austini" for "Austin," "Ambeguda" for "Amber," or "Torzo" for "Tor." You might say something like, "You won't believe it, but Austini is a lot like you." Then proceed to note the central character's hair, eyes, size, and age. These, of course, are described as being very similar or identical to your child. You also may talk about other characteristics that the hero (or heroine) has in common with the child listening to the story (e.g., being very active, having a younger sister, living in a big city, living on a farm, and so on). Thus, to tell the first part of the story, you simply need to create an appealing character with whom the child can identify.

Step 2: Tell About the Problem.   Children need to know their problem is not totally pervasive. Let the child know that the main character in the story is lovable and has many admirable strengths but has this one problem that is not getting better. For example, the child learns that the main character is having a problem with toilet accidents or is getting into frequent fights with siblings, and so on. It helps if the story provides some dramatic exaggeration of the problem to highlight the child's understanding of his or her predicament. The child in the story has a goal but has encountered a significant roadblock.

Step 3: Talk to a Wise Person.   Because the problem is not getting better, the main character (generally with their supportive caregiver involved) goes to see a wise person in order to get some assistance. The wise person totally accepts the child and gives unconditional love. This person shows support and understanding for the problem while also providing the child with a new way of thinking or acting that may be helpful. For example, the wise woman or man might say it is important to "remember what you *can* do rather than what you cannot do," or "a little boy could *never—ever— ever* be the boss of his parents." A sense of mystery or intrigue provides a nice touch for the wise person. Thus, the family might call upon a "wise man" or a "wise grandmother" who lives in a magic tree house or a stone hut high on top of a mountain. The wise person is special.

Step 4: Try Out a New Approach. In this section, the lead character generally thinks a great deal about what the wise person has said. He or she begins to explore flexible plans and strategies (waypower) in order to evaluate them. The main character is curious enough to look at the issue from different perspectives. Willpower lessons related to increasing persistence may be learned. This section of the story basically tells the child that the hero listened closely to what the wise person said and here is what happened. Instead of receiving a lecture, the story character learns through actual experience.

Step 5: Summarize the Lesson. A good story has enough repetition to highlight the hope lesson in a clear manner. A happy ending helps to amplify the impact of this lesson. After the story ends, you may give the child a chance to ask questions, make comments, or give alternative suggestions.

At this point, a real-life intervention for your child now can begin. Parents or teachers may want to refer to the story during the week whenever it is appropriate. If the child is beginning to have a temper tantrum you might say, "Oh-Oh! We should probably remember what happened to Tommy in the story." At times, you might use only a prompt or cue, such as mentioning the name of the character ("Remember Austini") or providing a code word to help the child remember an important point. Sometimes you pose a question such as, "I wonder what the wise man would do now?" These are all ways to have the story continue to be prominent in the child's thinking in real-world situations where it is important to remember the salient details.

The above description provides an outline for how you might tell any story. It is a generic pattern that can be utilized in many different ways. In the next section, we will look at an actual story reduced to the bare essentials in order to further illustrate this process.

The Story of Susie Q

This is a simple narrative about a little girl who dawdled in the morning and was late for preschool; in turn, her mother was late for work. The story is divided into the five-step process.

Step 1: Introduce the Main Character(s). Once upon a time there was a little girl name Susie Q. Susie Q was four years old, and she was a wonderful little girl. In fact, she had blonde hair and blue eyes just like you. Stand up and let me see how tall you are (the adult then puts a hand over the

Susie Q

child's head and measures her height). Yes, as a matter of fact, Susie Q was just about the same size as you. She had a wonderful smile, and she loved to play and laugh and have fun all through the day.

Step 2: Tell About the Problem. The only problem was that Susie Q had a very hard time getting ready to go to her preschool. She did not want to get dressed, and she was never ready to eat her breakfast. It seemed like she would never brush her teeth or comb her hair unless her mother reminded her again and again. Both Susie Q and her mother usually were very grumpy in the morning. Getting ready for preschool was not much fun.

Step 3: Talk to a Wise Person. Susie Q's mother decided to talk to a wise grandmother who lived in their neighborhood. This grandma was the cleverest person in the whole town. She seemed to be able to figure out almost everything. The wise grandma held Susie Q on her lap and listened to the whole story. Then the grandma said, "Susie Q, if you don't want to get dressed, don't do it. If you don't want to brush your teeth, don't do it. If you don't want to eat, don't. If you don't want to comb your hair, don't. Try it out and let's see what happens."

Step 4: Try Out a New Approach. The next day Susie Q's mother used the ideas the wise grandma had given them. She said if Susie Q did not want to get dressed for preschool, she could wear her pajamas. If she did not want to brush her teeth, she didn't have to! If she was not ready to eat breakfast, she could skip breakfast, or perhaps she could eat her oatmeal at the last minute in the car. Further, Susie Q did not have to comb her hair *unless this was what she wanted.*

Susie Q smiled. She was very happy. She thought it would be wonderful to do whatever she wanted, and she decided that she would not put on her clothes, brush her teeth, comb her hair, or eat her breakfast for that matter. When Susie Q did just as she had planned, her mother smiled and seemed very calm. Mom was not at all worried. When it was time to go, she put Susie Q's clothes in a paper sack and asked her daughter if she would like some oatmeal to eat in the car. Susie Q ate some of the oatmeal, but it was cold and felt like an ice cube in her stomach. When she got to preschool, some of the other kids looked at Susie Q in a funny way because she still had on her pajamas. One of her girlfriends said Susie Q's mouth smelled like "dragon breath." Another of her friends said her "ratty hair" did not look very nice. Susie Q did not feel so good. She wasn't very happy about being free to do whatever she wanted to do. In fact, she felt miserable.

Step 5: Summarize the Lesson. The next day Susie Q decided to try something different. She put on her clothes as quickly as she could. She ran down for breakfast and gave her mom a big smile. She loved eating her nice, hot oatmeal, and she was quick to brush her teeth after she was finished. She asked her mother if they could braid her hair in a special style. When Susie Q went to preschool that day, she was so happy. Everyone told her how nice her hair looked, and no one said her breath smelled like "dragon breath." Her breakfast felt nice and warm in her stomach. Susie Q was so proud of herself! She felt like a big girl. And that was the story about the time Susie Q decided to get herself ready for preschool because she didn't like cold oatmeal, dragon breath, or ratty hair.

This story is borrowed from the mother of a client. This mother was given a kernel of an idea, and she then told the above story to her daughter. As you might imagine, the daughter was fascinated by the story and listened closely. She did not need to have a sad day at preschool with cold oatmeal in her stomach, dragon breath, or ratty hair. She got herself ready the next day and reportedly has been doing so ever since. She was able to learn the lesson without going through the actual experience. This is an excellent example of how stories can engender hope in children. The real "Susie Q" was able to set *her own goal* of getting ready in the morning. The story helped the little girl develop a plan for achieving this goal (way-power) and the motivation necessary to achieve it (willpower). Further, the little girl apparently sufficiently identified with Susie Q that she "owned" this as part of her personal self-narrative.

Parents often find it helpful to use the same main character for most of their therapeutic stories. Children love routines, and this makes it easy for them to get to know a character very well. In this process, of course, they also are getting to know themselves better. Thus, if you have a daughter (or son, for that matter) like Susie Q, you could routinely tell "Susie Q stories."

If your main character lives in the jungle, have him or her travel occasionally to visit cousins around the world. The main character could have relatives who live in Alaska, Canada, Mexico, and so on. Thus, your stories become a wonderful integration of social studies, psychology, philosophy, and racial and gender mixtures, as well as spiritual values. If possible, try to start and end the stories in the same way wherever possible. The beginning gives a picture of what will happen ("This is the story about the time Susie Q went to visit her Eskimo cousins who lived in snow houses in the far north of Canada."). The ending has a familiar ring that might go something like this: "And that was the time Susie Q learned how to walk with her mother in the store without having to go out to the car for a break." In this way, one can develop a whole series of stories with the same main character, a routine beginning and a familiar ending.

The prescriptive remedy of your story should be grounded in the theory of hope that has been described previously in this book (see especially Chapters 1 and 2). Accordingly, ask yourself questions such as those listed below:

- What would a hopeful person do in this type of circumstance?
- What goal does the hero want to achieve?
- What kinds of flexible plans will be required to move closer to the goal (waypower)?
- What type of commitment is necessary to use the plans to reach this goal (willpower)?

As the hero of the story talks with the wise person, possible answers to the above questions are discussed. Gradually, a coherent plan unfolds, and energy is applied to that plan. This provides the basic content of your story.

You now know how to create a tale of hope. Stories using this five-step process are most appropriate for children in the three-to-eight-year age range. We will close this chapter with a description of an additional technique for creating stories. It is easily applied and very popular with children.

Turn-Taking

Our final approach for telling a story involves starting with absolutely no idea in mind except to allow the child to help tell the story. We call this process "turn-taking."[4] The only rules for this turn-taking process are the following:

1. Say the first thing that comes into your mind.
2. Trust the process; it will actually work.
3. When either the parent or the child cannot think of anything else to say (or merely because they would like to give their partner a chance), simply point to the other person and it is now his or her turn to continue.

These kinds of stories can be fascinating. They often give us a tremendous insight into the thought processes and, occasionally, some of the obstacles that are blocking a child's thinking about goals. Consider a recent example involving a delightful young girl who was quite fearful at night. Neither the therapist nor the girl had any idea what form their story might take, but here is the resulting creation.

THERAPIST: Once upon a time there was a . . .

CHILD: dragon.

THERAPIST: And this dragon decided to take a walk. As he was walking down a path, he saw a . . .

CHILD: baby bear.

THERAPIST: The dragon was all ready to scare the baby bear . . .

CHILD: but the baby bear said it was a magic bear that could change itself into anything it wanted to be, and it would eat the dragon if the dragon wasn't nice.

THERAPIST: The dragon and the magic bear became friends, walking along the path until they saw . . .

CHILD: an eagle.

THERAPIST: The dragon said it would scare the eagle . . .

CHILD: but the eagle said it would pluck out the eyes of the dragon if the dragon tried to scare it.

THERAPIST: Then the eagle became a friend of the dragon and the baby bear. Finally, as the three animals were walking along, they saw . . .

CHILD: an ant.

THERAPIST: The dragon was happy, because at last he had found something to scare . . .

CHILD: but the ant said it was a fire ant. The ant said it would light the dragon on fire if it tried to scare it. Then the dragon, the baby bear, the eagle, and the ant all became friends.

THERAPIST: As the dragon, the baby bear, the eagle, and the ant were walking along, they saw two very scary monsters. The monsters said, . . .

CHILD: "We are going to eat you." But the eagle flew into the air and said it would pluck out the eyes of the monsters. The fire ant said it would land on the monsters and burn them. The baby bear said she would turn herself into a scarier monster. The dragon began huffing and puffing and blowing fire out of its nostrils. Then the monsters were scared and ran away.

THERAPIST: The dragon, the baby bear, the eagle, and the fire ant all laughed and joined hands in a circle. They sang and danced and played, feeling very safe that no monsters would ever be able to harm them again. And that was the story about the day the dragon made three special friends, and they all learned how to scare the monsters away.

As soon as the therapist completed this story, he felt hope for this young girl. She had many resources for coping with fears.

The turn-taking format may be good for days when you are tired and not feeling particularly creative. This approach works particularly well for children between the ages of five and ten. If your child is pestering you for a story on these days, it is an excellent opportunity to say that you are willing to tell a story if the child is willing to help. Because there is little pressure involved in this technique, most children love the approach, and with practice they grow in confidence. Interestingly, this turn-taking approach also inherently trades on the concepts of hope theory. One reason for this is that such stories, while exceedingly creative, do not ramble on in a totally goal-less fashion. Children know that stories, like life, lead toward goals or end points. When one of these end points is reached, the parent can stop and review how the goal has been reached, emphasizing the pathways that were taken (waypower) and the manner in which the protagonist became energized to use these pathways (willpower). Then, the parent can close by asking how the story may relate to the child's own self-narrative.

Stories as Hopeful Blueprints

The storytelling techniques described in this chapter provide blueprints for creating hopeful tales for your children. These kinds of stories typically teach children that goals can be established and achieved. They encourage waypower thinking by having children try out options in order to evaluate the outcome, and they provide clear models for flexible problem solving to overcome impediments. Finally, the heroes of the stories exemplify willpower in that they do not give up; moreover, they are courageous in that they manage to get themselves started and continue in their quests. These heroes bring to life our concept of hope.

Now that you are familiar with the basic process of creating hopeful tales, it is time to apply these skills to help children with a variety of common developmental issues. This will be the focus of our next chapter.

6

Parents Building Stories of Hope: Normal Problems

*O*UR CHILDREN NEED HOPE-FILLED STORIES to instruct them in coping with life's difficulties. In the first part of this chapter, we examine common problems such as picky eating, bedtime difficulties, sibling rivalries, social conflicts, and fears that can be dealt with through stories.[1] In the second part of the chapter, we discuss how stories can be used to find new goals, waypower, willpower, and self-acceptance. The many story examples are meant to provide general ideas that you can then individualize for your particular situation. Although some of our examples come out of our experiences with clients, we emphasize that it does not take a mental health professional to implement these. Parents are admirably equipped to use the approaches we outline for instilling stories of hope.

Common Problems

Some problems are so frequent that anyone with children will probably encounter them. How many of the subsequent issues have visited your family?

Picky Eaters

We have had many experiences with so-called picky eaters. It is amazing to see the lengths to which parents will go in order to coax such children to eat. Meanwhile, the kids are yelling and screaming, and the situation approaches hand-to-hand conflict. In such situations there often is a vicious circle, that is, the more the parent tries to get the child to eat, the more the child resists. Does this sound familiar? In these kinds of situations, a particular story might have some benefit.

One of our favorite finicky eater stories is about a little girl named Tori. She hated pizza, tacos, and almost everything else, except for sweets. A wise woman named Mrs. Hartwell came to visit the family, bringing snacks for everyone. However, the glass she filled for Tori only had a tablespoon of juice in it, and Tori's piece of cookie was the size of a fingernail! Tori got angry. She liked apple juice and cookies and wanted more of each. Mrs. Hartwell said she was sorry, but she did not think Tori would like "cowboy cookies" made of oatmeal and nuts. Further, Mrs. Hartwell said the apple juice was squeezed from apples that had very little sugar. Tori tried the juice and decided it did taste a little funny. When she found a small piece of nut in her cookie, she stomped her foot and ran out. Mrs. Hartwell helped Tori's parents to see that "Tori should eat because she is hungry, not because we want to fatten her up." Tori's parents started to give their daughter only very small bites of food. They gave her a magnifying glass so she could see the tiny pieces on her plate.[2]

Because the old dance had been changed, Tori began to beg and plead to have more food. Now she had an appropriate goal, which was to take care of her own hunger. As she established new eating patterns to work toward her goal, Tori was able to solve her own problem (waypower), and her sense of enthusiasm for eating was enhanced (willpower) because this was *her* goal. As Tori's hope grew, so too did her parents' hope increase.

Bedtime Difficulties

Given that this is such a common problem, we will offer three story possibilities.

A Monster Under the Bed.   In this story, an adorable little girl named Greta develops a fear about monsters under her bed. She tells her kindergarten friends about the problem during show-and-tell at school. The children want to see the monsters. Greta decides to invite them to her house for a sleep-over so that her friends can see the monsters and perhaps help her to figure out what to do about them.

On the first night, the children sit on Greta's bed and wait. When they hear creaking and groaning sounds in the house, they slowly lean over the bed to peak at the monsters. All that her friends can see are some cobwebs and an itsy-bitsy spider. Greta tells her friends that they each need to go to

GRETA

the eye doctor to get glasses so they can see better. Then they can come back the next night to see the monsters.

On the second night, the same scenario unfolds and the children look with their new glasses, but all they see are cobwebs and the tiny spider scurrying across the floor. Greta decides it must be too dark to see, so she tells the children to return the next night with flashlights.

On the third night, the children shine their flashlights under the bed, but again all they see are cobwebs and the itsy-bitsy spider. Greta had thought the monsters were having a party under her bed, but they could not be found. The children laughed and laughed about looking so hard but not being able to find the monsters. Finally, they went to sleep as Greta realized she had lost the fear that had kept her awake. Her playful interactions with peers had revived her hope in solving life's difficulties. This story not only highlights the importance of humor in helping to sustain hope, but it also reveals that friends can be wonderfully helpful for building hope.

The Dream Girl. This second story involves a different type of bedtime problem. The heroine was Katie, a bouncy little girl who was full of energy. Katie loved to jump, climb, hop, and swing. Late at night, when Katie's parents were tired and ready for bed, Katie was still going strong. Katie's parents eventually took their daughter to see Katie's grandmother, who lived down the street. Grandma told Katie that she had not yet learned about all the exciting, fun adventures that she could have after she went to bed and began to dream. Her grandmother told her, "You can go anywhere, do anything, and see everything that you want to see." Grandma helped to stir Katie's imagination toward the magic of dreams.

Grandma told Katie about some of her dreams that related to flying bicycles and secret treasures that could only be seen during a dream. Grandma helped Katie look forward to going to bed so she could have fun, exciting dreams. Katie's grandmother told her that it took practice to remember dreams. Katie learned to lie quietly in her bed each morning before she got up so she could remember the dreams and then tell her grandmother about them later in the day. Katie began to look forward to bedtime. It was her time to let her mind go free so that she could "go anywhere, do anything, and see everything." Now Katie had a new goal for bedtime—wanting to be able to dream. Because she was committed to pursuing this goal (willpower), she eventually learned how to get to sleep (waypower).

Unhappy Children in Disguises.   A third bedtime tale called "The Untold Story of the Monsters and the Cupcake" is borrowed from psychologists Joyce Mills and Richard Crowley.[3] In this story, the child is told that monsters are really "make-believe disguises for unhappy children who had no friends." These unhappy children tried to make friends, but everyone ignored them. No one would give them any attention. They went off by themselves and felt bad until they figured out they could get lots of attention by putting on their disguises and scaring children. Eventually, the hero of the story feels sorry for the unhappy children (that is, monsters) and leaves them a cupcake at night. In this process, the poor monsters eventually make friends with the hero of the story.

The beauty of this story is that it gives parents a new approach to their children when fear is being experienced. Rather than always trying to calm the child down or provide reassurance, parents can instead refer to the story. With a twinkle in her eye, the parent can remind the child of the story of the cupcakes and suggest that she go downstairs and get some cookies and cupcakes to lay out for the monsters who are feeling so sad. Using this technique, the child's view of monsters is altered significantly. In terms of hope, the goal still is to go to sleep, but the child can apply himself or herself to this goal (willpower) because of assurances that the monster is not so bad and actually is more interested in eating cookies than kids (waypower).

As these various stories attest, numerous opportunities for hope unfold as the child begins to explore new options in the bedtime routine.

Sibling Rivalry

Sibling conflicts are normal and present in virtually all families with two or more children. An only child has a very clear role (i.e., "the baby"). When a new baby arrives, however, the role of the first child is dramatically changed. Instead of having his or her needs readily tended to, the first child encounters the parents' ministrations to the newborn as an interference in the old and cherished routine of attention. This often will lead to jealousy and strong emotional reactions. Children need support from parents to know that these feelings are normal, but they also need guidance in order to move past these feelings and to rediscover (regain hope) that their desires can be met. The following two stories provide guidance for such matters.

Brothers. Imagine, if you will, two brothers named Frankie and Harry, who spend most of their time fighting with each other. (It helps here to go into great detail describing how they scratch, bite, kick, and so on.) The boys are eventually taken to see their grandfather, a kindly old gentleman named Papa. Papa takes the boys for a long hike to watch mountain goats butting their heads against one other. He says very little, but eventually Papa tells the boys, "You're not mountain goats, boys. You're not mountain goats."

The children keep hearing this phrase go through their mind. They ask Papa to explain it, and he gives them a very powerful picture of brothers learning to talk with each other to resolve conflicts and help each other in life. The boys go to visit their grandfather each week for a whole year, and they begin to learn to be brothers.

The kinds of details you supply in this kind of story could be taken from your own experiences or from those of friends or relatives where sibling relationships were eventually resolved in a positive manner. An important parenting goal in this process is to move away from the role of being the "judge" who needs to hear the case of the embattled protagonists in order to give some kind of ruling. Once children are of school age, they can begin to resolve difficulties by themselves; several "Frankie and Harry" stories could be devised in order to provide examples of how to do this with specific problems (e.g., fighting over which television program to watch, arguing about one child disturbing something in the other child's room, and so on).

Children who chronically fight with each other have the misdirected goal of winning the battle against their siblings. The Frankie and Harry kind of story suggests a new model. There is no battle to win. The new hope-related goals of the protagonists are directed toward living cooperatively and being friends. In this context, hope can blossom once again. The goals can be shared, fulfilled for one sibling followed by the next in turn. The net result is cooperative thinking in which the needs of both siblings are met.[4] In this instance, the mere act of reworking the goals serves to unleash associated waypower and willpower thinking.

Kateroo and Mariboo. This example comes from a mother who requested help for her three-year-old daughter. The mother had given birth to a second child, and the older girl became very jealous. For several weeks, the three-year-old frequently had been biting her baby sister. Naturally, the parents were frustrated and confused about what to do. The older girl had heard many times that she was not supposed to bite her sister, but this admonition did not seem to improve matters.

A story can help even a three-year-old understand some of these psychological dynamics. The story devised for this case involved a mama bear, a papa bear, and a baby bear named Kateroo. Kateroo was the nicest, most wonderful little baby bear. She was very smart and loved her life until her new baby sister named Mariboo came along. Kateroo did not like her new sister because Mama bear was always holding Mariboo and feeding and playing with her. Kateroo didn't have anyone to hold her or feed her or play with her. She became very sad. She didn't like those sad feelings, and she started to get mad at Mariboo. She decided she would do something to make Mariboo go away and not bother her anymore. So, Kateroo began to bite Mariboo as hard as she could. Mama bear and Papa bear did not like this biting, but they did not know what to do to help Kateroo stop hurting her sister.

Finally, Mama bear and Papa bear took Kateroo to see her wise Grandma bear. Grandma bear told Kateroo she was going to tell her two secrets so Kateroo would be able to get over this problem of biting Mariboo. First, Grandma bear whispered in Kateroo's ear and told her it was never, ever, ever, ever, ever, ever okay to bite another bear, because her teeth were too sharp and too strong. Then Grandma bear said she would teach Kateroo how to bite on huckleberries, how to catch fish and eat them for dinner, and how to climb to the top of a tree to get honey to eat. Thus, the first secret was that Kateroo could go to "bear school," where Grandma bear would teach her what she *could* bite.

Next, Grandma bear asked if Mama and Papa bear were playing with little Kateroo. They said they were so busy that they did not have time. Grandma bear said that Mama bear and Papa bear had to spend some special time every day with Kateroo. Grandma bear then whispered that the second secret involved Kateroo and her parents doing some very fun things together.

Kateroo liked the new attention she was receiving. She learned the lesson about what she could bite and what she could not bite. If she forgot and bit Mariboo, she was taken out to the kitchen to chew on some cereal rather than given a lecture. Eventually, Kateroo went for two weeks without biting Mariboo, and all of the animals in the forest had a big party to celebrate Kateroo's growth and success.[5]

Fortunately, the real three-year-old girl who heard this story went through a nearly identical process. Her needs for love and security had been threatened by the very presence of a baby sister. The story taught the older sister how to cope with her sibling. She also learned how to find new pathways to meet her basic needs (waypower) and how to apply herself to those pathways (willpower). Such stories of hope help children fulfill their desires and to do so in a manner that respects the needs of the other people around them.

Social Conflicts

Benito II. All children come into conflict with other people. Sometimes they are teased and harassed by other children. In these cases, we find it helpful to use the tale of a very inventive boy named Benito.

Benito lives next door to a scientific wizard named Einstein. Together, Benito and Einstein create a life-sized robot named "Benito II." Benito II is a wonderful robot that can do many things. It has several dials and controls. On the back of Benito II, however, is a large button that can activate all of Benito II's movements at the same time. This causes Benito II to go "wild and crazy" (it helps here to gesture and demonstrate what Benito II looks like in this scenario). Einstein cautions Benito to not let anyone push the big button on the back of Benito II.

Benito takes his robot to school. The other children are fascinated by Benito II. Eventually, one of them discovers the forbidden button. Soon, everyone begins to sneak up and push the button in order to see Benito II go completely out of control. Benito is beside himself. The other children are wrecking his robot. Eventually he takes Benito II back to Einstein and they disconnect the wires so that this button will no longer work. When Benito takes his robot to school the next day, the children continue to push the button many times until they see that it will no longer work. Eventually, they begin to play with Benito II in a more appropriate manner.

This metaphor can be very helpful when children are in a situation where someone is "pushing their button." Oftentimes children in these situations "erupt like a volcano." The story of Benito II helps them see how they can disconnect their button and no longer overreact. It is nice to have someone as smart as Einstein to rekindle our hope by using creative waypower.

Tojo and the Rap Music Rules. A second story idea for dealing with relationship problems involves learning basic conflict resolution skills. These can be woven into many stories, but one favorite involves a boy named Tojo who loves rap music.[6] Tojo and a wise man work out some rules to help children solve social conflicts at school. Tojo sets the rules to rap music and they go like this:

1. "Use my name, but don't take it in vain!"
2. "Say how you feel and then we'll get real!"

3. "Say what you want like the wise man said, or the refs will show
   you the light that's red."

In the above scenario, the children have peer referees to help them learn
to talk about how they feel and what will help them feel better. If they engage in name-calling or attacking kinds of comments, the referees hold up
a red circle that signals they have broken the rules.

To make this story come to life, all that is needed are a few examples of
common school problems. One possibility we have used involved a child,
Brandon, who was excluded from play activities with a group led by Andy.
When Brandon initially talks with his antagonist, he is angry and tells
Andy, "You are so mean. I hate you!"

The referees merely hold up their red circles. They do not tell Brandon
what to say, however. The wise man can provide some mediation suggestions, such as, "Brandon, I wonder if you could tell Andy what would help
you to feel better."

In this way, the children learn to talk to each other in a more reasonable
manner and to brainstorm solutions and compromises to their problems.
In our story of Brandon and Andy, the eventual agreement is that Brandon
will be allowed to participate in the group activities, but he must "Play fair,
not bother everyone, and follow the rules." Then everyone can feel good
about the outcome. Conflict resolution may be best conceptualized as two
parties agreeing to devote their combined energies toward a common goal.
In this context, both sides can share hope. Indeed, there is a strong communal quality to hope.

Fears

It is very common for children to develop fears and anxiety in response to
challenging situations. For example, children may be afraid to put their
head in the water when taking swimming lessons. They may be afraid of
the first day of school. They may be attacked by a vicious dog and become
afraid of dogs. If they are in a car accident, they may be afraid to ride in an
automobile again. In such cases, we have found that it is useful to tell a
story that involves a very simple desensitization type of format. In the beginning of the story, the child is able to go to a trusted wise person to talk
about their feelings. Next, the child begins a hopeful journey in which he
or she gradually works through the fear using real-life experiences. For example, if a child is afraid of water and swimming, the hero of the story
might go through a progression such as the following:

1. Sitting in a chair next to the pool.
2. Sitting on the flat surface next to the pool.

3. Being able to touch the water with a toe.
4. Leaving that toe in the water for one minute.
5. Putting one whole foot in the water.
6. Putting two feet in the water.
7. Sitting in the water up to the waist.
8. Sitting in the water up to the chest.
9. Walking in the shallow water, and so on.

A similar process can be used to help children begin to cope effectively with a variety of other common fears. In our experience, a story is the best way to teach this progression to children in order to inspire them to follow the hero's example of perseverance, as small steps are taken to achieve the long-range goal. Further, it should be noted that our research on high-hope people reveals that they also employ this one-step-at-a-time approach to achieving their goals.[7] Indeed, the segmenting of long-term goals into small steps appears to be an essential aspect of waypower thinking. It has the added willpower bonus of increasing a child's willingness to get moving toward the goal because success can be experienced at each step, giving encouragement to continue, rather than beginning with a task that seems so large as to be impossible to accomplish.

Using the Components of Hope

In this half of the chapter, we will move away from specific problems and teach you how to use the components of hope more generally in the stories of children.

Finding a New Goal

The Story of Caitlyn. Caitlyn loved her Grammy almost more than she loved anybody else. Her Grammy was very old; she was Nana's mother, and Nana was Mama's mother. Her Grammy couldn't play ball with her, or ride bikes down to the river, or climb the apple tree on the edge of the cornfield, but she could tell wonderful stories and sing wonderful songs, and Caitlyn loved to just sit in her lap and rock.

Grammy always sat right next to the woodstove in her big wooden rocker because it seemed like she was always cold. She said it was because she was getting old, and her bones were hard and cold, but Caitlyn still thought she was snugly and soft.

One day when Caitlyn was sitting with Grammy, Mama came and sat with them. She was knitting something a beautiful shade of blue.

CAITLYN

"What's that, Mama?" asked Caitlyn.

"This is a blanket for the baby your Aunt Tina's expecting," said Mama. "He will be born in November, and it will be cold, so he will need lots of soft, pretty things to keep him warm."

When Caitlyn was in bed later that night, she thought of the pretty blue blanket and said to herself, "Grammy could use a warm, soft pretty blanket, too. She could wrap it around her, or put it over her legs to keep warm. I'll bet I could learn to knit and make a blanket for Grammy!"

The next morning, Caitlyn asked, "Mama, could you teach me to knit so I could knit a blanket for Grammy?"

"Why, Caitlyn, I think that's a lovely idea. Knitting is not so difficult, if you use simple stitches. I think it would be easy for you to learn. Maybe instead of an elaborate pattern, you could use a really pretty yarn," suggested Mama. "Then the plain stitches would show off the yarn better. Why don't you go with me this afternoon, and we'll look for something special."

So Caitlyn went into town with Mama to look at the different yarns, and almost immediately she saw the exact one she wanted. It had very many colors, like a rainbow, but they were soft gentle colors, a blue like the sky, a pink like a rose, a pale, pale yellow. Here and there among the yarn was a tiny silver sparkle, as if someone had thrown a handful of stars into the rainbow. And the yarn was soft and fuzzy, too. In some ways it seemed like Grammy.

"This is the one I want, Mama. Grammy will like this one!" she pronounced.

"That yarn is very expensive, Caitlyn," replied Mama. I don't know if we can afford it." Mama thought for a while. "Well, we won't have to buy knitting needles, because you can use some of mine. If I buy this yarn for you, will you feed the chickens for me this summer? That way, I can give you part of the egg money to pay me back."

Caitlyn hated feeding the chickens because they smelled bad and pecked at her. But she thought of how beautiful Grammy would look wrapped in her new blanket, and she knew she had to do it.

When they got home, Mama showed Caitlyn how to start the blanket. Caitlyn worked hard the first week. Many times she had to unravel what she had knitted because she made a mistake. Sometimes she was tempted to just leave the mistake in, but then she thought of Grammy and how much she loved her, and how she wanted her blanket to be perfect. So Caitlyn carefully unraveled her mistakes and reknit the yarn. At the end of two weeks, she had her first square. Mama showed her how to finish it, which was called "casting off," and Caitlyn held the tiny blanket in her hand. It was soft and fluffy, with big loop stitches and beautiful melting colors. Caitlyn was so excited. But she had 29 more squares to make!

Caitlyn worked harder. Sometimes it was difficult, because she didn't want her knitting to take away from her time spent with Grammy. But she didn't want Grammy to see what she was doing, either. She faithfully fed the chickens for Mama, although she never got used to the smell, and summer passed by quickly.

When Caitlyn had finished her ninth square, she ran out of yarn.

"Mama, I need to go back to town with you and get some more yarn," she said.

"Caitlyn, I don't have any money to buy more yarn," said her mother. "You will need four more skeins of yarn. I think you'd better talk to Daddy about this."

Caitlyn explained the situation to her father.

"Caitlyn, that's a lot of money. But you're doing a good thing for Grammy, and I do need someone to help me feed the new calves. If you will feed them for the rest of the summer, I will pay you the amount of money you need to buy the yarn."

Caitlyn didn't mind feeding the calves. They were sweet, with big brown eyes, and rough, pink tongues. She agreed to feed them, and Daddy gave her the money.

The next day Caitlyn and Mama went to town. They went back to the fabric store, and Caitlyn looked for her yarn. She couldn't find it anywhere!

Caitlyn spoke to the sales clerk. "I'm looking for some more yarn like I bought about three months ago. It has a lot of soft pretty colors and a little tiny silver thread running through it. It was right here!"

"Oh yes, I know just the one you mean. It has been discontinued by the manufacturer. We just had a little left in stock and now it's all gone. We won't be able to get any more."

Caitlyn couldn't believe her ears. What was she going to do? She walked out of the store in shock, and when she got home, she went to her room, threw herself on the bed, and cried.

After she had cried until she had the hiccups, Caitlyn sat up and began to reconsider the problem. The main thing was to make something warm for Grammy and to do it herself. She thought about using a plain color of yarn for the other squares and putting the pretty colored squares in as accents. That idea didn't sound too good. It seemed sort of second best.

She got up from the bed, got the squares out of the drawer where she kept them hidden, and laid them on the bed, trying to think of a solution. They were so beautiful! Tears welled up in her eyes as she thought of Grammy and the beautiful blanket that never would be. All of a sudden she had an idea. She laid the squares end-to-end and then ran to get Mama.

"Look, Mama, what if I stitched the squares together like this?" she asked. "Then this could be a scarf for Grammy's neck. I could knit her a blanket out of some other yarn."

"This would be a wonderful scarf, said Mama. "Just think how pretty these colors will look next to Grammy's face and with her soft white hair. I think that's a great idea, and I will help you do it."

So Caitlyn and Mama stitched the squares together end-to-end, and Caitlyn carefully wrapped the scarf for Grammy's birthday.

Grammy was so thrilled when she saw it. And she did look beautiful with it wrapped around her neck. Best of all for Grammy, it was very, very warm. But best of all for Caitlyn was that she had made it herself!

The New Goal in Review.   This story and ones like it show the importance of flexibility in reworking one's desires when the original goals are no longer possible. High-hope children appear to know when persistence in the pursuit of a truly unreachable goal is folly. In this sense, high-hope children are smart investors of their time and attentions, and they find an alternative goal that meets their needs.

Waypower and Problem-Solving

At this point, we would like to share a generic story that can be used to help children solve a wide variety of life's challenges. The basic plot line for the story is that two children go to visit a wise woman (or man) because they are trying to solve a problem. The wise woman tells them that she has hidden a golden key. If the children can find the key, they will be able to solve their problem. The children have to search very hard until they find the key. When they take the key back to the wise woman, she lets them open up an old wooden treasure chest that sits on her dining-room table. Inside are three golden P's.[8] The wise woman says, "These three P's will help you solve your problems."

P_1 On the back of the first P are the words, "What is the problem?
P_2 On the back of the second P is the question, "What are all your
  possibilities?

P₃ On the back of the third P, the children read, "Pick one and try it out. See if it will work!"

Next, the wise woman has the children try out the three P's by looking for a coin that has been hidden by something made of wood. The wise woman asks if they want to give up, but they are quick to shout, "No—never!" The children think of all the possibilities and eventually solve the problem on their fifth attempt. The wise woman helps them see that this is how they can solve problems in life. If they keep trying and do not give up, they can think of all the possibilities and eventually pick the best one to solve their problem. The three golden P's stay in the wise woman's treasure chest, but the children are able to take them home in their minds and use them forever.[9]

Willpower in Action

The Story of Carlos. The need for persistence to achieve goals has been emphasized throughout this book. Some of the children we have worked with are very willing to attempt to solve a problem, but only for a day or two. Sometimes we tell them the story of a four-year-old boy named Carlos who knew he was musically gifted and wanted to play an instrument.

Carlos decided to play the piano, so his parents bought him one. He played quite well on his first day, but he was not perfect, so he quit. Carlos then decided he would play the trumpet. He blew many beautiful notes, but some had a slight sour tinge and he again quit playing the trumpet after only one day. Finally, Carlos decided to play the violin. Again, he played well, but with some screeching and scratching sounds. Carlos was ready to give up, but he sensed a quiet voice inside of him that said, "It's okay. One day is not enough. Practice and you will receive your full gift."

Carlos continued. He was better on the second day, better yet on the third day, and even better on the fourth day. By the end of the month, he was a pretty good violinist. Over the years, Carlos was able to master several instruments and became a great musician, all because he listened to the voice inside of him that said, "One day is not enough. Do not give up on yourself so easily."

On Hanging in There. Previously we have noted that high-hope children can abandon a goal when it appears to be unreachable. But if there is a chance that effort will help in the attainment of desired goals, high-hope children—such as Carlos—will go all out. In many situations children encounter, moderately difficult goals are not achieved without considerable effort and persistence.

Self-Acceptance

The Story of Tiffany.   Some children accept themselves too much. They become self-centered. Sometimes we have used a story about a girl named Tiffany who invented magical glasses. If she pushed one button, the glasses would enable her to see ten miles away. With the push of the other button, they could be used to look exclusively at herself.

Tiffany looked at many things in the world, but eventually she decided to look only at herself because she enjoyed this the most. Unfortunately, Tiffany lost all of her friends because she spent every minute of her day looking only at herself.

One day, Tiffany's grandmother talked to her about her magical glasses. The grandmother helped Tiffany realize that there was no joy as great as friendship. She helped Tiffany begin to shovel snow and mow the grass for an elderly neighbor woman. Then Tiffany began to bake and share cookies with her new friend. Every day after school they would sit on the front porch, have long visits, and share stories. Eventually, Tiffany learned that giving to others can be the greatest gift we ever receive. Tiffany's grandmother taught her to find self-fulfillment as the indirect by-product of cultivating friendships and giving of oneself.

This story mirrors that which we have found in our practices—high-hope children cultivate friendships in which the needs of both partners are met. Hopeful thinking is neither a one-way street nor solitary in nature.

On Being What You Are.   As parents, we all want our children to develop hope-filled perspectives about themselves. There are many fertile possibilities for teaching such perspectives. For example, some children become jealous of their peers. Accordingly, we might tell them the story of a squirrel who gets a sore neck trying to be like a giraffe, who eats nuts by craning his neck up from the ground. Conversely, there is a giraffe who becomes sore and bruised trying to climb the tree to get food like the squirrel. As the squirrel and giraffe learn from their experiences, they begin to see how their own unique abilities allow them to be successful. A major factor in sustaining hope in children is to match their goal-related thinking to their natural talents. To be what you can be is to hope; to try to be what you cannot is an exercise in hopelessness.

Hope Is a Story, and Vice Versa

Our desire is that the story ideas in this chapter stir your imaginations and, more importantly, the imaginations of your children. Indeed, you may become inspired to tell stories to your own children. Remember, if you start the process, your children will want you to continue. Although this is a challenging process, it could be one of the most exciting ones you will ever experience.

Children generally do not like lectures or nagging. The theory of hope described in this book is very powerful, but it cannot simply be explained to a child in a didactic manner. Stories, in comparison, provide a method of explanation that allows children to gradually integrate lessons and incorporate hopeful strategies into their lives. The story examples in this chapter teach children what to do when they encounter barriers. They show children how to set new goals, how to produce the pathways (strengthening waypower) related to attaining those goals, and how to begin the journey and sustain themselves along those pathways (fortifying willpower). Children probably want you to tell them stories first and foremost because they are so enjoyable. Additionally, and often beyond their level of awareness (at least for very young children), stories provide guides that allow children to emulate the particular hero or heroine that they admire. As children hear these stories, they cannot wait to see if they can be as inventive, as persistent, and as successful as their story heroes. In this process, fears and problems need not be debilitating; rather, they come to represent opportunities waiting to be unlocked. The stories of life offer the keys.

7

Parents Fostering Stories of Hope: More Difficult Problems

Now that you know how to tell stories to help children with a variety of common, everyday problems at home and at school, we will begin to look at the process of creating stories to deal with more significant psychological difficulties.[1] First, we will discuss stories that help children cope with emotional problems. Next, we will provide story examples that can be used to help children with behavioral problems. Emotional problems typically reflect internalized conflicts whereas behavioral problems involve problematic external behaviors. Sometimes these problems overlap, but different stories are required in these two areas.

Before proceeding, it is important to comment on the issue of parents' capabilities to deal with more difficult psychological problems through stories. It is advisable to secure the input of professionals when your child is undergoing significant difficulties, especially those that are not being resolved. We also believe, however, that parents are capable of helping their children through the use of stories. Whether you work in concert with professionals or not, implementing the following approaches can produce benefits for children.

Guidelines for Working with Emotions

Opening Our Children to Feelings

Children need support in trusting their feelings so as to cope with emotional conflicts. These feelings can be difficult, terrifying, or overwhelming, but they are real. In our experience, children can be helped to more readily accept, express, and learn from their feelings.

Emotions really are a barometer for what is happening in the pursuit of our desires. As we have discussed previously in this book, positive emotions indicate that a person is experiencing success in goal pursuits. Most children are well aware of their positive, "good" feelings, and they communicate them both verbally and nonverbally. Negative emotions are equally important because they help children see where they are unsuccessful in their goal pursuits.[2] This awareness is often the critical first step in resolving the problem and establishing a more hope-filled path of action. If children attempt to deny their negative emotions, they are likely to remain frustrated and low in hope.

The following story examples provide safe contexts for seeing that emotions have value in helping children open themselves to "negative" feelings and the goal blockages that underlie them. By sharing such stories, we can gradually help children deal effectively with their emotions by finding new ways to focus their willpower and waypower toward goals that they want to achieve.

Story guidelines for helping children with emotional conflicts involve the following themes:

- Trust the feeling and learn to value it.
- Express the feeling to an empathic person in a safe setting.
- Realize the feeling tells about a problem that needs attention.
- Gain awareness of what is blocking a goal.
- Establish a plan and use it to achieve the desired goal.

Sample Stories for Children with Emotional Difficulties

Following are seven examples of stories to help children resolve emotional difficulties.

Grieving. Children need clear models for how to cope with significant losses. Whether it is a close relative, friend, or beloved pet who dies, the child experiences a loss that is painful and difficult (or impossible) to understand. Children in these situations need to be helped to begin a grieving process, the stages of which are (1) shock and denial; (2) anger; (3) sadness; and (4) acceptance and resolution.[3]

The grieving process is not a simple matter of moving from one stage to another. Children slip back and forth between these states in unique ways. It is easy to run away from the strong feelings provoked by grieving, but when children can express these emotions and let others help them reestablish hope, it is almost always a growth-enhancing experience.

One of our favorite stories relates to a little girl named Cynda whose pet goldfish, Matilda Fish, died unexpectedly. Cynda had loved Matilda Fish very much. When Matilda Fish died, Cynda felt so much grief that she thought it would never end, and she couldn't think about anything else. Eventually, she went to a wise man who helped her value her tears. The wise man said that Cynda's tears showed her love was as deep as the ocean and that she needed to let out these tears rather than keep them inside.

With the wise man's help, Cynda buried Matilda Fish in her garden and planted a sunflower seed over her. Every day she went out to the garden to cry. As she watched the sunflower seed grow into a flower, she gradually moved through the grieving process.

At the end of the summer, Cynda roasted the sunflower seeds from her flower and took them back to the wise man as a present. Cynda learned to see the connections between life and death because she was supported in this process by her parents and the wise man who loved her unconditionally. Matilda Fish had died, but Cynda had rediscovered how to move on and hope about that which was living. She had lost a cherished goal object—Matilda Fish—yet she had learned from the loss and had begun to focus on the other desired and attainable objects in her life. In our experiences, and consistent with hope theory, a child must not be hurried through the grieving process because this actually can prolong the period until new goals are set.

Depression.   Children who are depressed lose interest in everything. They lack the energy to climb trees or ride bikes. These children become fixated on how badly they feel and see the world negatively. They perceive themselves as having little success in achieving their goals, and they feel blocked. Children who are depressed can benefit from physical exercise, positive accomplishments, and fun experiences, especially those involving other people. Unfortunately, these are the activities that a depressed child usually avoids, and this is why stories can be helpful.

A story we have used with depressed children involves a little boy named Freddie who goes to see a wise Native American grandmother. Grandma Sits-in-the-Sun helps Freddie see that he is the boss of each of his fingers. He also learns that he is the boss of his legs, arms, mouth, eyes, ears, and everything in his body. Grandma helps Freddie realize he has a great power inside of him waiting to come out if he truly wants to use it. Grandma asks Freddie to walk each morning to the top of a small hill behind his cabin so he can think about what he wants to do that day. She tells him, "No one else knows what is best for you. Only you can decide."

Without any pushing or prodding, Freddie begins to explore. He listens to the birds sing and eventually decides he wants to play music. He asks his father if he can play an old violin that belonged to Freddie's grandfather. It is hard and frustrating, but Freddie starts to use the power inside of him to learn to play the fiddle. Slowly, Freddie begins to develop his interests and expand his activities. He still has some sad days, but he grows very close to Grandma Sits-in-the-Sun. Freddie learns to tell her about his sad feelings as well as the good things that are happening in his life. He is no longer stuck in his depression; rather, he is able to find and attain goals that are his.

An important consideration for helping depressed children is to know if the depression is related to environmental circumstances or a biochemical imbalance. If a child has a severe type of depression, professional help always is indicated. Some children may need antidepressant medication and professional psychotherapy along with help from their parents, teachers, and family. For many forms of depression, however, stories such as the one noted above could be a good starting point for increasing motivation so that new interests and self-fulfilling activities can be attempted once again. Likewise, stories can be an excellent adjunct intervention approach for professional treatment, even for depressions that are largely biological in origin. In this regard, hope theory suggests that many childhood depressions reflect the child's profound sense of not being able to attain desired goals, or not being able to set meaningful goals that are reachable. Stories help them get back on the track and to feel more energy.

Anxiety. Children worry and become nervous in many situations. It is important, in this regard, to help children find ways of dealing with anxiety without getting locked into chronic, self-defeating patterns. Children with significant symptoms of anxiety are "frozen" or paralyzed with inaction. They may know what they want, but they expend most of their energy in considering all of the associated problems. They are low in hope because they cannot find viable strategies to solve the problems that stand between them and their desires. Accordingly, it is important to help such children to understand, talk about, and resolve the problem. Anxious children are afraid of their symptoms and will do anything to keep them from occurring.

Stories that take place in a jungle setting are excellent for dealing with anxieties. Children seem to enjoy this format, perhaps because the context is novel and far removed from their own lives. In one such story, a little girl named Kayia worries about small problems, such as whether or not a banana has a tiny brown spot on it. She has a large number of worries, but she eventually goes to see a wise man who asks if she could "possibly worry just a little bit more?" The wise man gives Kayia some things she could worry about, such as making sure her shoelaces are exactly the same length.

Kayia thinks this is pretty funny at first. She tries to worry about these little things, but she finds it tedious. She goes back and tells the wise man

KAYIA DREAMS OF THE RIVER

she does not want to worry about little things anymore. The wise man then teaches Kayia a relaxation approach in which she learns to close her eyes and pretend her mind is a beautiful, smooth flowing river. Kayia learns to put her worry thoughts into a bubble so she can watch them float down the river. Kayia is no longer paralyzed by her anxiety. She begins to let go of her worrying so that she can have time for enjoyable activities. Thus, Kayia develops a new way of thinking about her worries and learns a technique to use so the anxiety no longer controls her.

This story encourages the child to "try to worry more," which is a paradoxical approach that often leads a child to conclude that small issues are not so worrisome. In the process, the child is freed to initiate more productive courses of action. This combination of willpower and waypower thinking, as told through story form, can help Kayia and children like her to move forward with high hope.

Coping with Emotional Trauma.   Children can be victimized by a wide variety of traumatic experiences, including car accidents, natural disasters, and physical, sexual, or emotional abuse. Symptoms may include nightmares, avoidance of previous activities, physiological arousal, and both recurrent and intrusive thoughts about the traumatic experience. The child trauma victim can be easily overwhelmed by his or her negative emotional experience.[4] It is difficult to have hope when a child has looming fears. Thus, the child perceives that all goals are blocked, nothing will work to change things, and the only coping strategy is to avoid the feared stimulus.

Here again, tales of hope provide excellent models for considering alternative approaches. An example of a useful story is one we call "When Cleo Met Chloe." The plot line is simple. Cleo is traumatized by a vicious dog attack and decides to hide in her room all of the time. She is startled if she even hears a dog barking outside. She cannot sleep at night. Cleo's parents take her to visit a wise grandmother who encourages her to express her fears and listen to them. Gradually, the wise grandmother helps Cleo get to where she can watch a Great Dane puppy named Chloe through a window, then progress to look more closely at the puppy, pet the puppy, play with the puppy, and eventually take the puppy home. In this story, Cleo learns to stay away from mean dogs so that she can protect herself. Later, she begins to rely on her own dog, Chloe, to protect her when she is walking down the sidewalk. Thus, the dog becomes a protector rather than a stimulus for fear. Chloe and the wise grandmother have helped Cleo find a way to overcome the traumatic fear. Hope is an antidote for the things that produce fear in children. As the fears abate, hope provides new goals and the waypower and willpower to go with these goals.

Coping with Foster Care. Children in foster care face a monumental task. Their emotional loyalties are divided between their biological parents and their foster parents. Caregivers are a prime source of hope, but to which ones are children to attend? Being loyal to one generally means being disloyal to the other. On this point, children in foster care can profit by hearing the story of a boy named Rama who tries to be loyal to his biological mother. Rama visits his mother on his birthday, but she does not have any treats or presents for him. To make matters worse, the mother spends her time talking to a boyfriend and has little time for Rama. After such visits, Rama goes home feeling very angry. He hits his foster sister and steals money from his foster parents.

If Rama were to attach himself to his foster parents, he would feel disloyal to his biological mother. He is in a bind. In the story, Rama goes to see a wise man named Solomon (the prototype of the "wise person"). He tells Solomon that his mother does not call him or give him any attention. He also expresses some of his feelings. Solomon has Rama stand up. He stretches Rama's legs as far apart as they will go. Solomon tells Rama that he has one foot in one town with his foster parents and one foot in another town with his mother. Solomon then states, "It is time to put both feet together, or you will be pulled apart." Very slowly, Solomon helps Rama to start to put his feet together. Rama does not know where he will be living in ten years, but he knows where he is living right now. The metaphor of "putting his feet together" helps Rama to settle into his foster home and establish a more positive relationship with his foster family as he waits to see what is going to happen with his biological mother. Solomon has helped Rama find a way to fulfill his needs for security and nurturance from adults. Incidentally, our research reveals that the fulfillment of these security and nurturance needs are important for high-hope children.

Physical and Emotional Abuse. Abused children have a problem similar to that seen with Rama: It is very hard for them to attach themselves to anyone because they do not trust others. For such children, the story of Ivy the Kit-

Ivy ᴛʜᴇ Kɪᴛᴛᴇɴ

ten can introduce a new model of hope. Ivy was abused and neglected. She was missing one ear and her tail. A young girl saw Ivy on a school playground and tried to go up and help, but the kitten was very scared. However, Ivy was willing to take one small risk. She followed the little girl down the street to her home. Somehow, the kitten had a survival instinct that allowed her to seek assistance.

In her new quarters, Ivy was so scared that she slept under a bed for one whole year. She would not let anyone touch her. Whenever people were around, she hid. Ivy came out only for food and water. She protected herself because she needed to let her wounds heal. During the second year, Ivy sat on the kitchen refrigerator, watching and learning how a normal life might work. Ivy was still protecting herself, but she was beginning to reach out.

During the third year, the cat came up to family members to be petted for short periods of time. Ivy no longer ran when someone offered her food. During the fourth year, Ivy allowed nearly anyone to pet her. She finally had learned to trust others.

The story of Ivy gives children permission to protect themselves. It also gives them permission to move slowly as they let their wounds heal, learn to trust others, and work toward new goals. It allows them to see the value in letting adults help. It acknowledges their pain and allows for a slow process of healing rather than demanding arbitrary changes over a short period of time. We need to remember that hope comes slowly for abused children.[5]

Vinny's Mask. At the beginning of this chapter, we noted that children with emotional difficulties may want to run and hide from their feelings. For such children, the story of ten-year-old Vinny is hope inducing. Vinny had many strengths and abilities, but he could not face stress, teasing, or conflicts. Therefore, he developed an ingenious invention. He always kept a mask in his book bag. Whenever a problem came up, Vinny would immediately take the mask out and put it on to close himself off from the world and protect himself.

Vinny went to see a wise man who taught him that he did not have to hide. He could talk about how he felt. After expressing his thoughts and feelings, he could decide how to solve the problem. He did not have to believe what others were saying about him; he could believe in himself. Very slowly, Vinny began to try out these new approaches. As he found success, Vinny began to need his mask less and less. In fact, he was outgrowing it, so he put the mask on a bookshelf in order to save it as a memory. Vinny had learned to grow up and cope with the challenges the world brought him. This story is a good example of how we help children develop hope by facing and resolving the underlying emotional issue.

Guidelines for Helping with Behavioral Problems

Many years ago, a colleague asserted that parents who do not provide *any* discipline for their child in the first 12 months of life could expect to spend the rest of their parenting career trying to "catch up." In our experience, this has been true. We believe the appropriate goal is to provide some very simple and effective limits for children at an early age (e.g., 9–12 months) so they learn that they cannot have everything all the time, whenever they demand it. An analogy that has been useful in communicating with parents over the years is to think of the limits for a child as being originally confined to a bassinet or cradle. As the child grows, she is able to graduate into a crib. Eventually she moves into a playpen, and between 6 and 12 months she is able to enjoy the freedom of a room. In the toddler years, she begins to explore the entire house. As the preschool years dawn, she begins to discover the many exciting aspects of her yard. Eventually these limits expand to a block, a neighborhood, a community, and so on. It is much easier to expand limits than it is to provide all of the privileges (generally without any of the responsibilities) for young children and then have to take them back. By gradually giving children more freedom as they have demonstrated responsibility, we build a very solid foundation that can actually prevent some of the tumultuousness in the adolescent years. This process reinforces the likelihood that children will continue to develop hope strategies for life's difficulties based on past patterns of success.

Our job as parents and teachers is to put ourselves out of business. We need to prepare our children for life by giving them the freedom to make mistakes, to learn from their mistakes, and to begin to accept responsibilities for the consequences of their actions.

Research has shown that children need both kindness and firmness.[6] The major challenge of parenting is to find the right balance between these two variables in order to specifically match the temperament and special needs of a particular child. The story ideas in the remainder of this chapter may provide some new inspirations to meet this challenge.

The psychological issues involved with behavioral problems can be very different from the dynamics related to emotional conflicts. Children with behavioral problems frequently have been able to achieve some degree of power over their parents and do not want to surrender it. In other words, they pursue and often attain their desired goals without having to attend to the rules or needs of others around them.[7] It can be very hard for them to cooperate with adults and learn from their parents. Although learning how to accept rules and limits is difficult, it is essential.

Story guidelines for helping children with behavior problems generally involve the following themes:

- Put parents in charge of the family. Typically this means ensuring that children do not control the parents or the mood of the family.
- Establish consistent rules and limits.
- Utilize natural or logical consequences so children can learn from experiences.[8]
- Have children experiment and discover that they are happier when they cooperate with and allow their parents or caregivers to teach them.
- Let children relax because they no longer are responsible for bossing their parents.
- Gradually expand limits as children experience success and develop new skills for achieving important life goals.

Sample Stories for Children with Behavior Problems

The following six story ideas are designed to help children see the rationale for *wanting* to change their own behavior. The story heroes find productive ways to achieve their goals that do not interfere with the rights of others.

Oppositional Defiance. Oppositional children demonstrate noncompliance, arguing, and temper tantrums. Parents and teachers need to help these children learn that their tantrums no longer will force adults to give in to unreasonable demands. Parents also need to have a way to ensure that the child will not disrupt the family through tantrums or have the satisfaction of making parents angry. Once a child consistently sees that tantrums will not work, change can begin. Stories are invaluable in speeding this learning process.

One story we tell is about a girl named Teresa who had the worst temper tantrums in the world. Teresa even hit her mother when she would not do what Teresa wanted. Teresa visits a wise man who listens to her and then whispers very softly in Teresa's ear as he tells her a sad secret: "A little girl can never-ever-ever-ever-ever-ever be the boss of her mommy and daddy."

After the wise man gives this message a chance to sink in, he proceeds to tell little Teresa about a family of bears living in the nearby woods. He explains that the mama bear teaches the baby bear where to find huckleberries and how to fish. He goes into detail as he describes how the mama bear teaches the baby bear to climb trees in order to get honey out of beehives. Then he asks Teresa what would happen if the baby bear tried to boss the mama bear. Gradually, Teresa (who is very smart) is able to see that the baby bear could not really survive if she did not let her mother and father teach her. The wise man agrees and tells Teresa that she is "trying to do something that *no* little girl can do. You are this big (gesture), and they (the parents) are this big (gesture). It is time to let them teach you."

The wise man tries to help motivate Teresa in this process. He describes another child who was so smart that she was able to learn this lesson in just two days. He explains that most children take longer, and he asks Teresa how much time she might need to learn the lesson. In the story Teresa still tries to boss her parents on some days, but she lets them teach her on other days. In about one week she is able to learn the lesson and goes back to see the wise man, feeling quite proud of her accomplishment. Teresa feels emotionally secure now that she has accepted a role that is appropriate, that is, being a child who allows her parents to guide her.

Children who hear this story develop hope, possibly because they want to prove that they can be as smart as Teresa and follow in her footsteps. This story also can impart to oppositional children that their adult caregivers (parents and teachers) really do have useful things to teach them. If they allow themselves to learn from their elders, they can become more effective in procuring their goals (waypower).

Stealing. Young children need to learn that stealing is not the way to achieve their goals. They need to know they will be caught and will experience consequences. Children need to understand that alternatives always are present to acquire a desired object in a more appropriate manner (waypower). They also need to learn to empathize with the victims of theft.

For such children, we like to tell a story about "Billy's Bike" that was adapted from a true story. In the story, Billy wants a new bicycle, but he believes his parents will not get him one. He steals a bike on the very day his father has brought a new bicycle home as a surprise for him. Billy feels very bad when he learns this. Although it is very difficult to do, Billy is able to tell his parents about the problem. He then takes the stolen bike back where it belongs and apologizes to the owners. Deep inside, Billy knows he has learned a lesson that he will never, ever forget. Breaking rules is not the way to accomplish our goals (unacceptable waypower).

We have used a variant of this story with a teenage boy who impulsively stole whatever latest item of clothing he wanted. Caught in this pattern, he

HOPPER THE RABBIT

was facing sterner penalties from the law. When he came for treatment, he was told the story of a young man who, being very hungry, approached an old fisherman and demanded his morning catch. The fisherman, in response, offered to teach the young man how to fish. The young man accepted the offer and quickly learned the angling skills. The old fisherman told the young man that he not only could feed himself now but probably could catch his fill in the future. This story produced a starting point for teaching the teenage client about how to get a part-time job so that he could buy the new clothes he desired.

Attention Deficit Hyperactivity Disorder (ADHD).   Children diagnosed with ADHD have a very complex and challenging problem. Many of these children benefit from a total approach that involves a physician, a therapist, parents, and school personnel all working together. These children find it very difficult to slow down and think before they act. As one child put it, "I want everything right now!" Children with ADHD have difficulty talking themselves through a given situation. They also have a hard time anticipating the consequences of their action. Therefore, they need a great deal of structured practice in order to develop these abilities.[9]

We have found it helpful to tell children with ADHD stories about a rabbit named Hopper who is always hopping, bouncing, and jumping. For example, when Mama Bunny is trying to wash clothes in the creek, Hopper jumps in the creek and lands on top of Mama. He knocks her down and sends all the clothes flowing down the creek. When Papa Bunny is trying to dig some dirt in their house to make a new room, Hopper tries to help, but he sprays dirt into Papa's eyes. Everyone gets mad at Hopper and tells him to go away. Next, Hopper finds Brother Bunny and Sister Bunny jumping rope. He cannot wait until Sister is done jumping, so he hops under the rope, knocks Sister down, and gets both Brother and Sister mad at him.

Finally, Hopper's parents take him to see old Uncle Thinker Bunny, who loves Hopper very much. He tells Hopper that it is time for Hopper to learn to "stop and think" before he acts. He gives Hopper many examples of how to do this and then starts to follow Hopper around in order to remind him to "stop and think." Eventually, Hopper learns how to help his mother wash clothes without knocking her down or losing the clothes. He learns how to help Papa without spraying dirt in his eyes. He learns how to wait his turn so that he can have fun jumping rope with Brother and Sister. Very slowly, Hopper learns how to "stop and think" even when Uncle Thinker Bunny is not with him. Gradually, Hopper becomes almost as smart as old Uncle Thinker Bunny.

Although the technique illustrated in this story does not cure the problem (ADHD), it can certainly be a helpful component in working with the many issues that are part of this syndrome. In the Hopper stories (or scenarios), ADHD children are repeatedly exposed to a model that teaches them to "go slow and stop to think." Here again, it is important to reinforce this concept with a subtle prompt or cue in relevant real-life situations so that the child learns to practice this important skill. The "stop and think" strategy provides the waypower component of hopeful thought so that Hopper can revise his previous disruptive behavior patterns.

Aggression. Many children who come for professional help are angry and aggressive. They appear self-centered and frequently fight with their families and friends. It does no good to tell these children to "be nice." In addition, punishment rarely motivates them to attempt more positive behaviors. Our greatest success has come through inspiring these children to explore the benefits of friendship. In this regard, we have found that hopeful children can and do work well with others and do not feel as if other people are "in their way," that is, are obstacles to overcome.

Many aggressive children have strong personalities. They can be helped to channel this strength in a more constructive manner by being a true leader with their peers. One approach we have utilized is to tell these children about an Eskimo boy named Alekehaw who is self-centered and demanding. He needs to be the first to get in a kayak. He has to have the best place to fish. He forces the other children to do what he wants them to do.

Alekehaw is taken to see a wise man named Old Kaluk. Alekehaw tells Old Kaluk that he has no need for friends, but Old Kaluk replies that Alekehaw is missing the two most important secrets of life. Old Kaluk does not expect miracles right away, but he has Alekehaw come back to visit him each day to listen to stories handed down by other wise men from many years ago. The stories tell about a man who happily lays down his life to save a friend. They also tell about two boys who fought side-by-side to scare away a polar bear that had attacked their village. One story was about a young man who spent a whole year making a special present for the woman he wanted to marry. When he finally gave it to her, it was the happiest day of his life.

Eventually, Alekehaw learns that the two secrets of life are friendship and love. Alekehaw listens quietly as Old Kaluk says, "The people will only follow a leader they love. They will never follow anyone out of fear!"

Because Old Kaluk is getting up in years, he has difficulty fishing and caring for himself. Old Kaluk asks Alekehaw to help him, and Alekehaw begins to bring fish every day to feed the old man. Gradually, Alekehaw is no longer talking about the two secrets of life; he is practicing them. Note that the story does not emphasize punishment but rather provides a strong degree of motivation for the hero to want to make constructive changes as he begins to see others as allies and sources of personal fulfillment. High-hope children show respect for their friends. They see and use friendships as a vehicle for both partners to meet their goals.

Anger Control.   Most people know from firsthand experience how difficult it can be to deal with significant anger control issues. A story can be very valuable in helping children have hope that they can learn to manage their anger. A good one involves a girl named Sally Smart.

Sally had a major problem with anger, so she went to see a wise woman.[10] The wise woman helped her see that this "big anger" was sneaking up and getting her into trouble. The wise woman suggested a contest. Who was going to win, Sally Smart or big anger? If Sally was truly smart, she might find a way to kick the big anger out of her life so that it could no longer sneak up on her.[11]

Sally decides to use her brain so she can win the contest. The wise woman helps Sally realize that she can solve problems rather than just get upset. She starts to see herself as being very competent to use her brain so as to solve life's many challenges. Eventually, Sally learns to talk to other children and to adults to solve problems "without hurting anybody." Sally's parents help her. Sometimes they give her a choice when problems are arising. Does she want to hurt someone, or would she rather use her brain? At the end of the story, Sally states very clearly that she has learned from the wise woman that she can be the boss of herself and she is not going to forget it. She will no longer let the big anger sneak up on her and get her into trouble. In hope terms, she now has waypower tools to use in place of anger.

Trust Mountain.   In the earlier part of this chapter, we noted that many abused children find it hard to trust others. In contrast, when a child has significant behavioral problems, it is often difficult for adults to trust the child. For example, if children have been lying and stealing, their parents will find it hard to believe them or trust that their valuables will be safe. In these situations, a story can help children see that they can be hopeful about regaining their parents' trust.

In the story of Trust Mountain, little Amy is determined to climb to the very top of a metaphorical cone-shaped mountain drawn on a chart at home. Each day that she goes without lying or stealing, Amy is able to color in a slice representing one-thirtieth of the mountain, starting from the bottom and working upward. To get to the top requires 30 days, a full month without lying or stealing. Trust does not come easy; it takes time. If Amy slips, she falls all the way back to the bottom of the mountain and needs to start over.

In this story, Amy tries hard, but she does slip once or twice before she finally learns the lesson. At last Amy is able to kick the lying and stealing out of her life forever. When she gets to the top of the mountain, Amy and her family celebrate with a party and some new privileges that help Amy see the benefits of the trust she has gained. Her hard work has enabled her to climb to the top of a most difficult summit.

The preceding stories provide an excellent starting point for helping young children with behavioral problems. It is important to emphasize that professional and school help also may be necessary to provide a complete regimen for these children. The message to parents and teachers alike is that "Once the story ends, the intervention continues." Thus, it is generally important to be prepared to follow through with the use of the stories whenever possible. Generally, the child will be motivated to be like the hero in the story; this gives caregivers a major advantage in attempting a home intervention program to help the child. The stories can help transform the home into an environment that brings hope to the most important participant—the child.

The Rest of the Story

In Chapter 5, we described a five-step process for creating an individualized story for your child. We also have discussed applications of stories for common developmental issues (Chapter 6) and more significant psychological problems (this chapter). The stories you have read are meant as models. We believe that you will be able to combine the basic principles of hope theory and the five-step storytelling process to create individualized stories that are most appropriate for your particular child. We will now summarize a few additional strategies that can be used to construct the basic content of a story to match the circumstances of a particular child:

- If the child has a goal that simply cannot be achieved, the hero of the story may learn to select a new goal that is more appropriate and reachable.
- If the child is determined to accomplish a goal but has few plans or methods for how to do so (i.e., the child lacks waypower), the story hero may develop a very flexible attitude that involves considering a variety of plans and options in order to pick the very best one to try out.
- If there is limited willpower or commitment, the story heroes may need to go through experiences that help them become more motivated and determined to achieve their goal even if it takes a great deal of hard work and effort.

As you combine the principles of hope theory with storytelling, you gain access to a very powerful tool to assist children with many diverse needs. All we can add is encouragement. Relax and enjoy the process. Try not to be too serious. Develop a picture in your mind of the hero in your story working through the challenges and difficulties that are being presented. In this manner, the story can tell itself. All you have to do is talk about the picture in your mind and apply some of the basic principles you have learned in this book. As we said in Chapter 5, it's not that hard; you can learn to do it. In the process, you and your child will have a great deal of fun.

8

A Teacher Needs Hope

*F*AMILIES AND SCHOOLS EXERCISE the two greatest influences on children's lives. In Chapters 5, 6, and 7 we saw how hope messages are conveyed through the family environment to increase hope in children's lives. This chapter and the next two focus on teachers and the roles they play in influencing hope through the crucial school years. The intent of these chapters is to provide teachers with a means for assessing their own hope and looking at what goes on in their classrooms.

We examine how high- and low-hope teachers establish classroom atmospheres that either encourage or discourage students' hopeful thinking. We will follow two teachers who epitomize high and low hope both in and out of the classroom and see how a teacher's level of hope influences their teaching styles and the lives of their students. An adult's own level of hope has a powerful effect on how he or she interacts with children. Accordingly, we trace the childhood events of the teachers in order to understand their personal stories. The chapter concludes with a review of ways to use personal stories to assess hope in oneself, and suggestions of ways to increase hopeful thinking.

Subsequent chapters address bringing hope to the classroom. Because cognitive abilities differ so greatly between elementary and secondary school children, the approaches used for presenting hope also must be different. Chapter 9 explores methods for incorporating hope into elementary curricula, and Chapter 10 concentrates on secondary school.

In Loco Parentis

Consider some impressive facts—children are in school six or seven waking hours a day, five days a week, roughly nine months a year. Many children are in school or child care for even longer hours; consequently, they may spend as much time with their teachers as they do with their families. Along with parents, therefore, teachers have an enormous impact on children.

As parents, we may not fully comprehend the complexity of the world in which most children live. Crime and violence abound, drugs and alcohol are prevalent and accessible, divorce rates are very high, and many youth face a dismal employment outlook. In their daily contact with students, teachers are keenly aware of the world that surrounds and awaits these young people. These teachers may feel caught between the pressures and demands made by the school system and community on the one side, and the needs of the students on the other. They often come to know their students well enough to be aware of family problems, poverty, single-parent households, and other conditions that affect the child's school and social life. Indeed, teachers have the daily task of providing substantial structure and guidance to children.

For the past several years, we have been constructing an approach for training hope in the classroom.[1] The lessons learned and techniques developed are presented here and in the following chapters, but first we would like to show why it is so important for the educator to have high hope.

The Infectiousness of Hope in the Classroom

High-hope people infect others with a sense of enthusiasm and a belief that they too can achieve their goals. By the same token, low-hope people often leave others with a sense of futility, as if something crucial were missing. Therefore, it is vital that teachers and child-care workers send hopeful messages to their young charges. In order to do this effectively, one must become aware of one's own hope and, if it is low, implement means to raise it. In Chapter 3 we described various instruments to measure hope. In this chapter, stories are presented to illustrate how an individual's level of hope can be determined from a personal vignette. These stories also illustrate the effect of high and low hope on the classroom environment.

As soon as you walk into a classroom, you get a sense of what the atmosphere is like. Some classrooms are neat and orderly, others are disorganized; some are colorful, others are drab. The students also will give you a sense of the atmosphere. Are they enthusiastic or bored? Free to explore ideas, or constrained? Let's look at two classrooms and see how the teacher has set up either a high- or low-hope atmosphere. As you read about each classroom, think about the level of hope displayed by each teacher. Is it high or low?

Ms. Brimm's Classroom

Ms. Brimm teaches third grade at an inner-city school. Her class of 19 students is drawn from an especially low-income area in a large midwestern city. Frequently the children come to school inadequately dressed, without necessary school supplies or their homework. Having spoken with parents as well as students, Ms. Brimm suspects that parental supervision and family resources may be scarce because parents are working several jobs. Accordingly, Ms. Brimm takes extra care to deliver all the structure and encouragement she can provide during the six hours each day children spend in her classroom. In part, it is this challenge that drew her to teaching as a profession.

Ms. Brimm, as you probably have guessed by now, is a high-hope person. She loves challenges, but she sets realistic goals and usually can figure out how to solve most of the problems she encounters. She has a lot of energy and enthusiasm for the things she is doing, one of which is creating a classroom environment where each child can experience goal setting, problem solving, and success. In short, she strives for a classroom where children can hope.

Because so many of her students begin with an "I can't" attitude, Ms. Brimm starts with very small goals that are determined individually with each student. In this very early phase, she guides each student in the process of learning to set realistic goals. An individual goal might be to learn one new word each day for two weeks. Ms. Brimm also has the students set classroom goals so that they develop the habit of working together. An example of a classroom goal might be for all supplies to be put away at the end of the day.

Ms. Brimm knows she must teach the children to solve problems; she also knows that those problems cannot be allowed to reignite the "I can't" self-talk. To do this, she encourages children to discuss their problems with her, thereby giving her an opportunity to help them think through difficult situations. Developing waypower is learning to look for options, or creative solutions, that are not readily apparent. Children often lack the information to do this alone, and a thoughtful adult can be of great help. When Ms. Brimm brainstorms with her students she is teaching that it is all right to have problems and that these problems need not spell defeat.

Another special aspect of Ms. Brimm's class is that she makes every effort to get to know each child's primary caregiver. This means she deals with a variety of people, including moms and dads, grandparents, aunts and uncles, and older siblings. Ms. Brimm always assumes that at least one adult can be found who cares about the education of each child. In a school where parent-teacher conferences are unusual, they are the rule rather than the exception in Ms. Brimm's class. Often, if the parent cannot make a conference, she arranges a telephone conversation. Her assumption is that parents and teachers can and must work together for the benefit of the child. Just as she elicits hope in her students, to some extent she is also able to do the same with parents.

Of course, students in Ms. Brimm's class do not always reach their goals. When they don't, however, she always points out that they tried hard and that the lessons learned can help in the future. There is as much praise from her when a student tries but does not succeed as when the student does succeed. The atmosphere in this third-grade classroom is one of busy activity where children can focus on the work at hand. Ms. Brimm is clearly an "I can" person.

Mr. Downley's Science Class

A different sort of classroom is run by Mr. Downley, who teaches sixth-grade science. He also has the best interests of his students at heart and is aware that these children have many problems. He likes to keep his class-room well organized and have his students listen quietly to his lectures. He believes he is providing a structured environment they do not get elsewhere and that this is the best way for his students to learn.

Long ago, Mr. Downley accepted the fact that most of his students would never leave the inner city and would continue on the same road traveled by their parents; therefore, he determined not to set unduly high goals for his students that would lead them to disappointment. Likewise, Mr. Downley has long since stopped trying to interact with students' care-givers because he perceives that they either are too busy or don't care about their children's education, or both.

One of the assignments given to sixth-grade science classes is to prepare science fair experiments. Three of Mr. Downley's students came to him with a novel and difficult idea for a project. It would involve a lot of time and some equipment that was only available at another school. Although it might have been possible to complete this project, Mr. Downley could see difficulties ahead. He envisioned the students getting bored and not being willing to put in the extra required time. He believed that there would be no parental support in getting the necessary supplies. He also imagined that the science department at the other school would not be willing to loan him the equipment. Because of these potential problems, Mr. Down-ley discouraged the original idea and suggested that the children should pursue a much simpler task.

Though he believed he was saving his students from disappointment, Mr. Downley was sending them several important negative messages. He was telling them that problems are reasons to quit rather than challenges to be conquered. He was putting a damper on their creativity and potential interest in science. He was stifling a goal they were attempting to set for themselves and, most importantly, he was reinforcing an "I can't" ap-proach to life.

Both Ms. Brimm and Mr. Downley believe they have the best interests of their students in mind with their particular teaching approaches. Ms.

Brimm is aware that she has a positive attitude and is high in hope. Mr. Downley believes that he is being realistic in his response to his students' life problems. Occasionally, these two teachers meet in the lounge and discuss what is happening in their classrooms. Usually, Mr. Downley comes away thinking that Ms. Brimm is a Pollyanna, and Ms. Brimm believes Mr. Downley is doing his students a disservice. Ms. Brimm has seen the changes that can happen when children are encouraged to hope, and her encounters with Mr. Downley only serve to strengthen her belief in her approach to teaching.

Hope is contagious in a classroom, but so too is its opposite—hopelessness. One reason hope is infectious is that high-hope people thrive on passing it on. A high-hope person truly enjoys seeing another person alight with enthusiasm over an idea. Ms. Brimm derives most of her satisfaction in teaching by knowing that she is lighting fires and turning on light bulbs in those little minds. Mr. Downley, in comparison, does not enjoy his work to the same extent. He began his career with high hopes for the social good and positive changes he could bring about. However, the demands and pressures have worn him down to the extent that he no longer has hope that he can change lives. The process of losing hope Mr. Downley experienced is referred to as "burnout," and it is one of the major ways individuals (particularly those in the helping professions) can experience a loss of hope.

Losing Hope Through Burnout

Recalling Ms. Brimm and Mr. Downley in the teachers' lounge provides a good example of burnout in action. It is clear that regardless of his present attitudes, Mr. Downley wants the best for his students. If we were to have visited with him when he was a new teacher, we would have found him to be enthusiastic about bringing change into students' lives. He even chose to teach in the inner city precisely because he wanted to go where he could do the most good. Mr. Downley seems to have forfeited his dreams and goals. What happened along the way?

One of the insidious characteristics of burnout is that once people have succumbed, they tend to explain their negative feelings in terms of external events or circumstances.[2] Mr. Downley encountered a number of problems when he was a new teacher. If he wanted special supplies or equipment so that his students could do even rudimentary experiments, he would have to buy them with his own money. He found that students often missed classes or assignments, or transferred out of school never to be seen again. Parents or caregivers seemed increasingly difficult to engage about their children's progress. As the years rolled by, Mr. Downley grew more and more negative about the prospects of educating his students. Occasionally he had a student whose enthusiasm for science was so great that his hope was rekin-

Jack

dled, but when that student graduated, Mr. Downley returned to his previous level of hopelessness.

If burnout were a natural consequence of encountering difficult problems as well as unusual stresses and demands, everyone in Mr. Downley's position would be having the same experience. This clearly is not the case, however. Why do some people, such as Ms. Brimm, cope with difficult conditions and remain hopeful while others, like Mr. Downley, appear to deflate under pressure? A large part of the answer lies in the role that hope has historically played in a person's life. Let us examine stories from the childhoods of Ms. Brimm and Mr. Downley to see what messages they received about hope.

Jack Downley and the Pinewood Derby

When Jack Downley was seven years old, his father announced that it was time for him to join the Cub Scouts and that he, Mr. Downley Sr., was going to be the troop leader. This pleased Jack but also caused him a great deal of anxiety. He rightly assumed that his father would expect him to be the best at everything the troop did. Jack's father had high expectations for his children in both their school and social activities. For example, when Jack's older sister brought home a report card with two C's instead of all A's, Mr. Downley was greatly displeased and let everyone know about it. Jack was the son, named for his father, on whom his father had placed the fulfillment of many of his own dreams. This had been conveyed to Jack in a variety of ways: Everyone called him "little Jack," and his father often remarked that Jack reminded him of himself. There were bedtime stories of Mr. Downley Sr.'s days as a high school football star, trophies from athletic events, and merit badges and awards from his Eagle Scout days. It was clear to Jack that he had much to live up to so as not to disappoint everyone, including himself.

Cub Scouting went well for the first few months. Jack's father organized good meetings and fun activities. Jack's mother frequently sent tasty snacks, and Jack was enjoying popularity as the leader's son. One big event was the Pinewood Derby in which each boy was to make a small car out of wood. Cars were to be aerodynamically constructed so that they would race down a wooden ramp, with the fastest one being the winner. The cars were to be made by the boys themselves, but it was a widely known secret that fathers usually helped. Jack, however, really wanted to make his car by himself, believing he could win the race.

Jack purchased the wooden block, wheels, weights, paint, and decals and set to work. It was harder than he thought, and the final product didn't look quite as he had envisioned. He reasoned, however, that it was speed and not beauty that counted. He shaped his car and applied his weights just so, trying it out on a variety of surfaces, until he finally had what he thought was a speedy car. He knew it didn't look as slick as some of the cars constructed with the fathers' help, but he was proud because he had made it by himself. Mr. Downley Sr. offered to help a number of times, but because he was a judge for the contest, he did not press the point.

On the evening of the Pinewood Derby, the church where the event was held stirred with activity. The fathers were every bit as excited as their sons. One by one, each boy set his car on the top of the ramp, allowing it to run its course, then having the time written down by Mr. Downley. Jack decided to wait until last so that his extra fast car would be a surprise to everyone. When Jack set his car on the ramp and let it go, however, it rolled only three quarters of the way down and stopped. He was allowed to try again, and the car completed the ramp, but rather slowly.

Jack was devastated, and it was hard for him to keep from crying. On the way home, Mr. Downley lectured about the folly of trying to do things that were clearly too difficult. He told Jack that he was sorely disappointed and that he wanted this to teach him a lesson. Unfortunately, it did.

Jack never forgot the Pinewood Derby, and although he was a bright and naturally inquisitive boy, from then on he was always very cautious about doing independent creative work. He was keenly aware how horrible it felt to disappoint oneself and others, and he avoided all situations where that could happen. Consequently, as a teacher he believed he was doing his students a favor by protecting them from the feelings he had suffered.

One does not necessarily develop low hope, of course, on the basis of one experience. It is true however, that some experiences continue to be salient story memories, and their repetition reinforces the negative belief. Jack Downley's story may not be one he tells his children, but it is likely he repeats it to himself often.

Interestingly, his story easily could have been a high-hope one if handled differently by his father. All high-hope stories do not have happy endings. In this case it is the goal setting, the determination evidenced in Jack's hard work toward the goal, and the way in which he attempted to solve the aerodynamic problems that indicate his level of hope. Had his father been able to praise Jack for his efforts, to be understanding of his embarrassment, and to explore ways with him to build a truly fast car, Jack might

have learned very different lessons—that it is all right to try and not succeed, that one always can try again, and that self-esteem and the esteem of
important others will not be lost just because something didn't work as
planned. Importantly, he also would have learned hope.

Linda Brimm Produces a Ballet

Linda's father died when she was six years old, leaving her mother with
many medical bills. Linda had no brothers or sisters, and her mother
worked long hours as a secretary in order to pay the debts, support the two
of them, and save enough money for Linda to attend college. Linda was
alone each day after school, and consequently she had to learn how to
amuse herself.

By the time Linda was ten years old she had become thoroughly stage
struck. She took ballet classes every Saturday and in all her daydreams
imagined herself dancing and acting in leading roles. One rainy day, as she
was playing in the garage, she realized that by hanging a sheet across the
back part of the space, she could contrive a stage. This gave Linda the idea
of assembling the neighborhood children and producing a ballet. She
would be the choreographer, director, and costume and set designer. When
rehearsals were complete she would invite the neighborhood mothers to
buy tickets and attend.

The first step was convincing the other kids to participate. Some of the
older ones thought the idea was downright silly, but Linda was able to con-
vince four younger children that it would be a lot of fun. For music Linda
chose Johann Strauss's *Tales
from the Vienna Woods*, and
she could just imagine the
garage turned into a bower
of leaves and flowers. This
was accomplished by using
branches trimmed from
small trees, flowers from the
garden, and grass clippings
from the yard. The costumes
were diaphanous night-
gowns the children bor-
rowed from their mothers.
The production was taking
shape.

Next, Linda had to cho-
reograph the ballet. This
took some thought and plan-

LINDA

ning because most of the steps she wanted to use were too complicated for children with no training. In the end, she settled on several simple poses and turns that allowed her to be in the forefront dancing a more complex set of steps. They practiced for several days, and in between dance rehearsals they decorated the stage. At last the production was ready.

On the specified afternoon, dining-room chairs were moved into the garage and mothers paid ten cents admission price. Some of the older children in the neighborhood also bought tickets, mostly out of curiosity. Linda got the most pleasure from knowing that her mother took time off from work to attend the performance. The ballet was very successful, and because it was so short, the children were asked to perform it four additional times! After each performance, the audience applauded loudly and many bows were taken.

Later that evening, Linda and her mother discussed the initiative and hard work it had taken to produce the ballet. Mother was very proud, and Linda was pleased with herself. She thought the whole thing had been fun from beginning to end, even through there had been problems to solve. Especially important was seeing the enthusiasm in her younger friends and knowing that she had sparked a flame. Putting on plays and ballets was a new game in which they could all participate in years to come.

This story has all the markers of high hope. Linda had an idea, a goal, that filled her with energy and drive. She encountered a number of problems related to all the aspects of the production that had to be decided, but for each problem she was able to discover a solution. She demonstrated both high willpower and waypower. Very important in maintaining Linda's high hope was her mother's encouraging attitude. It would have been easier for Linda's mother to put a stop to the production, saying that it would be too much work and would interfere with her busy work schedule. Instead, Linda was permitted, indeed encouraged, to go ahead with her plan with the caveat that she would clean up whatever mess was caused. Mother demonstrated trust in Linda's responsibility as well as her ability to pursue her goal. A very valuable lifetime lesson was learned that day, and a family story, retold many times in later years, was created.

Changing Your Hope Messages

In light of the information you have from the present chapter, you may wish to review your own stories. In fact, we encourage you to write a number of personal narratives because they provide valuable information that is difficult to get in other ways. If you write about your childhood, you are examining the hope messages you received from your family, school, and social situations. If you write about present-day events, you are examining the current hope messages you are giving yourself. Although the messages you give yourself are rooted in your past, it is only in the present that change can take place.

Now that you have a general idea of your own level of hope, you may want to increase it. Whether you are experiencing low hope because of professional burnout or because of messages you received in the past, the suggestions recommended for increasing hope will be effective. If you believe yourself to be a high-hope person who has experienced a loss of hope because of burnout, there are some specific suggestions for you. Whatever the source of the loss, increasing hope in your life requires a shift in your thinking. To do that, you will have to examine the messages you currently tell yourself as you pursue goals and encounter problems.

To begin this process, write a brief story about a current life event in which you wanted to accomplish something and then stopped working for it, or how you settled for something far less than you originally wanted. Be sure to record how you felt about achieving the goal, both at the beginning and at the point where you stopped working or began believing it was just too difficult. This critical point may have come when problems began to arise, or perhaps you took no action toward your goal and simply lost interest and energy. It is important to note at which point you gave up, and also how you felt at that time. What messages did you tell yourself? If you lost energy to work toward the goal early in the process, you may have told yourself that it was just too much work and that you couldn't do it anyway. You probably rationalized quitting. If you didn't quit until you began to encounter problems or roadblocks, you may have told yourself that these were insurmountable.

Keeping track of where you begin to give up is important because it tells you which area of hope is low, and thus which area needs the most work. If you run out of steam before you begin to work toward your goal, this indicates that the willpower portion of hope is low for you. If it is the roadblocks and problems that defeat you, it is an indication that your waypower is low. It is possible to be low in both areas, in which case you would find yourself with both diminished enthusiasm and the know-how to discover solutions to roadblocks. The Hope Scale is a first step in assessing your hope; the story you write provides an example of your hope in action.

The next step in the change process is to become aware of how you work toward daily goals. It is true that each day we have a number of small goals, such as getting to work on time, getting the family fed, or doing the grocery shopping, in order to complete many of these goals we operate on an automatic pilot of sorts. Our hope may not be as visible in everyday things as it is when we decide to do something different. For example, suppose you have decided that you should exercise several days each week. Perhaps this was a New Year's resolution. Unless it has become a habit, part of your routine, you may experience a battle with yourself each time you do, or do not, exercise. In this situation, you have an end goal, whether it is to become healthier, to lose weight, or just to feel better about yourself. Examine the message you tell yourself as you resist working out. You may say that you don't have time, that you are too tired, that you'll do it tomorrow, or that maybe it isn't so important after all. Allowing yourself to give up your goal in this way indicates low willpower.

If you have a strong desire to exercise but fail to do it because you encounter problems, such as competing tasks or bad weather, you may be lacking waypower. A high waypower person would find ways to schedule the exercise at low-demand times such as very early morning, or to prioritize other demands to allow for exercise. If the weather is bad, the person with high waypower would find ways to exercise inside, such as joining a gym or using an exercise tape. These are a few examples of how hope may operate in your life. Think of your own examples. Examine how you do, or do not, achieve what you set out to attain for yourself.

Becoming aware of situations such as those described here is a large part of the battle if you wish to increase hope in your life. It is advisable to keep a notebook in which you record your goals, thoughts, and feelings as you work for those goals and, most importantly, what you tell yourself as you go through the process. You can determine at which point you begin to experience less hope and, in response, begin to think of alternatives to the "quit" messages.

In psychology there is a method known as restructuring, in which the person keeps track of recurring thoughts every day, then, with the help of a therapist, devises more adaptive thoughts to counter the problematic ones.[3] Our suggestion is similar but is specific to situations in which you are clearly embarking on a goal. Here you are asked to record thoughts and feelings that limit your ability to achieve what you desire. As each of these thoughts and feelings become clear to you, so too do the ways you can reverse them. If your willpower thinking needs increasing, the longer you can continue to work toward the goal, the stronger the willpower becomes. Using exercise again as an example, the more often you actually work out, the more you will want to work out. You will begin to feel better and see the changes you are accomplishing, and the motivation to continue will grow. Interestingly, if your willpower for this goal is high and you encounter problems, you also may be more eager to find solutions that will keep you on track.

Increasing your waypower thoughts involves a willingness to look for solutions in less obvious places. It is important not to work in a vacuum when you have problems. Find out how other people might solve the same problem, and ask for ideas. Our culture of individuality teaches us that we are responsible for our own lives; hence, we should solve problems on our own. This cultural value can get in the way of really creative problem solving because it does not permit us to use other people's experience to the fullest extent. In this regard, our research reveals that high-hope people solicit lots of advice from their friends.

Another factor in increasing waypower is getting beyond the familiar. You may need to consider unconventional ways to solve problems; you need to have an open mind about such solutions. Don't be afraid to take a few risks. In the case of the reluctant exerciser who allows bad weather to stop her, one solution, that of using an exercise video, carries with it the risk that her family may laugh at her efforts. The risk is worth taking for the long-term benefits it confers. It also serves to model hopeful behavior to the rest of her family.

If your hope seems to have deteriorated because of burnout, there are some specific things you may consider. The authors have conducted research to determine specific correlates of burnout. The single most important finding was that individuals who experience burnout appear also to experience a lack of control in their lives and jobs.[4] Success in helping individuals who were complaining of this phenomenon appears to be greatest when they can be shown how to regain control of such factors as hours spent on the job, communication patterns with employers and fellow employees, and most importantly, time spent doing constructive and interesting things for themselves. Teachers need to examine all of these latter processes. Let us take those days when the normally upbeat Ms. Brimm feels drained. What does she do? She takes care to make sure that she builds in time for the goals that she enjoys and values. She sets aside some quiet time just for herself. She lights up her "slug buster" sign in her mind. This is a figure of a slug with a slash drawn through it (borrowed from *Ghost Busters*). She makes sure that she does things that enable her to laugh more that day. She goes for a walk. In short, she breaks the pattern so that the beginnings of burnout are erased. In fact, she has one final approach where, in her mind, she places all her problems on the blackboard and erases them one by one. Perhaps it is fitting that a teacher should use an eraser as a means of wiping out fatigue and providing refreshment for her work.

A Lesson for Teachers

Teachers often feel controlled by the needs of their students, administrators, and fellow teachers. Yet teachers are among the most important members of our society, carrying as they do a large part of the responsibility for shaping and guiding each new generation. Hopelessness need not be a consequence of the stresses and pressures placed on teachers, but taking control and changing one's personal messages requires an active decision to do so. It isn't easy once inertia has set in. Nevertheless, once action is securely in place, momentum can take over. Young people look to teachers as beacons of hope; teachers are role models with a great deal of power to influence young minds. Because hope is an infectious process and teachers with hope beget hope-filled students, it is worth the effort to increase your personal hope. The rewards will be great, both in your personal and your professional life.

9

Teachers Infusing
Tales of Hope:
Primary School Years

Getting Started

Elementary school sets the tone for children's later education. As was noted in Chapter 8, teachers have key responsibilities for children's lives during this period. As children grow, their attentions focus on peers, who may exert more influence than teachers or parents. For the young ones in primary school, however, teachers are absolutely central. Whether a teacher is high or low in hope can determine how a child will experience a day, a week, a month, and even an entire year. In this chapter, we will give examples of how teachers can use stories about high-hope children to transmit hopeful ideas to their young students. We'll present several of the stories used in our research and provide examples of high-hope and low-hope classrooms to further illustrate the impact a teacher can have on a child's view of life.

Lest parents feel they can skip this chapter, *we want to stress the vital importance of parent participation in their children's school activities.* Teachers need and welcome parents as teaching partners. When children know that the significant adults in their lives stand together in efforts to help them, they have a secure base from which to grow and develop.[1] The stories of Maggie and Matt, presented in this chapter, supply good examples of parents acting as teaching partners.

Establishing a High-Hope Kindergarten

Going to school for the first time is both awe inspiring and fear provoking for many children. From the very beginning, children must be helped to have positive experiences. It is helpful to let children know that they have faced a challenging experience by going to school on the first day, and that they have shown courage and determination. From day one at school, it is important to help each child go home feeling that he or she has done something about which to be proud. One way to point out this accomplishment is to ask children to draw pictures of how they felt coming to school that day. The teacher can then discuss how the first day of school is full of new activities and how brave they all were to be there. The children can then take these pictures home and tell their parents of their accomplishments. This process is akin to hope theory in that the child has a goal of having a good first day, encounters some barriers (i.e., all the new and difficult stuff), and with effort and thinking is able to succeed (and feel good in the process!).

Children need to know what is going to be expected of them and how they are to behave, even though such things may seem a bit difficult for them to remember. High-hope teachers have a structure that is consistent yet flexible enough to allow for individual differences.[2] Expectations should be stated in a positive way during the first days of kindergarten. Depending on how teachers present what is to come, children can be enthusiastic or anxious. Classroom behavior rules are important because they constitute a major part of children's early socialization. A high-hope teacher does not tolerate situations in which children tease or bully others; these behaviors diminish other children's hope. High-hope teachers base classroom rules on kindness, caring, and helpfulness. To illustrate these points, let's look at the experience of Diana as she enters a high-hope kindergarten classroom. We will then contrast Diana's experience with that of Powell, a child whose experience in a low-hope environment had negative consequences.

Diana

Diana had never been to preschool because she had been in the care of a nanny while her mother and father worked. Diana's only experiences with other children were at Sunday school and with the children of her parents' friends. As she and her mother approached the school for the first time, it looked very large and intimidating; the school seemed even bigger because it was attached to the church where they attended mass. One comfort was that Diana had on a uniform, a navy blue jumper and white blouse that were exactly like the ones worn by all the other girls.

When Diana and her mother entered the classroom, quite a few children already were playing with toys and looking at books. Sister Veronica immediately came over and told Diana how happy she was to see her. Diana then was introduced to several other little girls, none of whom knew each other previously. As soon as Diana got comfortable, her mother said she would be back later and left. After a few more boys and girls arrived, Sister Veronica had the children sit in a big circle on a rug. First, she asked everyone to tell their names and ages. Then, she assigned a desk to each child, saying that this could be decorated with paper cut-outs however the child liked. As the children drew things for the fronts of their desks, Sister Veronica went to each child to talk about what kindergarten was like. When it was her turn, Diana said that she very much wanted to learn to read but that she was afraid it would be terribly hard. Sister Veronica told her they would take it in small steps and that if Diana tried hard and did not give up, she certainly would be able to read by the end of kindergarten. They would set small goals together, and when the going was difficult, they would figure out how to get past the hard parts together.

When Diana went home that afternoon, she shared her excitement about learning to read. Mother, Dad, and Nanny all said that they too would help. Diana looked forward to going to school and had a positive view of learning something new. Sister Veronica's approach was that each child should have a goal and should learn the meaning of working toward that goal. If a child did not know what he or she wanted to learn or to do, Sister Veronica would explore ideas and perhaps make suggestions, and together they would determine a goal, even if it was a very small one. For some children, a first goal was learning to print the alphabet, then printing their names. For somewhat more advanced children, the goals had to be greater, such as learning to read or do arithmetic. Above all, Sister Veronica was consistent in that each child would have a goal, but the approach would be flexible enough to allow for growth and individual differences. In her words and deeds, Sister Veronica set up a classroom of hope, not just for some, but for all students.

Powell

Powell was nine years old and in the fourth grade when he first went to a public school. His kindergarten and first three grades had been at a private school with only a few students per teacher. He was an extremely bright boy and ahead of his class in most subjects; however, he was very tall for his age, extremely thin, wore glasses, and had braces on his teeth. At his private school the children had been kind and the teachers had made sure that no teasing took place.

Powell changed schools when his father moved to a new city to take a lower paying job. Initially, Powell was a curiosity to the other children, but soon they began to tease him because of his size, glasses, and braces. The teacher, Mrs. McBride, rarely interfered with the teasing, even in the class-room. Powell's grades began to suffer; in particular, he had an exceptionally difficult time with his multiplication tables. To make matters worse, Mrs. McBride appeared to take pleasure in asking Powell multiplication questions he could not answer.

POWELL

After the first teacher and parent conference, Powell's parents concluded that for whatever reasons, Mrs. McBride did not like their son. They worked with Powell on his arithmetic and had frequent talks with Mrs. McBride. At the end of the first semester, Powell was placed in a nearby parochial school and his grades improved. For years thereafter, however, Powell felt badly about his intelligence and his appearance. Although he matured into a handsome young man, he still imagined himself as the skinny, incompetent, and tormented fourth grader.

Teachers like Mrs. McBride leave trails of personal doubts in the minds of their students. When they do not attend to their classroom social climates, they do students a disservice. In considering how hope is integrated into the classroom, we must take into account all the types of things that children learn to do at school. The example of Powell concerns learning about getting along with others and the development of self-concept. His negative fourth-grade experience strongly influenced how he saw himself and how he believed others saw him. In addition to basic facts and operations, children learn a myriad of details about other people and themselves. Most of us remember elementary school as a critical time when we learned to relate to others and to find out who we were. Teachers often choreograph this real-life drama. Unfortunately, when the script is low in hope, so too will be the students.

Using Hope Stories with the Primary Grades

In carrying out our research on incorporating hope into classroom curricula, we have seen a variety of classrooms and observed many atmospheres. Generally, the learning environments we've observed have been positive, and teachers have relished the idea of encouraging their students to have higher hope. Most of our classroom work at the elementary level consists of setting aside blocks of time to share stories about and discuss hope. Children of all ages love to hear stories, and in the elementary classroom a story provides a pleasant break from the other, more demanding activities. So, when we come into the classroom and announce that each week we will be reading stories, there is great excitement. We tell the children that we are going to read about, talk about, and think about hope. In the upper grades, we also ask the children to write about hope, but for the lower grades (kindergarten through third grade) we concentrate on reading stories aloud and discussing their meaning.

We obtain a measure of hope (Children's Hope Scale) on the first and last sessions we have with the children. During the other weeks of the semester, we practice a regular pattern that becomes familiar to the students. We come to the classroom at a set time every week. When the children see us, they put away what they are doing and sit on a nearby rug. We first explain the definition of hope in this way: "Hope is something you can feel inside of you. It has two parts. One part is feeling and *knowing that you are able* to reach your goal, that you can do or get what you want. The second part is being able to *think of lots of ways* to reach your goal. When you have problems, you can think of ways to solve them. *So hope is feeling able to do a thing and finding ways to do it.*"

The children are encouraged to discuss this definition and give examples from their own lives. This hope exercise is repeated each session for the first four weeks. After the discussion, we read a story. Many of the stories we tell are sprinkled throughout this book. Two of the longer stories we use to illustrate high-hope models follow in this chapter. The first (Maggie) is for the lower grades (first through third) and the second (Miguel) is for the upper grades (fourth through sixth).

In order for stories to be effective in teaching hope, they must be understood. To ascertain whether the students get the main points of the story, we ask them to identify the main characters, name the goal, and tell how the central character reaches his or her goal. Important lessons are emphasized, and concepts the child does not understand are explained. (See subsequent "Discussing the Hope Story" sections later in this chapter for specific questions pertinent to the early and later primary grades.) In particular, we go over the story to show how the central figure sets a goal, feels empowered to reach it, and then has obstacles to overcome before reaching the goal. In some stories, the story hero finds that the original goal must be changed, and in others he or she does not reach the goal but discovers an unexpected benefit from putting forth the efforts. Children learn that one can be successful even if a specific goal is not reached. Key lessons are to be learned from trying, with or without success, that will be helpful the next time a goal is set.

Because the stories we use are about real children doing things most children could do, the jump from story to real life is easy. We ask the children to think of times when they set goals, overcame problems, and then achieved an outcome, whether or not it was what they expected. Even the youngest students can think of good examples. Some describe learning to roller skate or to ride a bike without training wheels. Many of the older children describe learning to swim and dive, and others talk about doing chores to earn money to buy something special, or learning to sew. As they tell us and each other what they had learned to do, we see pride and pleasure in their faces and hear excitement in their voices. Teachers also express pleasure and surprise, saying that this exercise uncovers a side of the children they seldom see.

All of the stories used throughout the semester depict actual high-hope children. They each follow a pattern of goal setting, determined work, and problem solving that leads to a satisfactory resolution (which may or may not be the original goal). Accompanying many of the stories are line drawings that can be duplicated and colored by the students. The stories we use are taken from a variety of cultures and socioeconomic levels so that all children can identify with the characters. Here is one of the stories we use with very young children.

Maggie

Maggie ran home from school with tears streaming down her face. It was her first day of school, ever, and the day had not gone at all the way she thought it would! She raced home and rushed straight to her bedroom, where she threw herself down on the bed and cried and cried.

Maggie's Aunt Ethel followed her into the room, and Maggie could dimly hear her aunt shooing her sisters, Belinda and Martha, outside to play.

"Maggie darlin', what on earth is the matter?" Aunt Ethel stroked Maggie's dark curls. "Did you have a bad first day at school?"

"Oh, Aunt Ethel, it was terrible!" cried Maggie. "My teacher, Mrs. Garfield, hates me! And all the other kids laughed at me!"

MAGGIE

"What on earth for, Mags?" asked Aunt Ethel, continuing to hold her close.

Maggie was so upset she couldn't even talk anymore. She just cried and cried as she remembered her terrible first day. Aunt Ethel just held her, rocked her, and rubbed her back until finally Maggie's tears began to dry up.

"Now honey, tell me what this is all about," Aunt Ethel said as she wiped Maggie's face with the corner of her apron. "What was so terrible at school today?"

"Mrs. Garfield just hates me," cried Maggie. "All day she was mean to me, and she said if I couldn't sit still and be quiet, she would send me to the principal! Then she said she would make me sit in a chair at the front of the room all by myself, and that's when all the other kids laughed at me." Maggie's eyes teared up again as she remembered how embarrassed she had been.

"Maggie, it sounds like Mrs. Garfield was upset, too. What were you doing that made her angry?" asked Aunt Ethel.

"I didn't do anything. I was just going to help Jeannie draw her tree on the board, 'cause she wasn't doing it right, and tell the answers to the questions 'cause I knew them all, and she told me to raise my hand and wait my turn, but she never called on me, and I kept forgetting."

"Maggie, I know it's hard for you, being the youngest child," said Aunt Ethel. "At home, whoever is the loudest and fastest with the answers usually gets the attention. Here, I can spend more time with you, because your brothers and sisters are older and need me less. But Mrs. Garfield has to make sure that everyone in her class gets some of her attention. That's her job. So she has rules about raising your hand to talk and taking turns so that everyone gets a turn."

"It will be hard to remember," Aunt Ethel admitted. "You are used to doing things a certain way, and you will have to learn to act a new way. But school is for learning new things, and I think you can learn this, just like you learned your ABCs. Do you think you can try?"

Maggie agreed to give it a try, and her Aunt Ethel hugged her and told her she was proud of her. And Maggie did try. But it was so hard. It seemed like every time she knew the answer, Mrs. Garfield would call on someone else, and Maggie would sometimes blurt it out before the other person could answer. Mrs. Garfield frowned at her when she did that, and Maggie felt very bad. But it was hard to remember to wait until she was called on when she knew the answer.

When it was time for Maggie's first report card, Maggie made very good grades. But in the behavior section, Maggie had a "U" for unsatisfactory, rather than an "S" for satisfactory. Mrs. Garfield wrote on the back, "Maggie is very smart, but she needs to raise her hand when she wants to talk, and let the other children have their turn." Maggie felt very bad.

Signing her report card, Aunt Ethel said, "Maggie, I just don't know what to say."

"Aunt Ethel, I really am trying," Maggie promised. "It's just so hard."

"As long as you keep trying, that will make me happy," said Aunt Ethel. "Sometimes it takes a while to learn something new. You just keep working at it."

Maggie tried to think of ways she could help herself remember to keep from shouting out answers in class. She knew that if the other children could keep still, she could learn to do that too. She tried to imagine herself sitting quietly at her desk with her hands in her lap. She could do that for a while each day at school, but soon her impatience to tell the answers got the better of her.

When Maggie got her second report card she didn't have a "U" in behavior, but she didn't have an "S" either. She had an "N" for "needs improvement." Mrs. Garfield wrote, "Maggie is getting better at taking turns in class, but she still forgets to raise her hand sometimes."

Aunt Ethel said "I'm proud of you, Maggie, for working so hard on this," and gave her a great big hug. Maggie felt better about the "N," but she still wanted to see an "S" for her behavior on her next report card. So, she worked even harder at raising her hand and waiting her turn.

"I know," thought Maggie. "Whenever Mrs. Garfield asks a question, I'll zip up my mouth before I raise my hand. And I can't unzip it until she calls on me, and I put my hand down." So Maggie turned this into her private game. Although the other kids looked at her strangely, it did help her to remember. And so she worked even harder at raising her hand and waiting her turn.

One day in December, Maggie was surprised to see Aunt Ethel at the classroom door just before lunch. Maggie wanted to go see what Aunt Ethel was doing there. Aunt Ethel came into the classroom and began to talk to Mrs. Garfield, and Maggie wanted to hear what they were saying. But she hadn't finished working on her numbers, so she stayed in her seat and kept on working. Aunt Ethel sat down on a chair at the front of the room.

"Okay class, let's put away our papers and get ready for lunch, " said Mrs. Garfield. "And before we go I have a special announcement to make."

Maggie put her papers in the desk and sat quietly waiting for Mrs. Garfield to call them to line up for lunch.

"Class, as you know, each month we have a Superkid Award for the best-behaved student in our class. This month, I am proud to announce that our award winner is Maggie Gordon, and her Aunt Ethel will join us for lunch today to help us celebrate." Mrs. Garfield held out a sheet of paper. "Maggie, will you please come and take this award, and then lead us to lunch?"

Maggie could hardly catch her breath, she was so surprised. But she calmly rose from her desk, walked quietly to the front of the room, and took the certificate from Mrs. Garfield, who gave her a big, beautiful smile. As Maggie led the way to lunch she whispered to Aunt Ethel, "I think she likes me after all!"

Discussing the Hope Story

After students in our research groups hear this story, they are asked a series of questions to help them to discover the hope in the vignette and to apply it to their own lives. The following questions are ones we have used with the story of Maggie.

1. Who was the main person in the story?
2. What did she want to have happen?
3. What did Maggie try in order to get what she wanted?
4. What were some of the problems Maggie had?
5. What was her plan at the beginning? How did it change by the end?
6. How did Maggie feel by the end of the story? Why did she feel that way?
7. Think of something you really wanted to do that was hard for you. What was it?
8. How were you able to do it? What things did you try?

9. What were the problems that got in your way? How did you
   solve the problems?
10. Were you finally able to do it? How did you feel at the end?

Even children as young as five are able to answer these questions, sometimes with some prompting or further explanation. The first three questions are posed to insure that the children understand who is the high-hope
person in the story, and the remainder examine the hope process. It is necessary that the students can identify Maggie's goal, which in this case is
learning to take turns in answering questions and thereby earning an "S"
on her report card. Students also must recognize the effort (willpower)
Maggie put into learning this new behavior. They should see waypower evidenced when Maggie finally hit upon the idea of zipping her mouth when
the questions were asked. It is helpful if the children can learn the
"willpower" and "waypower" terms, but more important is that they understand the underlying concepts.

Once children understand the process of hope, they can begin to identify
it in themselves. Hope does not always involve major goals—it can be seen
in small tasks as well. If students cannot think of something they have done
that was difficult, the teacher or parents can prompt with examples such as
learning to print one's name, learning to say numbers or the alphabet, and
so on. The important thing is that the children come to see themselves as
people who can achieve in the present and future, *because they already
have achieved in the past.*

Returning to the idea of parents as teaching partners, we see that Maggie's Aunt Ethel played an important role in helping Maggie achieve her
goal at school. The following story is about another high-hope child who
was temporarily derailed but helped back on track by his parents and
teacher working together.

Matt

When Matt was in the second grade his parents got a divorce and his father went to live in another city only a few miles away. The custody order
allowed Matt to visit his father every other weekend, which was less time
than either of them wanted. On those special weekends Matt and his father
did all their favorite things and thoroughly enjoyed themselves. There were
no rules for Matt with his father, and life was like a big party from Friday
night until Sunday afternoon.

Soon after this arrangement took affect, Matt's schoolwork and his class
behavior began to show signs of strain. Matt often failed to pay attention
to what the teacher was saying, gazing out the window or daydreaming instead. On the days before and after a visit with his father, Matt was restless
and often blurted out answers and comments in class. Matt's teacher, Miss

Gold, called Matt's mother one evening to discuss the problem. The next afternoon Miss Gold and Matt's mother and father, who had taken the afternoon off from work to attend the conference, all sat down with Matt to discuss what could be done about the situation.

Matt's mother and father had already agreed that he should see a child psychologist for a while so that he could have a private place to learn about his feelings. In addition to this they agreed that Miss Gold would work out a checklist of behaviors that Matt should be doing each day. These included such things as paying attention, waiting his turn to speak, and doing any assignments sent home. These were all things Matt had readily done before the divorce.

Matt's mother agreed to initial the checklist every night Monday through Thursday, and his father agreed to initial it on Fridays. If the checklist showed good behavior for the day, then Matt was entitled to a treat such as a special food, extra time reading with Mom, or a video. If the checklist was not satisfactory, those special things would not happen. Matt agreed to this plan. In fact, he embraced it willingly because he did not want to do poorly in school. He felt very happy that his parents were working together in a cordial manner for his welfare. Miss Gold was pleased, too, because she knew she had Matt's parents' support and cooperation.

Teachers and parents both can feel isolated in their respective responsibilities. *It is our experience that when they begin working together, even in a situation as potentially difficult as Matt's, the outcome is always beneficial to the child.* Matt's parents and his teacher showed high hope in their approach and determination to help Matt with his problem. This served as a model for Matt's hope in the future, showing him that problems can be surmounted and that the important people in his life were there for him.

Stories about high-hope children provide wonderful examples for discussion, but there are many other things that can be done in the elementary classroom that foster hope. Ms. Brimm's classroom, described in Chapter 8, showed how a teacher can help children achieve both large and small goals while teaching them to have higher hope. Recall that Ms. Brimm helped each child identify one goal that he or she specifically wanted to accomplish. After the goal has been determined, teachers of young children need to monitor progress and give children assistance or reminders where needed. In this way, the teacher can praise the student as progress is made and also be aware when problems arise. Let's look at an example of how this might work.

Jimmy

Jimmy has decided that he wants to learn to keep his desk clean and orderly because he has been losing many of his papers and pencils lately.

Each afternoon before school is over, Ms. Brimm looks in his desk to see whether it is orderly. If the desk is neat, she praises Jimmy for remembering to keep it tidy. If the desk is messy, she gives Jimmy a gentle reminder. She notices that some days, particularly those with a large amount of paperwork, are more difficult for Jimmy than others. Ms. Brimm discusses with Jimmy how he might keep better track of his desk items. Together they decide on a system of folders with labels. Within several weeks, Jimmy has learned to keep his desk neat all the time, for which he receives lots of praise.

Ms. Brimm plays a very important role in this example. It is she who encourages Jimmy to decide on a goal. She checks on his progress, problem-solves with him, and finally sees that he incorporates his achievement as hope. Although this process takes time and attention, the end rewards to both the child and the teacher are great. For Jimmy, the immediate reward is that he has his papers and supplies when needed and does not use teacher or class time searching for them. The long-term rewards are that he learns to monitor his own progress as he builds his successes, and that teacher input can decrease. High-hope children have a strong desire to succeed and can cope well with problems. In this instance, in addition to the other benefits, Jimmy received a self story of hope.

For children from kindergarten through grades three or four, depending on their language skills, we recommend frequent readings that feature high-hope role models. To be most effective, however, each story should be accompanied by the types of questions detailed previously under "Discussing the Hope Story," and group discussion should take place to reinforce the concept of hope. In addition, the goal-setting model should be used. Together, these two techniques provide young children with a good start for hoping.

Hope in the Upper Elementary Grades

The story of Maggie is suitable for the early grades because the main character is beginning school. Maggie's goal of learning to take her turn could be a goal shared by many kindergartners or first-graders. For children in the upper elementary grades, where language skills are more developed, we recommend both reading and writing hope stories. For these students, a suitable story is read, the concept of hope is again discussed along with appropriate questions, and children then are asked to write their own hope stories. Here is an example of this method.

Miguel

Miguel came to San Diego from Mexico when he was nine years old. First, his father went to California and got a job as a gardener in the yard-care business of Miguel's uncle. Soon Miguel's mother was able to join his father, because she too had the promise of a job. While his mother and father were working in California, Miguel and his brother and sister lived with their grandmother in a little village called Las Palmas, in central Mexico. Miguel liked the small town, but he longed to be in San Diego with his mother and father. Then, one day Miguel's father came to get the children. He said that Miguel's mother had just had another baby, a little sister, and that the new sister would be a United States citizen. Because of this, as well as the fact that Miguel's mother and father had jobs, Miguel could join them in San Diego.

Saying good-bye to his grandmother and the village was sad, but the trip to California in their father's old car was fun. Miguel saw parts of Mexico he had never seen. The children were quiet with wonder, especially as they got close to the large city of San Diego.

The house Miguel's parents lived in was very small, but it was bigger than his grandmother's house in Las Palmas. There was a yard with no grass, but it was a place to play. Lots of children were in other yards and in the street, and when Miguel and his brother and sister got out of the car, many of the children crowded around them. Miguel stood in a circle of noisy boys and girls who all seemed to be asking him questions he could not understand, and he was frightened and confused. Miguel's older brother put his arms around him and told the other children, in Spanish, that he did not understand English. It seemed that many of these children could speak both Spanish and English. Maria, a girl about Miguel's age, told him that he would have to learn to speak English before he could go to school.

Miguel and Maria became good friends, and because it was summertime, they had a lot of time to play together. But they always spoke Spanish when they played. Miguel's mother and father spoke Spanish at home, too. Miguel felt as if he were still in Mexico, not in San Diego. He could see that if he was going to become part of the United States, he would have to find a way to learn to speak English. And, he would have to learn fast, because summertime was half over. Because Maria could speak both languages, however, Miguel knew he could learn too. He began to form a plan.

Miguel asked Maria to give him English lessons; in turn, he would teach her something she wanted to learn. But what could he teach Maria that she couldn't already do? He had to think hard about the things he could do well. He had learned to ride a bike, but she could do that too. He could throw and catch balls, but so could she. He could climb trees, but she was even better at that than he was. What did he know how to do that she didn't?

He thought about his former home in the little village. Since he had been very small, he had danced the traditional dances of Mexico and played the castanets (small wooden clappers that fit onto his thumb). Las Palmas always celebrated holidays with festivals, and Miguel knew people enjoyed watching him dance. Miguel had brought his castanets to San Diego. He showed Maria how he could use them and dance the Mexican folk dances.

MIGUEL AND MARIA

Maria thought it looked like fun, and she agreed to give Miguel English lessons if he would teach her to dance and play the castanets. The rest of the summer, they worked and played together. They had English lessons for one hour each morning, and dance and castanets lessons for an hour each afternoon, using music from the local Mexican-American radio station. Between lessons they played and did chores, with Maria speaking English to Miguel. It was very hard, and sometimes they got angry when they weren't learning as fast as they expected. But both were determined to reach their goals. Miguel was determined to begin school knowing enough English to understand the teacher, and Maria wanted to be able to dance in their own Mexican-American holiday celebrations.

Eventually September came, and it was time for school to start. On the first day, Miguel was able to tell his teacher about himself and where he had lived in Mexico, all in English. His teacher was very pleased with his English and said she thought he had learned very fast.

Meanwhile, Maria and Miguel kept practicing their castanets and dancing. When it was time for the community fiesta at Christmas, Maria's mother made her a red, lacy, full-skirted dress to go with the costume Miguel had brought from Mexico. Maria and Miguel danced the Jarabe Tapatillo—the Mexican hat dance—and kept time with their castanets. They got lots of applause, and their picture was in the local newspaper. All of this was wonderful for Miguel. What he liked best was that he now felt like a real Californian, but he could still keep his wonderful Mexican culture.

Discussing the Hope Story

As with the younger children, it is just as important to discuss the hope story with the fourth-, fifth-, and sixth-graders. The story of Miguel is more complicated than the story of Maggie, and it presents opportunities for learning a wider variety of information. For example, if the students are unfamiliar with Mexican-American culture, this story enables them to learn about different customs and to begin to understand what it would be like to be from another country. It also allows for a geography lesson by showing a route from central Mexico to San Diego. Because of the amount of information in the story, however, it is important to check the children's comprehension of the basic ideas before proceeding to a discussion of hope. The following questions are some we use with fourth- through sixth-grade students. The first six questions determine how well the story was understood, and the remaining questions are designed to explore hope.

1. Who was the main person in the story? Who was his friend?
2. What did Miguel decide he needed to do? What was his goal?
3. How did Miguel decide to achieve his goal?
4. What did Maria want to do? What was her goal?
5. How did they work toward their goals?
6. What happened in the end?
7. Miguel believed he could accomplish his goal, and he had a strong desire to do it. Talk (or write) about a time in your life when you wanted to do something that was difficult, but you believed you could do it. Talk (or write) about what the goal was and how you felt as you thought about working for it.
8. Talk (or write) about the problems you had as you worked for your goal. What were all the ways you thought of to solve those problems?
9. Talk (or write) about how the situation ended. Did you achieve your goal? Did you change to another goal? Did you give up?
10. Whatever the outcome was, talk (or write) about how you felt and what you said to yourself about being able to reach goals.

Upper elementary school students generally have the language skills to write basic hope stories about themselves. Young children often blur the line between what they have actually done and what they wish they had done, but it is our experience that even wishful stories are helpful in producing hope. Teachers and parents who read or listen to these stories should be able to tell the difference between fact and fancy and can respond positively to each story. While it is important not to accept something the child has not actually done as being real, it also is important to let the child know that the story is a good wish and that it might be possible. If the story is plausible, but you have doubts, it is best to treat it as fact. Writing the individual stories is an important way of incorporating hope into the curriculum. Along with addressing grammar, spelling, and sentence structure, teachers also can discuss how each child uses hope in his or her life.

In the previous chapter, we described how to examine the hope in your own stories. Teachers can use the same process in working with students, just as parents can when reading their children's hope stories. Be sure to praise the child for the accomplishment, or for effort if the goal was not reached. If the child reports having given up, it is important to brainstorm with the child other alternatives for problem solving or goal substitution. Even though this process is time consuming, it really is best to discuss your comments about the story individually with each child.

Parents can play an integral part in helping children write their own hope stories. Some suggestions have been given in previous chapters for helping children with stories. For example, the parents of the little boy in Chapter 5 who wanted to play the "thiddle" could help this child build a very interesting and high-hope story. Parents can help children recognize their hope by repeating stories of the things they have done. Such stories, as mentioned in Chapters 4 and 5, become family legends. Parents can discuss all the wonderful things that they and their children have learned to do over the years. Sessions of this type between parent and child are very positive and build hope. Children, caught up as they are in their daily lives, do not have the sense of perspective that a parent has about all the things the child has learned and accomplished *and what an achievement growing up really is.*

Summarizing the Hopeful Elementary Classroom

The architect of the hope-filled classroom is the high-hope teacher. Such a teacher approaches each student with an attitude that reflects both "You can find a way" and "You can do it!" The belief that each child can accomplish something worthwhile and learn something of value will carry over to the child and stimulate effort. We have suggested working individually with children to help them set goals, learning to monitor their own progress, engaging in active problem solving with them, and praising their efforts and accomplishments. Goals can be based on classroom behavior and daily habits, as in the case of Jimmy and the clean desk, but they also can be based on the curriculum content that must be covered in each grade. With a hope-laden approach, the child comes to view learning in the positive light of goal achievement. Learning to read, write, spell, do arithmetic, and understand all the other topics that are taught should *not* be presented or construed as occasions for failures; rather, *they become opportunities for students to succeed.*[3]

To supplement the hopeful approach to teaching content, stories are an excellent vehicle for examining and highlighting hope in children's lives. We suggest reading and discussing stories about high-hope children at all grade levels, with older children writing their own hope stories. Whether the stories tie into or supplement the language curricula, make sure that every story is processed individually so that the hope content is made clear and the child is praised for effort or accomplishment.

Some Final Comments on Feasibility

As you have read these suggestions for bringing hope into the classroom, you may have been thinking of how difficult they would be to implement in some schools. We recognize that a large number of schools are overcrowded, underfunded, located in dangerous places, and fraught with a myriad of social problems. Against this backdrop of concerns, however, remember this one thing: *The students who attend these schools are the ones who need the infusion of hope the very most.* We find that young children are often more filled with hope than older children or adolescents, so it becomes important to preserve what they have and to see that hope not only stays alive but prospers. The key is to start small. Student goals and personal goals for teachers must be realistic and manageable so that success is possible. In difficult classrooms it may be necessary to begin with the more cooperative students, allowing their successes to attract the more difficult students. Most children of elementary school age are still relatively tractable, willing to participate in activities and give your ideas a chance. Middle school, junior high and high school students pose more complex challenges. Ideas for teachers of these grades are presented in the next chapter.

Based on our past experience with teachers, we are willing to bet that despite your awareness of the difficulties involved in incorporating yet one more item into your curriculum, these ideas are attractive and exciting to your imagination. As you see the enthusiasm in the eyes of your students and their eagerness to embrace the hope process, your own fires will be kindled and your pleasure in teaching will be enhanced. Messages of hope are transmitted from teacher to student and, equally importantly, from student to teacher. Hope is a two-way street.

10

Teachers Nourishing Tales of Hope: Secondary School Years

Tweener Time

From the seventh through twelfth grades, boys and girls are changing from children, but they are not adults either. They are "Tweeners," crossing the tumultuous and exciting terrain of the teenage years. Increasingly over this time span, they are trying to put together personal stories that are coherent and understandable both to themselves and others. This is no easy task, however, as the Tweener is driven from within by raging hormones and from without by confusing social interactions. Oh yes, did we mention that these volatile creatures also are attending school throughout this period? No longer cute little girls and boys, they nevertheless are students who hunger for guidance through these "wonder years." In the present chapter, we will explore how teachers can use stories of hope to help Tweeners solidify their personal narratives. The goal: That our students and children, through the combined efforts of teachers and parents, will have hope-filled personal narratives as they travel from junior to senior high school. Ideas for solidifying stories of hope during these years will highlight extracurricular activities and the classroom.

Extracurricular Hope

Conferences between parents and teachers are not as routine in secondary school as in the earlier grades, but it is still possible to achieve communication between school and home, especially if the young person is engaged in a variety of school activities. Even parents who are not especially interested in their children's academic schoolwork may become fascinated by sports or club-related activities. As we reasoned in Chapter 9, the benefits of having parents involved are worth the extra efforts that are sometimes required to entice them to participate. An involved parent takes an interest in that part of the student's self-story that is created and lived out in the school environment.

A hope-filled tale in the context of school is one in which the student sees school-based activities as relating to his or her success, both now and in the future. Young people with hopeful narratives frequently have regularly scheduled activities such as sports, subject-related clubs, community service activities, and so on. They are not always in the high-profile activities such as cheerleading or football, nor are they always the most popular. They do, however, find an identity (or identities) through curricular or extracurricular activities. Having a sense of identity, as well as a sense of belonging, is critical to the positive adjustment stories of adolescents. Therefore, school-based activities not only help to structure time but also help to form healthy identities and hope-filled scripts to help avoid dangerous pitfalls and seek workable solutions to problems.[1] We will present examples of how this process can be fostered, but first, here is a story about a young man whose risk factors were creatively turned into preventative factors.

An Administrator Takes a Chance on Ryan

When Ryan was a young child, his parents suspected he might be hyperactive, but it turned out that he simply had a great deal of energy and was very intelligent. As Ryan progressed through elementary school, he developed a reputation as the class clown. He earned laughs but lowered his grades. Though he was likable, teachers began to peg him as a troublemaker and a potential problem.

Ryan's reputation followed him to junior high. His clever behaviors were no longer tolerated as they had been previously, and the number of his detentions began to mount. By the eighth grade, Ryan had accumulated many detentions, several in-school suspensions, and one three-day out-of-school suspension.

Ryan's parents were nearly frantic with worry. Ryan had begun to hate school and to feel he had been branded. This was in part true. The teacher grapevine was efficient, and teachers who had never met Ryan were prepared for his antics. Ryan's tricks and jokes had become so common that he was blamed for almost everything bad that happened in class. Sensitive to such unfairness, Ryan felt increasingly negative about school. Ryan's parents tried psychotherapy, which was helpful, but it did nothing for his negative attitude toward school. His frequent anti-authoritarian behavior remained.

Although a number of enjoyable after-school activities were available at school, from Ryan's point of view any minute spent at school after the final bell rang was a minute wasted. To make matters worse, the one thing Ryan really wanted to learn was not sanctioned by the school; in fact, it was frowned upon by school officials. He wanted to learn to ride a skateboard. Skaters, however, were considered one step away from gang members. They wore big, baggy pants and shirts that hung nearly to their knees. They frequently had shaved or buzz-cut hair, wore earrings, and had wallets attached to their pants with a long chain. This image conjured fear among many adults.

Looks can be deceiving, however, and serious skaters are seldom out on the street doing the things people assume. Learning to do the difficult skateboard tricks takes as much practice and concentration as learning to do any sport well. When Ryan began to make friends with the few other skaters in school, his parents invited them over for a pizza party. They quickly discovered that the boys were all "straight edge"—that is, they did not use any drugs, tobacco, or alcohol. Several of the boys were vegetarians and quite environmentally conscious.

Ryan's parents were pleased and supportive of his new interest. They bought him good equipment and allowed him to wear the requisite skater uniform. As the months went by, he was able to master several difficult tricks, and Ryan's mother videotaped him regularly to document his progress. Problems began to develop, however, when Ryan and his parents discovered that skaters have a very poor image among educators. As Ryan became a better skater, it was necessary to find more challenging places to skate, such as areas that had benches to ollie (when a skater jumps high and the board appears to stick to the bottom of the feet) up onto, and stairs to ollie down. These usually were public places from which the skaters were frequently evicted.

The situation threatened to become another malevolent encounter with authority for Ryan. Something had to be done. By now skating had become very important, and through it Ryan was developing an identity and a sense of belonging. He was determined to continue skating, even if it meant defying the authorities. Ryan's parents were completely supportive of skateboarding, knowing how much effort and practice it took to do well. They decided to take action to have this activity recognized as a legitimate sport, and they asked the school to allow Ryan to form a skateboard club. There would be at least six members to begin with, and perhaps more later. The school had steps and benches, in addition to smooth surfaces, that would make ideal skating areas. Each parent could provide insurance and sign a waiver of responsibility, just as was done with other student athletes. Further, Ryan knew a teacher whose son had been a skater, and she might be a faculty sponsor.

Because of Ryan's reputation, his parents went with him to talk to the principal. They agreed to let Ryan do most of the talking but to be backup support, if needed. Ryan presented an articulate case, stressing that the club would cover liability and damages done to the facilities. The principal was surprisingly positive about the idea but needed to discuss it with the school board. The next week the principal called Ryan to his office. This time the visit was not about some infraction but rather to share some good news: The skateboard club was approved.

Ryan and his friends were excited and especially pleased to have their activity recognized. Three days a week after the last class hour, they could skate at school. Soon, word of their skating got around, and other students stayed to see their tricks. Ryan was finding acceptable and rewarding ways of entertaining his classmates. As the school year progressed, Ryan developed a more positive attitude toward school, eventually joining the computer club and taking part in a fledgling rock band. His grades improved, and he began to look forward to high school. An additional perk from Ryan's point of view, but a dubious one from his parents' standpoint, was that he was now an idol of girls who kept the telephone line busy.

Despite his attention-getting behavior and his frequent brushes with trouble, Ryan was a high-hope child. Once he found an interest that was compelling, with the help of interested parents he reshaped his identity so as to set and achieve goals. A critical factor in the positive outcome of this story is that the school administrator was able to see beyond typical prejudices. He was willing to take a chance both on an activity and on a boy. In the long run, his risks and positive attitude paid off not just for Ryan, but for his friends who had moved from feeling alienated to perceiving that they had a place at school.

Wrong-Way Rhonda and Rules

A junior high school had a lot of congestion in the hallways during class changes. The administrators thought about this problem and instituted a rule whereby all the students would have to walk in one direction only. Rhonda, an eighth-grader, was given a detention for walking five feet in the wrong direction to get to her locker, rather than walking around the entire building and being late to her next class. Additionally, many seventh-graders, new to the junior high scene anyway, became so frustrated with all the incomprehensible rules that this "direction rule" was the last straw. A few students just stood in the hallway and cried. These students began to think of themselves as confused and ineffectual; their personal stories became tinged with hopelessness.

One of adolescents' and their parents' greatest frustrations is to come up against rules and regulations for which there appear to be no reasonable justifications. Some rules are obviously necessary, and usually these do not cause consternation. Other rules, however, border on the ridiculous. Students and parents alike recognize the irrationality of many school rules. Is it any wonder that many young people feel disheartened, alienated, and removed from such systems?

Many school rules deprive students of decision-making experiences. Such rules, although designed to create ease in school management, in fact produce more problems as students act out their frustrations in destructive and antisocial ways. Unfortunately, the approach taken over time in many school systems is to institute *more* rules and regulations. The logic of this thinking is difficult to follow. In contrast, giving thought and careful attention to rules and regulations and allowing some degree of student input not only can lessen frustration but also can provide a climate in which hope can flourish. Administrators, teachers, students, and parents must work together to find creative ways to solve problems that allow maximum respect for students.

Developing Fertile Ground for Growing High-Hope Students

The atmosphere of a secondary school can be sensed almost immediately upon entering the building. Are the secretaries and office staff friendly? Is the principal available and friendly? Is the counselor a helpful person who meets with students in a private and restful office? Do examples of students' achievements hang on the walls and fill the showcases? These elements are possible regardless of whether a school has money, and they are important signals to students that this will be a happy and positive—rather than a negative—experience for them. The atmosphere should be one in which students feel free to grow, set their own goals, and pursue their achievements. Teachers and administrators are available to assist in this endeavor and should be viewed as helping, not hindering.

How can a secondary school become a place for growing high-hope students? The first step has been discussed in Chapter 8, where teachers were encouraged and shown how to assess and develop their own levels of hope. Because we now have implicated administrators in the effort to develop high-hope–producing schools, we suggest that they, too, follow the processes detailed in Chapter 8 so that they will view the school environment from the same hope-engendering vantage point.

We recognize that new approaches are constantly offered to and required from teachers who may become cynical about the possibility of change. To effect real change, an important step must be undertaken by school personnel as a group or by individual teachers and administrators. *This is the decision to include hope activities in the school program.* In the schools in which we have conducted our hope-training research, the entire faculty have made decisions together. Once the idea of producing higher-hope students is explained to teachers and staff, there usually is an enthusiastic response. Teachers and administrators genuinely want to help students live happier and more productive lives. Our experience with teachers and administrators who work in lower-income schools is that they recognize the problems inherent in their students' lives and do not blame the victims. Indeed, we have found that these teachers are desperately searching for ways to increase hope in their students.[2]

Once teachers and administrators choose to introduce hope activities, each individual must then assess how to incorporate them into the individual classroom or school function. The ways to do this will be determined by the type of activity or the subject taught. For example, an English class could incorporate a variety of hope activities that would not be appropriate for the football coach or the school counselor. In the next section, we will illustrate hope-developing strategies for junior and senior high school subjects.

In the Classroom

The approach used in the high-hope junior and senior high classroom is similar to that used in elementary school. That is, there must be goal setting, problem solving, an outcome, and a developing sense of understanding the student's own empowerment through this process. What differs are the types of goals, the variety of pathways open to older students to problem solve, and the methods for teaching an understanding of the hope process. To illustrate some strategies a teacher might use, we will take English and basic sciences classes as examples.

English

This subject may be the easiest through which to convey hope because reading and writing stories fall into its purview. Throughout this book we have stressed the use of stories to foster hope in children, and this remains important for adolescents. The nature of the stories will be more complex and the protagonists will be older, but the process of using stories to illustrate high-hope situations remains the same. Young people read works of literature at school to become familiar with excellent writing and to learn the enjoyment of reading. Do they also experience reading as a way to learn about themselves? They will do so if teachers give assignments that require self-examination in light of the insights provided in the literature. For example, young people can examine their own reactions to adversity after reading Anne Frank's tender memoirs. Tom Sawyer, though mischievous, provides a good example of a high-hope young man. The protagonists in these and other books demonstrate high hope, and they can spark students' introspective imaginations about their personal approaches to setting and securing goals.

One type of assignment is to ask students to write about an adventure from their own lives. A student who feels she or he has had no such adventures may make up a story in which the student plays the central role. Although spelling, punctuation, and grammar are important to the student's learning, creativity might be enhanced if the assignment is not graded and if errors are simply corrected. To highlight and develop hope through this assignment, it is important that the central character's behavior be discussed according to the hope concept as described throughout this book. Similarly, the student's written adventures should be discussed in these terms.

A related way of incorporating hope into the English classroom is to use some of the high-hope stories provided in this book. The story can be read to the class—accompanied by an explanation of hope—and then students can be asked to write their own hope stories. One such story appropriate for students in junior high school is given here.

Alice Discovers Tae Kwon Do. Alice, a tall seventh grader, was extremely thin and wore glasses. Although she didn't wear a pocket protector filled with mechanical pencils, she fit the "nerd" image in most respects. She spent her afternoons playing computer games or reading books, and she also liked to play chess. The few friends she saw outside of school were interested in the same things.

Alice's mother was a different character. She had played basketball throughout school and had even been on the college varsity team. She liked basketball, soccer, and swimming, none of which especially interested Alice.

One evening, Alice's mother announced that it was time for her to learn to play a sport and that it was going to be basketball, to take advantage of Alice's height. She was certain that if Alice gave it a good try, she would learn to love it. The next day Alice's mother called the coach to enlist Alice on the team. For the next few weeks Alice was miserable. She was neither quick nor aggressive, and she had little interest in competitive sports. Practice games were the worst. If she made if off the bench, the coach or other team members yelled at her because she missed a ball or a basket. She seemed all legs and feet when she ran, she couldn't shoot, and though she

ALICE

towered over the other players, whomever she was guarding seemed to spurt past her.

Finally, Alice convinced her mother that basketball was not for her, and she was allowed to quit. She gladly went back to her computer and books. Nevertheless, the pressure for Alice to choose a sport continued in frequent dinnertime discussions. Although playing a sport was not important to Alice, she loved her mother a great deal and wanted to please her. Because of this, she began to explore whether any particular sport might better suit her personality and interests.

Because some of the books and computer games that had interested Alice involved martial arts, she began to research the various martial arts available in her town, the costs involved, and most importantly, the philosophy behind each. If she was going to learn a martial art, she wanted one that was strictly for self-defense, not for aggression. She finally chose American-Korean Tae Kwon Do, and her parents agreed to pay for the lessons.

After purchasing the required pants, jacket, and white belt, Alice began her twice-a-week lessons. She was surprised to see so many people of all ages, shapes, and sizes at the class. With such a variety it was impossible for her to feel out of place. Furthermore, because she was in a beginner's class with all white belts, her lack of skill was not noticeable. Alice worked hard to learn the forms, practicing every afternoon. Within a month, she was able to pass the test and move up to a white belt with a yellow stripe. One more month and she was wearing a yellow belt. It was time to show her mother what she was learning.

Alice's mother had shown only mild interest in Tae Kwon Do thus far, not really considering it a sport. When Alice asked her to attend the next testing session, which also would be followed by competitions and demonstrations, she agreed. Alice performed well at the testing, earning an orange stripe on her yellow belt. The demonstrations of sparring and the bare-handed breaking of bricks and boards by the more advanced students were very impressive. So intriguing and impressive, in fact, that Alice's mother asked if she might also enroll in classes.

As Alice and her mother began studying Tae Kwon Do together, they became better friends. Alice had much to teach her mother and, for once, could demonstrate superior skill. Tae Kwon Do may be a martial art, rather than a traditional sport, but Alice's mother discovered how challenging it was to learn. She developed respect for her daughter's physical prowess and no longer pressured Alice to play a traditional sport.

Alice, the central figure in this story, was a junior high school student. In order to provide a character with whom senior high school students can identify, we offer the story of Drew, a young woman who seemingly had everything.

Drew Tests Her Capabilities. Drew was a fortunate young woman. She had two parents who loved her and could afford to give her whatever she wanted, and certainly everything she needed. She lived in a very large home on a lovely tree-lined street, and she went to a good school. In addition to all of this, Drew was also intelligent and an excellent athlete. Her grades were better than average, and she demonstrated real talent for field hockey and tennis. It seemed that fortune had certainly smiled upon Drew.

The problem with this apparently ideal life was that Drew felt there was something missing. She felt a little empty. Sure, she could have and do what she wanted, but where was the challenge in life? In books, she had read about people who built character through struggle. Even her own grandfather had worked very hard to build the successful business Drew would one day inherit. Drew loved her life, and she loved what she saw as her future. But still, where was the challenge?

Drew began to ask herself if things had always been easy for her, or if, perhaps, she had simply chosen things she knew she could do. Had she only picked activities where she knew beforehand that she could excel? Drew felt she needed to test herself. She needed a struggle. Could she achieve a goal that was difficult, one that she was not sure of beforehand?

There was one thing that Drew loved as much as she loved sports: She loved music. She knew all the current bands and went to all the concerts that came to town. When she wasn't at school or playing tennis or field hockey, she was in her room listening to music. Often when she listened, she would imagine herself playing in a band, but she usually dismissed the dream because she had never learned to play a musical instrument. Now though, as she sat in her room listening to a band she especially liked—one she knew had formed while still in high school—she began to wonder if this was the challenge that could make her life less empty.

The first thing Drew did was figure out which musical instrument she would most like to learn. When she listened to music, she often kept beat on the table top with pencils. Drums might be the thing for her. That evening at dinner she spoke with her parents about playing the drums. She didn't tell them that she wanted to form a band because she thought they might not approve. They did encourage her to find out where she could get lessons, and if she really liked playing the drums, they would see about investing in a set after a while.

Finding the drum teacher was easy, but learning to play the drums was far more difficult than Drew had imagined. There seemed to be so many rhythms to remember, and both hands and feet had to be working at the same time, often at different beats. But Drew was well coordinated and, most important, she was willing to put in the required practice hours. After several months her parents bought Drew a drum set and allowed her to set up a studio in the basement.

By this time Drew had met two young men, one who played bass and one who played lead guitar. They had begun to practice several afternoons a week in Drew's basement studio. Sometimes they played music written by established bands, but frequently they improvised their own music. None of them could write music, so they tape-recorded what they played in order to remember how it sounded, and they all thought they were improving.

After several months of practice, it became obvious that they needed a singer. One of the young men had a friend who went to a different school and who had once been a singer with another band. This worked out well because, as a new person with different talents, the singer brought life to the band. The singer not only could write music but had a number of songs that she had written herself. The band began to practice these songs, which gave them a unique repertoire.

As the band became more proficient at their songs, they began to think of performing for schools or small clubs. Because the original idea had been Drew's, and she had a good mind for business, she became the band's promoter as well as its drummer. She first borrowed enough money from her father to make a demonstration tape. With copies of that tape in hand, Drew visited the managers of many clubs, finally securing a spot in an upcoming show.

All four musicians were nervous the night of the show. They believed, however, that they had rehearsed enough to perform well, and after all, this could be considered a learning experience. Their band was the first on the bill, so there were not many people in the club yet, a decided relief to the four young people. The performance went very well, and the few people in the audience applauded loudly. Afterward, the club manager said he would like them to play the next weekend too, both Friday and Saturday night. This was a good beginning, and Drew was enjoying the success.

As Drew thought about how the evening had gone, about the applause, and about all the hard work that had gone into establishing the band, she felt really proud that she had accomplished her goal. She had set out to meet a challenge, had overcome the obstacles, and had succeeded. One of the best parts about the experience was that Drew felt more certain that she could set and achieve goals on her own, and not rely on her fortunate circumstances.

Instructions for Students Writing Their Own Hope Story.   After the high-hope story has been read, students should be allowed time to process the story. A check should be made to find out whether all students understand how Alice or Drew demonstrated high hope. Alice wanted to please her mother, and though she failed at basketball, she searched until she found a physical activity she was truly interested in. After deciding to learn Tae Kwon Do, Alice worked hard to achieve a level of success she could show her mother. Her mother was proud, but an even better outcome occurred—they developed a mutual interest. In the story about Drew, the goal was to test Drew's ability to master a challenge and achieve her goal on her own, without primary reliance on her favored family circumstances. Students should be able to identify the hope processes evidenced in these stories before beginning to write their own hope story.

For this assignment, it is important that students use actual events from their own lives. The event does not have to be major; accounts of small goals achieved where difficulties were overcome are a fine beginning. If a student cannot think of any high-hope experience, teachers can often elicit ideas after a brief conversation with the student about his or her life. Again, as with the previous suggestion, the story—not the writing style—is the focus. Students should practice the elements of written communication through this exercise, but it may not be necessary to strictly grade this assignment. Allowing the students some freedom will increase their creativity and enhance their interests in learning about hope.

The format for the story is simple. A student is to write about a time when she or he had a goal, felt empowered, and overcame difficulties in order to achieve a specific outcome. It is important to stress that the specific goal need not have been achieved. The goal may have been changed, or the experience of trying may have been success enough. It is difficult for young people to understand that success does not always mean achieving a goal. There is a tendency for "all or nothing" thinking in young people, and this is an opportunity to teach an alternative view: *There is much to be learned from trying and doing one's best.*

Once the stories have been turned in and read by the teacher, the next task in teaching hope begins. If the story is filled with hope, positive comments should be noted on the student's paper so as to reinforce the way in which the student demonstrated hope in the story, and thus, in life. If the story does not show hope, perhaps the student didn't really understand the concept. Whatever the cause, a one-to-one discussion is in order. During this discussion, it is important to help the student find some effort, goal, or accomplishment in his or her life that demonstrated hope. The student can then be asked to write a new story using this incident.

A Detailed Example of a Teacher Working with a Low-Hope Student: The Case of Marcia. Although teachers often convey their messages to students on a one-to-one basis, interactions with students about the hope manifested in their stories may verge, at times, on the kind of communication engaged in by counselors. Here is an example of how such a discussion with a low-hope student might look.

Marcia has told her teacher that she cannot do the assignment because she does not feel she has accomplished anything in her life worth writing about. Marcia's teacher, Ms. Green, is meeting with her after school to see what they can come up with together. Ms. Green describes it as a brainstorming session to Marcia.

MS. GREEN: Marcia, you are in the tenth grade now, so you have made it through elementary school and middle school. That really is an accomplishment in itself. Many kids drop out of school before this. You can give yourself a pat on the back for still being in school. Let's think of some other things you've done, even though you may think they are not very impressive.

MARCIA: Well, my Mom is always telling me I can't do anything right, so I honestly don't do a whole lot of things.

MS. GREEN: Tell me what your days are like, a little about your life.

MARCIA: I just get up in the morning, then I have to make breakfast for my two brothers and get them ready for school. After that I go to school and try to get my homework done in study hall because I have chores to do when I get home. My mother works until 6:00 P.M., so I have to have dinner ready when she gets home. After dinner I do the dishes and help my brothers with their homework. If I have time, I listen to music in my room or read.

MS. GREEN: It sounds like you are taking care of your whole family. That's a very big job for such a young person. It might be a good idea if you spoke with our school counselor about the amount of responsibility you have. But in the meantime, we have an assignment to deal with on hope. You say that you don't have any accomplishments, but I can see some important ones. You make good grades in school, and you also have more responsibilities than most of the other kids I know. You must be pretty determined to do well in school, and you seem to find ways to get all your schoolwork done.

MARCIA: I do want to do well in school because I want to go to college when I graduate. But I just thought everyone wanted to do that. And of course I find ways to get my homework done. I have to. What's special about that?

MS. GREEN: It's very special because it takes a whole lot of determination on your part to do it. Many people wouldn't want to work as hard as you do. And finding ways to do all your homework, even though almost all your outside time is used taking care of your family, must involve being inventive about ways to create time. I think you do have a high-hope story here, and I think you have a great deal to be proud of.

This is one example of how a teacher could help a young person see hope in her individual story. When people say they cannot think of things they have accomplished or goals they want to set, we have reason for concern. Ms. Green discovered that Marcia had problems with which a counselor might help. It is appropriate to suggest such a referral, but it is also appropriate to process the story in such a way that the student discovers aspects of hope of which she was not formerly aware.

Returning now to the classroom, written stories can be shared in small groups or read to the class. It is important to remember, however, that these are personal incidents, not all of which ended successfully. Until students have mastered the hope story assignment, it is best if the teacher responds individually to each story. If a student appears consistently lacking in hope (just as if a student wrote any assignment indicating serious problems), the student should be referred to the counselor or school psychologist. A lack of hope is a serious concern and warrants further investigation.

Basic Sciences

Another hope-filled subject area is basic science. Although many science classes focus on rudimentary knowledge and simple experiments, we propose that science can help in the development of high hope, in part, by teaching scientific method. Scientific method teaches the young person to examine what has happened in the past, to evaluate the outcome, and then to try alternative ways of reaching the desired end. This is, in essence, hope. Although it may be challenging for science teachers to help students see the applicability of the scientific method to their personal lives, it is vital that they learn to use this reasoning process.

Basic experiments can be designed to teach scientific method, but completing a project can also teach hope. In Chapter 8 we described Mr. Downley's science classroom, where a group of students wanted to do a difficult project for the science fair. Recall that those students were discouraged by Mr. Downley because he was concerned about their disappointment should the project not succeed. Recall also that Mr. Downley had a critical and demanding father from whom young Jack learned a fear of disappointing others. Several years ago, Jack Downley reached a low point in his increasingly negative attitude about work. At that point he decided to reassess his life in terms of what he still wanted to accomplish in his personal life and his profession.

In reviewing his life, Mr. Downley found that it was characterized by a fear of disappointing others and that this, in turn, produced an unwillingness to try new things and take risks. He first became aware of what he told himself when new challenges arose—for example, when students want to try difficult projects. He found that his self statements were always cautionary and usually ended with his discouraging the students. He consciously began to change these statements to ones of encouragement. Important also in Mr. Downley's change was that he began to explore how he had acquired low-hope messages. To do this he wrote his own stories, including the one about the Pinewood Derby, which was a very important event in his life. Through self-examination of his hope in personal stories and through his determined behavior change, Jack Downley rediscovered a hopeful approach both in his personal life and teaching. Let's take a look at Mr. Downley's classroom now and see what changes he has made, as well as how hope can be taught through science curriculum.

Mr. Downley—A Horse of a Different Color.   Kathy, Mary, and Paula, juniors in high school, have been good friends in and out of school since the sixth grade. Their friendship was cemented by the fact that all three girls were horse crazy, and all three own horses that are kept at the same stable. When Mr. Downley mentioned that the science fair was approaching and that students could work in groups, they naturally planned to work together and to do something involving horses.

The girls discussed a variety of ideas, but none of them sounded like scientific experiments. Finally, stymied, they decided to consult Mr. Downley. Now, Mr. Downley didn't know the first thing about horses except that they were large and potentially dangerous animals that he would just as soon avoid. His first inclination, but one he kept to himself, was to talk the girls out of a horse experiment. Seeing their enthusiasm, however, he began to brainstorm with them about what types of questions they could ask about horses and then put to a test. After considering such questions as whether horses are color blind and how many sounds horses can make, they decided to test the possible decline in hearing as horses age.

Mr. Downley said that he could locate a machine that would generate and measure sound; the girls would need to do some background research on hearing in horses. After first speaking with their local veterinarian, they made a visit to the state veterinary school in a nearby town, where they were able to find out such information as how many cycles per second a horse can hear. Mr. Downley located the appropriate equipment and even said he would supervise the project because the equipment would have to be used at the stable.

Over the following two Saturdays, Kathy, Mary, and Paula, along with a very cautious Mr. Downley, tested the hearing of 25 horses spanning a range of ages. The testing turned out to be a lot of fun for everyone, except perhaps the confused horses. The girls achieved their goal of doing an equine science project, and a very good one at that. Mr. Downley, who found out more about horses than he ever wanted to know, discovered the real pleasure of having and encouraging high hope.

Scientists as Examples of Hope Stories. Before we leave the science classroom and move to the counselor's office, one further hope-inducing activity should be mentioned. Most scientists are high-hope individuals. Their hope is what keeps them moving on into unexplored realms. They encounter many problems as they struggle to find solutions to the puzzles that engage them, yet they persist. Many famous scientists have marvelous biographies and autobiographies: Marie Curie, Albert Einstein, and Thomas Edison are but three. We encourage students, teachers, and parents alike to read about these high-hope scientists. They are models for us all.[3]

Counselors—The Wellspring of Hope

The counseling staff at any junior or high school serves many functions, most of which involve individual or group student contact of a helping nature. Counselors help students select coursework, colleges, and careers. They also give advice and support for a variety of personal problems. Counselors have an exceptional need for hope as they help students set goals for their futures. A counselor's advice can send students on either a downward or an upward course into young adulthood. Here are two scenarios of the same student being advised by a low-hope counselor and a high-hope counselor about the same concern.

Low-Hope Counseling

Our student is a young woman named Keesha, a junior in high school who has come to see Mr. Martin concerning the coursework for her senior year. Mr. Martin knows Keesha had a baby at the beginning of the year and that she is currently living with her grandmother on welfare. Before Keesha comes into the office, Mr. Martin reviews her record and sees that although she made excellent grades prior to the ninth grade, her grades last year were very poor. He also notes that she has not taken the usual college preparatory courses, such as foreign language. Mr. Martin decides before speaking with Keesha that her grades and her socioeconomic situation mean that college will be nearly inaccessible. When Keesha comes in, he advises her to take a noncollege program, telling her that she would have more time for the baby that way.

Keesha had, in fact, been giving some consideration to attempting to go to college, even though no one in her family had done so before, and she didn't know where she would get the money. Mr. Martin's words seemed to make sense to her. After all, she reasoned, just getting a high school diploma after having a baby was a big deal. Most of her friends already had dropped out.

High-Hope Counseling

Now let's replay this scene giving Keesha another chance. In this version Keesha's counselor is Ms. Mitchell, a high-hope person who has raised two children as a single parent. Ms. Mitchell also reviews Keesha's records and realizes that some of her poor grades were made during her pregnancy, when she missed a number of days of school. When Keesha meets with her they discuss how difficult it must be to have a small baby at home while Keesha is trying to go to school. Ms. Mitchell praises her for this accomplishment and then asks her what she would like to do after graduation. Keesha confides that she really wants to go to college, perhaps starting at the nearby junior college. She doesn't want to be on welfare for years, and she wants her baby to have a good life.

Ms. Mitchell confirms that this is a very reasonable plan and gives Keesha the name of a financial aid counselor at the junior college. They then proceed to plan out coursework that will help Keesha achieve her goals.

It is clear that hope should be, but isn't always, the stock-in-trade of school counselors. They, like teachers, suffer from the fatigue and burnout discussed in Chapter 8. But because counselors work specifically with students to plan future goals, it is all the more vital that they assess their own hope and provide hope-nourishing activities for themselves.[4]

Hope as a Boomerang and More

Any teacher, any administrator, and any parent or caregiver can foster hope in their charges. Most of the suggestions given in this chapter, indeed throughout this book, can be adapted to a wide variety of classrooms and situations. Use your own hope and creativity to discover the ways that you can bring hopeful thinking to children. Much like a boomerang, the hope that you throw out to your students will come back to you. Even more likely, in our experiences, your own hope will grow and you will be rewarded many times over.

11

Using Hopeful Stories for Children with Physical Problems

Myth Busters

Our image of children as vibrant, happy, playful, and perhaps most importantly, hopeful is put to the test when they confront severe and chronic physical illness. Beyond the usual developmental tasks, children with chronic health problems have to face other physical, social, and emotional challenges—challenges including pain, fatigue, limitations in daily activities, and changes in appearance. They also have to follow complicated regimens involving medicines, special exercises, and restrictive diets. And, most sadly, they sometimes must confront the ultimate challenge of facing their own impending death. Surely such children have more psychological adjustment problems than healthy children. Indeed, this is a widely held stereotype, *but it is wrong*. Based on our experience and research, chronically ill children are "myth busters." Far from being without hope, these remarkable children navigate their illnesses with hope. As we shall see in this chapter, there is much to learn from such children about hope. In turn, we can give them hope rather than gloomy stereotype-based expectations.

In her inspiring book on children surviving cancer, humorist Erma Bombeck observed,

One of the easiest tasks of writing this book was finding youngsters who had made up their minds to "run and win." They took personal pride in the fact that they were fighting something bigger than they were and stronger than they were . . . something that might even overpower them. But they still had something their enemy couldn't take away—hope. It's a formidable weapon.[1]

We agree! Hope helps us understand how children with chronic illness, as well as their families, can successfully cope with physical diseases. We can learn a great deal from observing those families that cope most successfully with a child's illness. First, they have clear goals, including the usual ones that are critical to daily life, plus goals specific to managing a chronic illness and containing its negative effects. They not only know where they are going but can alter their goals when necessary. Second, these children and their families can generate one or more pathways to their goals. This process, which taps waypower thinking, is crucial because diseases often present many obstacles. Third, these children and their families have the mental energy, commitment, and determination to use the pathways to their goals. In short, they have willpower.

Family members, teachers, and health care providers give hope to chronically ill children in many ways, the sharing of hopeful stories being a primary one. As you will see in this chapter, some of these hopeful stories come from the lives of physically ill children. These stories address the important question: *How do children with chronic illness maintain their hope in the face of threats to their physical and emotional well-being?* In this chapter we will discuss what children with chronic disease and their parents have taught us about maintaining hope under difficult circumstances.

When people ask about our interactions with physically ill children and their families, we are taken aback by a comment such as "that must be *very* discouraging work." On the contrary, our lives have been enriched by sharing in these children's stories of hope. We will explore the hopeful themes we have encountered and will incorporate them into stories that parents, teachers, and health care providers can use to help children and their families cope with specific challenges. In closing, we will explore the topic of death involving a young person. Even when death is inevitable and must be accepted, hope can be kept alive.

Acceptance: Getting Past "Why Me?"

When the son of one of the authors was diagnosed with asthma at age nine, his symptoms were fairly serious. Like many children with asthma, he had to cope with intermittent and sometimes unpredictable attacks that have been described as "trying to breathe with a gorilla sitting on your chest."[2] An active and athletic boy, he was frustrated that asthma had interrupted his active life. Soon after being diagnosed he asked, "Why did this happen to me?" In one sense, this is a rhetorical question because our knowledge of what causes asthma and most other childhood diseases is incomplete. In another sense, this is not really a question, but a way of asserting that "This is not fair, It should not happen to me (or my child)." Rabbi Kushner said it best in the title of his book *Bad Things Happen to Good People*. When these good people are also little people, these bad things seem particularly unfair.

How do children with chronic diseases successfully confront this "why me" issue? First, they express their "negative feelings" such as fear, sadness, and anger at the illness and how unfair it is for them to have it. Second, they are helped by their parents, teachers, and health care providers to understand that their illness is not a punishment for wrongdoing. Third, they come to accept the illness and treatment regimen as a part of their lives. Several good books that help children navigate these health coping stages are listed under various disease titles and are briefly described in Appendix B.

Jackie Joyner-Kersee

The story of Jackie Joyner-Kersee, the world-class Olympic track star, illustrates all three of these themes, but especially the acceptance of the reality of the disease. Diagnosed with asthma as a teenager, Joyner-Kersee was very reluctant to accept her illness and was not consistent in following her treatment program. Her wake-up call came one day when she was rushed to the emergency room after an extremely serious asthma attack. She could no longer ignore the realities of her illness. After this frightening experience, she focused on controlling her asthma instead of letting it control her. As she said, "Asthma is a part of who I am. If I want to continue to be great on the athletic field, I have to discipline myself to do things needed to win. Taking my medication every day is just one of them."[3] She discovered that lack of acceptance leads to lack of control. Hopeful children and families accept the realities of living with a chronic disease. They don't deny the negatives, *but they don't dwell on them either*. Their energies are directed toward doing what they have to do to meet the challenges of chronic illness.

Embracing Treatment

A major challenge for children with chronic disease is following medical treatment programs that are often complicated, not always immediately effective, and sometimes produce negative side effects. It's no wonder that about 50 percent of these children have problems consistently following their medical regimens. We believe that children with high hope are more likely to follow their treatments and that the hope that enables these behaviors can be cultivated by parents and health care providers in several ways. First, as active partners in their treatment, children can help set treatment goals in collaboration with their doctor, nurse, or therapist. This gives them a clear focus and energizes their efforts to improve and maintain their health. Second, parents and health care providers can provide structure and positive reinforcement, which helps to further energize children in their pursuit of health-enhancing goals. Finally, parents and health care providers can help children generate multiple pathways to reach their treatment goals, particularly when barriers are encountered. The following story illustrates how children can be helped to accept their illness and find ways to consistently follow medical regimens.

Cora Learns to Cooperate

"Who ever heard of kids having arthritis?" thought Cora when her doctor told her that's why her hands and fingers had been hurting. She knew Grandpa had arthritis that made his fingers stiff and painful at times, but Grandpa wasn't seven years old. Sometimes Cora felt sad and angry that she had arthritis. Why was she the only kid in the class with this problem?

Cora's doctor told her she was going to have to take medicine four times a day and do special exercises to make her hands work better. It didn't seem fair that she had to do many things that other kids didn't have to do. Cora didn't like taking medicine. Some of the pills were hard to swallow, so her doctor prescribed liquid medicine, and her nurse showed her how to mix it with cherry syrup so it wouldn't taste so nasty.

Cora didn't know much about special exercises, but she soon learned when practicing with the hospital physical therapist. To make her hands work better, she had to bend her fingers into a "cat claw" ten times. The first few cat claws hurt because her arthritis made her fingers stiff and hard to move. But Cora's therapist showed her how to soak her hands in warm water before doing the cat claws, and this made it much easier. She also found that some of her special exercises were really fun to do. For example, she got to work with play dough, rolling out "snakes" and using cookie cutters. She also got to string beads and make necklaces and bracelets for herself, her family, and friends.

As time passed, however, Cora sometimes failed to take her medicine and do her exercises at home. Some days there just were too many other things to do, and she forgot. Other days she felt so good that it didn't seem like she had arthritis at all, and so it seemed okay to skip her medicine and exercises. At this point, Cora's father helped her remember the medicine and exercises by getting a sticker chart that was taped to the refrigerator.

Each time Cora took her medicine or did her exercises, she got to put a sticker on her chart. She even got to pick out the stickers! Cora made things with the play dough so that her fingers could work better, and her father would sit with her and provide encouragement during this exercise. Cora's mother let her choose a special privilege if she took most of her medicine and did her exercises. Sometimes, they went out for ice cream, and at other times they played special games together. All these things helped Cora to keep taking her medicine and doing her exercises. Pretty soon, she hardly ever missed her medicine or forgot her exercises.

Cora began to notice something else that was important. She started feeling better, and her hands worked more easily. She could hold a pencil or crayon, open jars, throw a ball, and play her piano better without pain. That really made Cora want to keep following her treatment program. Cora even came up with a slogan: To Keep Arthritis Away, Take Medicines and Do Exercises Each Day.

Keeping a Sense of Humor

We have a saying that "If you don't laugh at yourself, you've missed the biggest joke of all." The health-restoring properties of humor have long been recognized.[4] Chronically ill children maintain a sense of humor about their illness and treatment that in turn promotes their sense of willpower in continuing to cope. The following anecdote illustrates a healthy sense of humor, which can sound somewhat macabre at times:

"A father told a story about his daughter who lost a leg to Ewing's sarcoma. One night, very late, a young orderly came to her hospital room with a wheelchair to take her to X-ray. Her face was ashen, her eyelids at half-mast. She had her legs crossed and her one remaining foot was sticking out. The orderly put her in the wheelchair, put down the flaps, and positioned her one foot. Then he began to grope for the other one she didn't have. Finally, she looked at him and smiled. 'Good luck!'"[5]

Humor is also helpful when having to cope with changes in physical appearance that can set children with chronic illness apart from their peers. Consider a story told to us by Laura, a girl with cystic fibrosis. One physical change caused by cystic fibrosis is "clubbed digits," where the tips of the fingers and thumbs become swollen and bulbous in appearance. Laura explained that these "fat" fingertips were usually not noticed by others, unless you painted the nails. On one occasion when she was a young teenager, she did just that and went to school. A child noticed one of her fingers and asked if she had slammed it in the car door. Instead of withdrawing or verbally attacking the other person, she saw the humor in this situation. She replied, "If that's true, I would have to be awfully clumsy, because I would have had to smash all of them in the door." She could laugh at herself and the absurdity of the situation. Instead of becoming beaten down and blocked by her illness, humor helps Laura and children like her maintain their energy for pursuing the goals of life.

Focusing on "Can Do's" Rather Than "Can't Do's"

We all have strengths and weaknesses as we navigate through life. It's not any different for children who are physically ill. A very important way to instill and maintain hope in chronically ill children is to help them focus on what they can do rather than what they can't do.

By focusing on what they can do, chronically ill children remain flexible in pursuing their goals. They shift to alternate activities that are within their capabilities and learn to excel in these new areas. We knew one young lady with arthritis who was a track star before she became ill. Because of the potential damage to her arthritic joints caused by the pounding and stress of running and jumping, she successfully shifted to a career in swimming, which satisfied her desire for athletic competition and was helpful in maintaining her joint function. Another young man with bone cancer in his leg was discouraged when he was first told he couldn't play football and the other sports he enjoyed. He said, "When they started discussing my not playing sports again, that's when it first got hard for me." But, instead of focusing on what he would not be able to do, he concentrated on what he could do and said, "I figured I'd just take up golf. I knew it'd be a new challenge." This is hope in action, remaining energized and finding new goals. The following story also illustrates how to help children focus on "can do's" rather than "can't do's."

Row, Row, Row Your Boat

Hiram was a ten-year-old boy who was born with cerebral palsy. He looked like other boys his age except when he attempted to run, jump, or walk on a balance beam. The cerebral palsy affected the coordination and strength in his legs. When Hiram tried to run, his legs didn't move smoothly, he couldn't go very fast, and he often stumbled and fell. When he thought about all the things he couldn't do, he got sad, sometimes angry, and definitely discouraged.

One day Hiram went to see a wise man in the neighborhood. The wise man looked at Hiram's arms and wondered if he would be able to row a boat. Hiram did so well at rowing that the wise man and Hiram eventually worked together on a long list of other things that he could do. Hiram learned to make his arms strong by going all the way across the school monkey bars. He also learned to build things with his hands, type on the computer, and play the trumpet. The wise man told Hiram he had learned an important secret—focus on what he *can do* rather than what he can't do.

Getting By with a Little Help from
Their Friends, Family, and Others

When children feel like they can't go on, they turn to other people nearby
in order to maintain hope. In this section, we will consider how important
support people impart hope to children with chronic disease.

Mothers

Mothers of chronically ill children have the usual tasks of caring for
their children plus additional challenges related to their children's disease.
The following "job description" captures this:

> WANTED: Woman to raise, educate, and entertain child for a minimum of
> twenty years. Be prepared to eat egg if yolk breaks, receive anything in hand
> child spits out, and take knots out of wet shoestrings with teeth. Must be ex-
> pert in making costume for "bad tooth" and picking bathroom locks with
> shish kebab skewer. Seven days a week, 24 hours a day, including holidays.
> Comprehensive dental plan, vacation, medical benefits, and company car ne-
> gotiable.

If the job description was for mothers of children with cancer, you would
have to add:

> An additional 40 hours a week set aside for reading magazines in doctor's
> waiting room, chauffeuring child to and from treatments and therapy, stand-
> ing in line getting prescriptions filled, and running errands. Sustaining guilt
> for not giving enough to other members of the family. Major worrying 24
> hours a day. Must possess maturity to realize that you can't "kiss cancer and
> make it well."[6]

So, in addition to the usual stuff they do for their children, mothers of
chronically ill children provide companionship, comfort, and encouragement to press on. A composite of what we have heard children say of their
mothers would be, "She just wouldn't let me give up! Without her, I
wouldn't be here." As these quotes suggest, mothers impart willpower, but
they also aid in the making of helpful goals and provide ways to reach
these goals.

Fathers

Like mothers, fathers can provide concrete and emotional assistance to
their children, such as being their advocate, staying with them in the hospi-

tal, and encouraging them to follow their treatment regimens. A father also provides indirect support for the children by supporting the mother. Having a child with a serious illness can make or break marriages. Those couples who "make it" seem to be able to share their feelings, comfort each other, maintain open communication, balance responsibilities, and find time for each other. In short, they energize each other (provide willpower) and help each other discover ways to cope with adversity (provide waypower).

Siblings

Siblings are a source of both care and conflict. We have observed both sides of this coin with children who are ill. Their brothers or sisters provide companionship by playing games, drawing, talking, and just hanging out with them, particularly when in the hospital or having to stay indoors. Such siblings support helps chronically ill children generate alternative pathways to social and recreational goals. Siblings also assist children with their medical treatments and encourage them to take their medicine, follow their diets, and do special exercises. To a lesser degree, we also have witnessed resentment among siblings of chronically ill children as their ill brother or sister often receives more attention from their parents. These resentful feelings are frequently mixed with guilt as siblings realize that the sickness is not their brother's or sister's fault. On the whole, therefore, most siblings provide companionship and direct assistance to their chronically ill brother or sister.

Grandparents

Grandparents are important in supporting children. Fortunately, health care providers have begun to recognize this and have allowed grandparents unlimited visitation in the hospital, as well as involving them more directly (with parental permission) in discussions about children's illnesses and treatments. We have seen grandparents providing affection and companionship and relating hopeful stories to their grandchildren. The lives of grandparents are full of hopeful narratives. Because grandparents also deal with physical challenges caused by illness and aging, they give living testimonials about getting around obstacles and living productive lives.

Friends

As the saying goes, a friend is someone who knows you and still likes you. Friends are an important source of companionship and intimacy for children. This is critical for chronically ill children because their illnesses can interfere with opportunities to develop and maintain friendships. One of the most important things friends do for chronically ill children is treat them "normally." They don't care if their friends have lost their hair from chemotherapy treatments or that they have a hard time keeping up physically. Because children with chronic disease often try to "protect" the feelings of their parents and other relatives, friends are sometimes the only people to whom they confide their frustrations and fears. Thus, friends can be hope-givers too. They help children with chronic illnesses to remain energized and generate alternative pathways to their social goals.

Teachers

With advances in treatments for once-fatal diseases, more children recover from serious illnesses and step back into the mainstream of life. School is an important part of children's intellectual and social life. As we discussed in Chapters 8, 9, and 10, school is also a place where hope can be nurtured, and teachers play a vital role in this process. Many medical treatment teams now include teachers who help chronically ill children keep up their schoolwork and provide valuable emotional support while they are in the hospital. Also, after chronically ill children have been diagnosed (or after lengthy hospitalizations), these teachers often will visit the children's classrooms to discuss the children's medical condition and encourage classroom teachers and students to treat them normally.

The classroom schoolteachers of chronically ill children also provide valuable support. They often arrange for their classes to send personal notes, pictures, and get-well cards to children when they are in the hospital. These messages communicate that their teachers and classmates have not forgotten them, still care for them, and will welcome them back when they return. Teachers also can share narratives that promote a positive and more balanced view of the effects of chronic illness: namely, that someone may have a serious illness or physical limitations but that does *not* mean they are any different as a person than they were before, or that they are to be pitied.

Health Care Providers

Children with chronic disease have regular contact with nurses and doctors. Most of this contact is supportive, but out of necessity some of it is painful and distressing. In this process, nurses are significant sources of support.

As an example of the role of nurses, let's examine the topic of pain. Nurses are at the forefront of efforts to assess and reduce children's pain from medical procedures and treatments. They were the first professionals to challenge the long-standing and unfortunate medical belief that children experienced pain to a lesser degree than adults and, therefore, didn't need as much pain relief. There has now been significant progress in assessing and relieving pain in children, and nurses have continued to be leaders in these efforts. Such advances are vital because unrelieved pain often leads to feelings of hopelessness and depression and can retard the restorative powers of the immune system. Nurses not only help relieve pain but encourage the following of treatment regimens, and they provide supplementary emotional support during hospital stays. Thus, nurses are significant givers of hope to children with chronic diseases.

Staying in the Hospital

Whenever feasible, children should be prepared for their stay by touring the hospital and obtaining information about what will occur during their stay. Even with such careful preparations, hospitals can be scary and frustrating. Painful things happen, unfamiliar noises abound, the food isn't tasty, the bed and room are strange, and it's hard to sleep because someone awakens you to take your temperature and blood pressure. In recognition of these perceptions, hospitals are making some changes. Parents can sleep in the room with their children, and as long as a favorite food will not compromise the child's health, it can be brought into the hospital. Siblings, family members, and friends can visit, and children can bring some of their prized possessions from home (e.g., a stuffed animal or a favorite blanket and pillow). Televisions, video games, VCRs, and classrooms in hospitals also help children enjoy their stay and keep up with their education. Children learn that there are special people in the hospital, such as nurses, recreational therapists, teachers, psychologists, and social workers, who will help meet their psychological needs. The following story is about a young girl with diabetes who is being admitted to the hospital and discovers that many supportive people there can help her.

Lindsey Goes to the Hospital

Even though she was just five years old, Lindsey knew something was wrong with her body. No matter what she drank and ate, she was still thirsty and hungry. She also had to urinate frequently, and sometimes she wet her bed (she had not done this for a long, long, time). Her parents took her to see the doctor. After some tests, Lindsey's doctor said she had diabetes. Diabetes is when your body can't use the food you eat to make energy. Lindsey's doctor said she would have to go to the hospital for a week so she and her parents could learn how to make her better. Lindsey knew about hospitals from books and television, and she even had a friend who had to have an operation at the hospital. But all that did not seem to matter—she was still scared!

Before her stay at the hospital, Lindsey, her mom, dad, and brother got to visit. They met a friendly nurse named Martye who took Lindsey and her parents to the part of the hospital where she would be staying. What a surprise! The hallway was painted in bright red, green, and yellow colors. There were pictures drawn by other children on the walls. In one big room, children were laughing, playing, and doing finger painting. Lindsey met some of the children and a very nice teacher.

Nurse Martye also told Lindsey and her parents that when she was in the hospital, Martye and some other people would teach them how to take care of her diabetes. Some things she heard about made her a little nervous—like poking a small needle in her fingertips to get some drops of blood so that a small machine could show how much sugar was in it. She also heard that her parents would have to learn to give her insulin shots two or three times a day. This would help her body use the food she ate. She even found out that one day she would learn how to give the insulin shots to herself, and she thought, "NO WAY!"

One thing she really didn't like to hear is that she could not eat any candy or sweets, except on very special occasions. Nurse Martye made Lindsey feel better about all this by telling her that many children her age have diabetes and learned to take care of themselves and even got used to the not-so-fun parts, like getting insulin shots.

The day finally arrived when Lindsey had to go to the hospital. After her parents filled out some papers, Lindsey and her parents took the elevator to the children's floor where she was to stay. When she got off the elevator, Nurse Martye was there to take her hand and lead Lindsey and her parents to her room. To Lindsey's surprise, a big banner hanging on the wall of her hospital room said "Welcome Lindsey!" Many of the other children in the hospital had drawn pictures of flowers, happy faces, and teddy bears on the banner and had signed their names. Lindsey got to bring her favorite blanket and doll. An extra bed in the room could sleep her mother or father if they wanted to spend the night.

Lindsey had many visitors while in the hospital. Grandma and Grandpa came to see her and sat with her and read stories. Her older brother, Nathan, came and played video games and cheered her up. She even got some get-well cards made by the kids in her kindergarten class and her teacher, Mrs. Kinskey. The hospital did not seem like such a scary place after all. Being in the hospital was like a new adventure. Lindsey worked hard to learn how to take care of her diabetes so she could run and play and feel better.

The Power of Hopeful Thoughts and Images

"For as he thinketh in his heart, so is he" (Proverbs 23:7). As this proverb illustrates, our thinking influences how we feel and behave. Our thoughts are the ongoing "internal script" of our life story. Chronically ill children and their parents have to "guard" their thoughts as they face situations that tax their ability to generate hopeful thinking. Catastrophic and pessimistic thinking, such as "This is awful," "I can't stand this," and "I'll never be any better," can lead to hopelessness and despair. We have observed that children with chronic disease and their parents avoid this destructive type of thinking. They do so by watching for negative thoughts, challenging them, and substituting more hopeful thoughts. When confronted with pain, for example, these children and their parents generate hope-giving thoughts such as "I don't like this, but I can stand it," "Don't make it worse than it is," "I'm just feeling bad now but this won't last forever," and "I'll feel better soon."

Pictures and illustrations are an integral part of stories for children, and so too are mental images important to children's thinking. We have found that children are particularly adept at transforming frightening and hopeless images into more hopeful ones. Take pain, for example. We often ask children with chronic pain to pick colors they associate with different levels of pain. Not surprisingly, they pick red or black most often to represent severe pain, and the more soothing colors of yellow or blue to represent no pain or less pain. We then ask them to picture the part of their body that is in pain as changing from the most painful color (red or black) to a less painful color (yellow or blue).

Doug, the Boy with a Vise on His Head

Children can also be asked to draw pictures of their pain. One boy named Doug had frequent and severe headaches. He drew a picture of his head being squeezed in a vise. We asked him to close

DouG

his eyes and visualize this painful image. Then, while asking him to relax slowly, we had him imagine that this vise was being loosened more and more, until his head was completely free of the pressure. With practice, this exercise became a mental script, a story that he could use to reduce the frequency and severity of his headaches.

To monitor their health and deliver some forms of treatment, children with chronic diseases have to undergo repeated painful procedures such as having their blood drawn, insertion of intravenous lines, spinal taps, and bone marrow aspirations. Such procedures have been described by children and their parents as the worst part of having serious illnesses such as cancer. Sometimes oral or topical medications can be administered to reduce the discomfort, but they are not always practical or may have unacceptable side effects. Through story formats, parents and health care providers can assist children in learning and using hopeful thoughts and images to reduce their discomfort, as is illustrated in the following story.

Betsy Learns to Be Brave

Betsy is an eight-year-old girl with leukemia. When she first got sick, everything was new and scary in her life. She got tired easily and had to rest and stay indoors. She also had stomachaches and threw up from the medicine she was given. The medicine also made her lose hair. After a while, she got used to all of these things but one: spinal taps. This is where they stick a big needle in your back when you are lying down all curled up in a ball. Everyone, including her nurse, doctor, and her parents, tried to make Betsy feel better about this, but she was still really scared and sometimes got sick to her stomach when her mom drove into the hospital parking lot on the day of the test.

One day Betsy decided to visit the wise old grandmother who lived in the neighborhood. The wise grandmother asked Betsy if she knew what it means to be brave. "It's when you do something hard, like get a shot at the doctor's office, and you are not afraid," she said. The wise grandmother nodded her head and said, "That's one way to be brave, Betsy, *but being brave also means doing something hard even when you are afraid.*" She then told Betsy that she would give her some magic ways to be brave when she was afraid or was going to have something painful happen to her. First, she told Betsy about relaxing her body. She taught Betsy how to take deep breaths and slowly let the air out, just like she was filling and emptying a balloon. She then had Betsy tense all her muscles—her face, neck, arms, hands, stomach, and legs—holding the tension for a count of five and then relaxing all of her muscles. Between tensing and relaxing, she did slow, deep breathing. After she finished this, she noticed how much more loose and relaxed she felt.

The second magic way was to use her imagination. The wise grandmother asked Betsy to close her eyes and picture in her mind a very relaxing place. Betsy pictured a park with a stream and lots of trees, where she and her family had picnics. She imagined all the sights, sounds, smells, and feelings that she remembered from the park. As she used her imagination, Betsy noticed that the park became more and more real, and she felt even more relaxed.

The third magic way was to think helpful thoughts. The wise grandmother explained that thoughts such as "This is terrible!" "I can't stand this!" and "I can't do this!" not only make kids feel bad but also make some things—like shots—worse. She taught Betsy to say to herself some comforting and helpful thoughts, such as "I will feel better in a little while," "Everything is going to be all right," and, "I don't like this, but I can do this because I'm brave!"

Betsy thanked the wise grandmother and went home to tell her mother about the magic ways to be brave. She and her mother practiced these every day. Several weeks later, Betsy had to go to the hospital for a spinal tap. She was still afraid—and she knew that was okay—but she used her magic ways to be brave and was not as afraid as she had been before. When she finished, the doctor and nurse told Betsy how brave she had been. Betsy felt very proud and happy.

Writing the Ending to Their Own Life Stories

"Whom the gods love die young" (Menander, 342–292 B.C.).[7] Most of us don't see it this way. Though almost all children with chronic diseases don't die, the unfortunate fact is that some do. And when this happens, it insults all of our sensibilities. Any parent may experience anxiety and vulnerability, realizing that this could happen to our own children.

For those of us who work with terminally ill children and their families, something else happens. We begin to appreciate that life is fragile and fleeting. As George Santayana said, "There is no cure for birth and death save to enjoy the interval."[8] We also learn from these families that hope never dies. As long as terminally ill children are physically able and conscious, they continue to "enjoy the interval" and often write, or live out in their particular way, the endings of their own life stories. The following story is about a young man who did just this as he faced the end of his life.

Danny's Story

Danny[9] was 19 years old when he was diagnosed with bone cancer in his left leg. The youngest of two boys, he was intelligent, handsome, athletic, and well liked by peers and adults. In December, he had surgery and was given prosthetic replacements for his removed left femur and knee. He did well through the next summer, until his regular checkup in August, when a tumor was found in his right lung. For the next year, he coped as this disease rampaged through his young body. Nevertheless, Danny's story is not about death. It is about hope.

Danny didn't dwell on "Why me?" questions. As he noted, "I've never said 'Why me?' Never, ever. This shouldn't happen to anybody. But like they say, there's a reason for everything. I'll just have to see what happens."

He focused on the good things in his life and saw the cancer as something that affected his body but not the essence of who he was. In his words, "My life has been great. When I die, I won't die from cancer. My body will die from it."

Danny didn't want pity. He was more concerned with how his illness would affect those whom he loved, particularly his parents. He commented, "The toughest thing for me is watching my parents. They hold a lot inside. I hate to see them hurting. They take everything ten times worse than I do."

Danny was a wonderful and supportive role model for other children with cancer. He would come to the hospital classroom and sit and color with a group of preschoolers who were also being treated for cancer. One day he lead a parade down the hallway of the children's ward in honor of one of the children's birthdays.

Near the end of his life, Danny continued to make plans for activities with his girlfriend, family, and friends. He was vibrantly living the life he had left and wouldn't allow anyone else to write the ending of his life story. Four months before he died, Danny was admitted to the intensive care unit in critical condition. The medical team didn't expect him to leave the hospital alive. During this stay, the attending physician called his therapist and asked if Danny would want to be resuscitated. She encouraged the physician to ask Danny about this.

In previous conversations, Danny and his therapist had talked about how he would know when he was ready to die. Later that day, she called Danny, fearing that he would be too weak to speak. Unexpectedly, however, Danny got on the phone. She asked him what was going on, and Danny said the doctors didn't think he would make it through the night. There was no dancing around issues with Danny. After asking for reassurance that he would know when he was ready to die, Danny asserted that he wasn't ready at that point.

Danny did survive, and he celebrated his next birthday with a new jeep. He visited friends and his girlfriend. He attended professional football games with the aid of a wheelchair and supplemental oxygen. Most of all, he talked with his family.

With his family at his side, Danny died at home early one Monday morning. He had made clear that his funeral was not to be a sad affair emphasizing his untimely death; it was to be a celebration of his life. Danny wrote the ending of his life story: It was about living life to its fullest and not dying before you are ready.

After his death, Danny wanted his family to continue to enjoy themselves to the fullest. As he reiterated to his father, "When I look down from heaven, I want to see you (Dad), Mom, and Rudee (his dog) fishing your butts off, because that's what would make me feel good."

Danny's story continues to inspire all who knew and loved him. He personified hope. He had a clear direction in life, and until his physical self gave out, he remained spirited and overcame enormous obstacles. In the final analysis, it is the story of hope that sustains our lives, even at the end of our journeys. Danny would want us to remember this.

Tips for Parents

There is no set formula for how young people face death and how their families can help them make this last transition in life. It is important to remember that young children have very concrete, rudimentary notions of death, whereas teenagers have views that match those of adults. Parents often want to know what to tell their terminally ill children. The answer is to tell children as much as they ask, no more, no less. It is critical to be honest with children and answer their questions as directly as possible. If a child asks if she is going to die, and death is imminent, parents can gently answer "Yes," but let their child know that they will be there. Just being with a child and offering a touch is often more helpful than what is said.

Children seem to know when death is near, and they want to be sure that they are not alone and that they will not suffer. Steps should be taken to assure that death is as pain-free as possible. Many families elect to have hospice care, a medically directed program that provides support, including pain management, in the home or an inpatient hospital setting.

Children often experience different stages of grief, but not necessarily in a set sequence or including all steps. These stages include denial (talking and acting as if nothing is wrong), anger (over their fate), bargaining (offering prayers to postpone the inevitable), depression (expressing sorrow), and acceptance (agreeing to their fate). Being supportive, empathic, and affectionate is often more important than the specific words that parents use to see their children through these stages.

Children may have specific goals they want to accomplish before they die. They may want to finish their current school year, write a story, or attend social activities with their friends. We should help them attain their goals whenever this is possible. As we have emphasized throughout this book, being goal-directed and remaining energized to meet our goals are important to a hopeful life story.

Cultural and religious traditions are often very comforting and hope-inducing for young people who are terminally ill. Various religious traditions emphasize hope in and beyond death. Children find solace in their religious beliefs and practices. The clergy also can be of great assistance to the children and their parents during this time.

We believe that those who live with hope will die with hope. At the end of their journey and as long as their physical self holds out, they will find the energy and pathways to pursue their goals. After their death, they will, like Danny and many others we have known, leave a legacy of hope to those whose lives they have touched. Indeed, they will leave this world a more hope-filled place.

12

Making Certain That the Hopeful Stories Last

Recapturing Hope: Across Enemy Lines

As we come to the end of our book about the positive role that hope-filled stories can play in guiding and buoying children and adults through the good times and the bad, it is important to examine the means by which these stories can be preserved. As is obvious by now, we think hopeful stories are a precious resource, a gift to be treasured and preserved. Consider the following story, told to one of the authors by his grandfather:

Grandpa's yarn was about a World War I army buddy. During long and scary nights in foxholes, this young man scribbled uplifting tales about how he had survived several precarious wartime adventures. On one occasion when enemy soldiers were advancing and threatening an assault, his unit retreated to a more secure position in a nearby village. Suddenly, however, one soldier bolted from the ranks and ran back into the night toward the very spot that had just been abandoned. Bewildered by this, his comrades feared for his life. After some time, he returned gasping and coughing, carrying his rifle in one hand and something else in his other hand. What was he carrying? What priceless object had compelled him to risk life and limb? It was the tablet of handwritten war stories that he unwittingly had left behind.

Hearing this story as a boy, the author was amazed and intrigued by the soldier's behavior. Four decades after this tale was told to him, he is more astonished that he can remember it than he is by the fact that the soldier embarked upon the dangerous rescue of the personal war stories. Perhaps the hero in this story was going to an extreme, but he was after the very thing that we will argue for in this concluding chapter—the preservation of hope stories.

Listening

Our listening means many things to our children. It means we think they are worth taking the time to hear. Listening means that we adults value and respect not only the child but their use of words as a means of communication. Listening gives the child permission to tell things the way he or she sees them. Although listening means remaining open to what our children have to say, it is not a passive process. On the contrary, good listening is an active endeavor in which the adult may need to prod the child to say more, to supply details, and to describe how he or she feels.[1]

What does such listening do to insure that our children's stories will endure? In our clinical experience, an attentive adult listener helps to solidify the initial impact of the story. As we discussed in Chapter 2, every story needs an audience. Although children always have themselves as an internal audience, it is the external audience that is more critical for implanting the story in children's enduring hope repertoire of personal narratives. One reason for this is that personal stories told to an attentive adult listener have an elaborative quality and are therefore more easily recalled by the child.

Inquiring: What Happened?

A mutual ally to the listening process is the adult's curiosity about children's adventures. Many a time our children may come running to us, obviously excited, surprised, angry, hurt, or experiencing one of a myriad of other emotional reactions. Under these circumstances, we must display some genuine enthusiasm for finding out what has happened. Don't become impatient, however, if children cannot tell the story in an absolutely lucid fashion. When they are aroused, it is difficult for them to talk coherently. Just remember the last time you were very excited about something and tried to tell your story. It simply is not always an easy process. Realize also that young children are new at this storytelling business, so help them bring their stories out.

Recall our earlier suggestion that positive and negative emotions typically reflect instances of successful or unsuccessful goal pursuits. With this clue in mind, if your child is displaying negative emotions, your questions may focus on what has gone wrong, what got in his or her way, and the like. Conversely, if your child obviously is experiencing positive emotions, your detective work may reasonably turn to questions about how a desired goal was obtained, what wonderful outcome has transpired, and so on.

One exercise that can be employed with children from about age ten and older is to have them play the role of newspaper reporter. Better yet, given the importance of television in the lives of young children today, ask them to play a TV broadcaster describing what has happened to them. Children love to pretend, and this is good practice for the process of storytelling that they will be engaging in for the rest of their lives. Another approach that teachers sometimes use is to have children give a written or spoken report about an event in their lives. Many of us have been through such assignments as "What I did with my summer vacation."

The net effect of such "What happened?" questions from adults is that children are given an opportunity to detail the events in their lives. The fleshing out of the story for the adult's consumption increases the likelihood that the event will be registered in memory by the child, and such stories may be remembered more readily.

Recounting: Would You Tell That One Again?

The logical extension of "What happened?" questions is to ask the child to retell some personal story. Selectively having the child recall instances in which he or she successfully worked for a goal allows for the reinforcement of that hope-filled story. Likewise, the requested retelling of a story in which the child surmounted obstacles to achieve his or her goal helps to build a sense of resiliency.

By periodically asking a child to retell tales of previous successful goal pursuits, we increase the likelihood that these stories will be recalled spontaneously by the child in the future. However, a prompt from a trusted adult is sometimes needed even after a child develops a collection of hope-filled stories that become a natural part of his or her coping repertoire. This tends to be the case particularly when a child is experiencing unusually difficult circumstances and cannot sense any hope in a particular situation. The parents' or teachers' task then is to remind the child about previous instances in similar situations where he or she exhibited hopeful thoughts and actions. The old story of hope may need to be rekindled, particularly for young children who do not readily understand how their latest predicaments resemble previous ones.

Scripting: Tying Actions to the Story Line

Many children are action-oriented and spend their days "doing." Much like the Energizer Bunny in the television advertisement, such children seemingly are in perpetual motion. Breaks in the action, such as dinnertime or preparing to go to bed (the infamous bedtime ritual) give adults the opportunity to talk to their children about what is going on in their lives. Similarly, teachers have opportunities to do this when children have finished with a particular unit or project. During these more quiet, reflective periods, the adult can point out how behaviors that the child has been engaging in represent a script of sorts. If the adult in this scenario can tie the actions to a "story line," there is the possibility of showing the child how he or she seems to be following a script of hope. The following example may help clarify what this approach entails. Consider the following scene in which nine-year-old Bobby is getting ready for bed.

DAD: You know, today I saw you doing something that is really great.
BOBBY: (Obviously pleased) Oh yeah? What?
DAD: Well, in the basketball game, you really seemed to be concentrating on getting the ball to the best open guy for the shot. And you know what else?
BOBBY: No, what?
DAD: You came up with some neat ways to get the ball to the other guys . . . sometimes dribbling over near them, sometimes making a good pass. And you kept at it the whole game, working real hard.

In this exchange, the child's concrete actions are placed in the context of a hopeful story line about goal pursuit and maintaining will- and way-power. It helps to end such an interchange with the adult briefly summarizing the hope script.[2] In this case, Dad says to Bobby, "What I like about what you were doing is this. You knew what you wanted, and you found a way to make it happen."

Exemplifying: You're At It Again

Closely related to tying the child's actions to a hopeful story line is the process of showing the child that these recent actions reflect a *recurring* theme of hopefulness. For instance, Bobby's father could continue by employing a technique that we call "You're at it again," pointing out how Bobby's approach to matters on the basketball court mirrors approaches exhibited in other areas of the boy's life. In this way, the given vignette is solidified as representing a larger tale of hope that is operating in the child's life. Eventually, the child will begin to see that there is an underlying "big story" of hope that describes him or her.

Remembering: Do You Recall When . . . ?

In the early days of television, one show particularly fascinated those of us who were novice viewers. "This Is Your Life" was based on the premise that some noted celebrity would be given a surprise reunion in which he or she was introduced to a string of people who had played important roles in the individual's childhood. The interest generated by this show depended in large part on the stories that the family and friends told about the person. Taken together, this patchwork of stories gave an insight into the life of the featured person. Almost without exception, the incidents that guests recounted took on a very similar, hope-laden form. The celebrated protagonist usually was described as being very desirous of some goal, only to run into hurdles that made the attainment of the goal more difficult but not impossible. In turn, the protagonists tried various solutions to achieve their goals, persevered against great odds, and eventually reached their goals. This made for riveting early television, but what is relevant for our present purposes is the importance of retelling the hope stories of childhood so as revivify them in the minds of the central participants.

There are several contexts in which the retelling of stories can be achieved. Natural times to do this are ceremonial occasions or holidays. With many family members gathered, these times are ripe for the rekindling of stories about certain individuals. As they tell these tales about each other, adults may not realize that the children at such occasions may hunger to hear about *their* escapades when they were younger. Therefore, it is helpful to make certain that the children present at such family gatherings are able to hear some vignettes about their own early years.

Certain marker events in childhood lend themselves to the telling of stories about the child by adults. Bar mitzvahs and birthdays provide two such occasions. Other child-oriented holidays, including Halloween, Christmas, Independence Day, and Valentine's Day, offer opportune times to take the youngster down memory lane. Such stories may include humorous or scary events, but their common theme is to retell some adventure that the child successfully navigated. Young children especially love such stories because they shower attention and love upon them. Even teenagers who sometimes appear to be embarrassed by anything that their parents say and do may be surprisingly open to stories about their "wonder years."

Story Albums

Caregivers go to considerable expense and effort in taking pictures and making movies of their children as they grow up. As wonderful as these photo albums may be for remembering given times, places, and people, we would recommend an even more useful type of album for children—the story album. To create a story album, a primary caregiver first secures a nice notebook for the stories. We would recommend a loose-leaf one where pages can be inserted and moved as desired. When a memorable event involving the child happens, it is entered in the story album through handwritten notes. It is important that the writing lasts, so a pen is preferable to pencil.

Although a story album takes work, compiling it can be a very enjoyable process for the caregivers. We would suggest placing the story album in a regular, easily accessible location. Then, as soon after the event as is possible, enter the story about that event. Don't concern yourself with the technical aspects of writing; just try to focus on the key elements of the tale. Include the time and place, the age of the child, and the names of other participants. Describe how the central protagonist in the story (the child) was looking, acting, and feeling. Have some fun with these entries.

The story album, perhaps enlivened with photographs, becomes a rich and vivid source of information about key childhood events and may be called upon for the simple joys of remembering, or perhaps to help the child with school assignments related to childhood experiences. This story album also makes a wonderful wedding present! The stories then can become sources of hope for the next generation.

Rooting: Family Ties

Although the traditional family structure has undergone changes in American society, nearly all children live within some type of family arrangement. Accordingly, each child has a lineage that can be traced for him or her by a knowledgeable adult. At minimum, there are stories about the child's ancestors that paint a word picture of what has been said and done by kinfolk. This information shows the child that he or she plays a part in the unfolding progression of humanity. Stories about ancestors at times may bear startling similarity to the circumstances faced by the latest generation. Further, with the contribution of genetics to most facets of personhood, there is a likelihood that the young child may approach things in a manner similar to that displayed by family members in previous generations. To some extent, the story of one's family provides a mirror in which children can look at their own neophyte sagas.

In our experience, there is a marvelous set of resource people who are admirably equipped to tell young children about family stories. We are speaking here of grandparents. Grandparents not only have the time to tell the stories but also may have better rapport with the child than do the parents. Grandparents can point out how the hope-filled actions that the young child is manifesting bear remarkably strong similarities to their parents' actions when they were children. Children love to hear stories about events that occurred when their parents were children.[3]

Keeping At It

A fundamental characteristic of high-hope children and adults is that they continue to apply hopeful thinking across events and over the course of their lives. Whatever a caregiver can do to instill the importance of persistently making goals, producing the associated waypower thoughts to reach those goals, and employing pathways to reach the goals will make the probability of actual success higher.

Perhaps a story of a high-hope individual in her later years makes this point most clearly. The story goes like this: A woman goes into a restaurant and immediately begins to stare at a man her same age who is sitting in a nearby booth. Finally, after she has stared at him for quite some time, the man says, "I cannot help but notice that you keep looking at me. What is that all about?"

"Oh," the woman replies, "you see, it's just that you remind me so much of my third husband. You have that same ruggedly handsome face and good physique, and your silver hair looks just great."

"Well, thank you very much!" beamed the man. "Do you mind if I ask how many times you have been married?"

"Twice," smiles the woman.[4]

Building Hope: Pockets of Goal Attainment

In order to preserve the viability of the previous approaches to maintaining hopeful personal stories in the minds of children, we adults must create environments where hopeful behaviors can flourish. That is to say, there must be some arena in a child's life where hopeful thinking can lead to successful achievement of goals. It is important to emphasize, however, that hopeful thinking is not some fragile thing. On the contrary, children with hopeful personal stories may have endured severe hardships (see, for example, Chapter 11 on the role of hope stories in the lives of children with physical injuries or disease). Even amidst seemingly hopeless environments, however, the child may find an oasis that serves as a powerful place for building or refilling hope.

To maintain hopeful personal narratives in children, it is important to recognize which arenas of their lives tend to be more filled with hope. For example, a child with learning disabilities related to language may not have encountered many successful goal pursuits related to English in school, but that same child may have much more talent and success related to music, mathematics, athletics, carpentry, or computers. In these latter arenas, the child may have readily available high-hope stories about him- or herself. When a child is feeling particularly down about difficulties in given areas, particularly if that area has been a source of difficulty previously, it is helpful to remind the child that there are places where she or he is more successful. Obviously, the more that the child can establish a way of life that places him or her in those arenas of success, the more likely that hopeful thinking will endure.

In general, our society tends to value goal pursuits related to intellectual matters, money, athletics, and appearance, and as such our children will seek these as the primary arenas for establishing their personal stories of hope. If the adult can help the child to find one of these societally favored goal-pursuit arenas where successful outcomes are possible, this naturally helps the child sustain hopeful stories to go along with these activities. At times, however, a child may not be well suited to pursue goals in one of these major, rewarded life arenas. In such instances, a good means of insuring that successful personal stories thrive in the child's life is to help the child secure some goal-pursuit activity that matches his or her talents and interests.

We do not believe that hope-filled personal stories can sustain a child indefinitely when there is a total lack of success in attaining a particular goal. In this sense, stories of hope are not a panacea that enable a child to sail toward any goal. Furthermore, it should be noted that it is difficult for hope-filled personal stories to develop in the first place if there is not some semblance of goal attainment for the child. Although there are examples in psychology of people who think well of themselves and perform miserably—just as there are examples of people who do not think so positively about themselves and yet perform admirably—*these people are the exceptions*. For the great majority of children, personal thoughts about oneself in the pursuit of goals match actual outcomes. An important additional point to remember here is that once the hope thoughts are in place, these thoughts predict how well children will do in both academic and athletic activities. even more remarkable is that a child's hope enables us to make accurate positive performance predictions *beyond what we would anticipate because of their basic ability and previous performances.* As such, stories of hope are powerful assets for children.[5]

Mentoring: Adult Models of Hope

High-hope children commonly have vivid memories of those adults who played critical roles in their lives. Such people often are parents, but these adults may be an older sibling, an uncle, a neighbor, a coach, or anyone who took the time to guide the child in a loving and caring manner. Recall our previous suggestions about using stories where the child with a problem is able to consult with a wise person (see Chapters 5, 6, and 7). The common characteristic of these stories and actual cases of children who recalled an adult model is the availability of mentorship by the older person.

What happens in such real-life mentorships? Typically, good mentors serve as positive models for hopeful thinking through the very manner in which they live their lives. In their words and through their deeds, mentors epitomize the processes that are inherent in hopeful thinking. These mentors often are willing to describe how they have tackled problems in the past, and they share stories that are rich in details about what they did to reach their goals. In this process, the mentor is not a perfect, infallible human being, but a person who makes mistakes and learns from them. Such mentors display a quality of humility about the struggles of life, yet continue in the face of adversity. Furthermore, they share their thoughts and feelings about important events.

A mentoring relationship often arises out of a child's bonding experience with his or her parent(s), teacher, or other important caregiver. Such bonding experiences typically involve a trip of some duration (a week or more) where the child and caregiver are together for long periods of time in a novel and challenging environment. It may be camping, white-water rafting, skin diving, or any of many other exciting activities. The key is that the child and caregiver share an experience that is meaningful to both of them. In the process, they undergo some difficulties and conquer many of them. Throughout the process, they talk about the experience and themselves. The journey becomes a special private story, or series of stories, that have hope as their central theme. The child and caregiver set goals, encounter road blocks, find alternative pathways or solutions, and apply themselves to these solutions.

The mentor must be willing to open up and talk freely about him- or herself, but he or she also must be a good listener. The adult mentor must pay attention to what the child is saying. A high-hope mentor thus *rejects* the old maxim that "a child is to be seen but not heard" and as such attends to the child's stories. Such active listening involves letting the child tell the story without fear of reprisals from the adult no matter how difficult or "negative" the content of the story may be. Research shows that telling one's story about a traumatic or difficult event is good for us in and of itself.[6]

Children make many mistakes as they strive to make sense of the world and find their place in it. If children can safely talk about mistakes with a caring adult in an open and safe atmosphere, they are more likely to learn from their misadventures. *Sometimes a personal tale is remembered because of what it taught us about what doesn't work.* If the mentor can tell such tales and highlight how hope-filled thoughts helped him or her, the child is more likely to learn from the adult model.

From MTV to the Library

Our children today are bombarded with "easy" input. By this, we mean television, movies, and radio, all of the electronic mediums that can render the viewer a passive, sponge-like consumer of someone else's stories, values, and products. In addition to the restoration of the oral tradition that we have advocated in this book, and the focusing upon the child's personal stories, we suggest that reading is a marvelous source for enlivening the story in the child's mind. Read as much as possible to your children and take them to discover the library. Off with the MTV, and into the library!

There are literally thousands of children's stories sitting on the shelves of your local library. With a little detective work on the part of you and your child, you will find stories that bring hope to life. Although we do not pretend to know what stories may be best for inducing and sustaining hope in your particular children, we have taken the liberty of including an appendix at the end of this book where approximately 140 children's books are listed according to content category. We believe that these stories are especially useful in working with children. Obviously, however, they provide only a taste of the many empowering tales that children can hear or read. The beauty of such stories, of course, is that our children can import and "own" them as applying to themselves as they pursue life goals. The personal tales that are showing in the theaters of young minds will be much more engrossing and helpful to children than all the latest attention-grabbers that are showing at our local movie houses or on our television screens.

Creating a Hope Chest: A Gift That Keeps Giving

Perhaps it is fitting to close this book with the most famous story about hope. In Greek mythology, the mortal Prometheus stole fire from the gods. Angered by this theft, Zeus created the maiden Pandora as the courier for his revenge. Sent to earth with a dowry chest, Pandora was warned never to open it. In what may be the earliest example of reverse psychology, Zeus knew full well that Pandora would be overcome with temptation and open the treasured box. When she did this very thing, a swarm of creatures flew out to torment humankind forever afterward. Included were gout, colic, and rheumatism, as well as envy, spite, and revenge. Rushing to return the lid to the chest, Pandora supposedly found only one item remaining inside—hope. The legend is vague, however, about whether she closed the lid in time to contain it.[7]

Not surprisingly, we prefer to conclude that hope was unleashed from Pandora's box onto the world. How else would it be the case that history is laced with hopeful stories that chronicle the tribulations and joys of humankind? Indeed, the pages of this book are filled with but a small sampling of these tales of hope. Ironically, although Zeus may have sought revenge through the sources of misery that he loaded into the box, he also appears to have given us hope. We cannot document it to be the case, but this may well be the very tale that produced the term "hope chest." Therefore, this ancient story of hope is really a gift that keeps giving.

THE HOPE CHEST

Our generation has used the gift of hope time and again. We must re-member, however, that this present needs to be passed on to our offspring. As adults, our best gift is to prepare our children for the journey of life. Our privilege and responsibility, as we have emphasized throughout this book, is to share our stories and help children to speak, write, and hold onto *their* own hopeful stories. In time, they will recount these stories of hope, first to themselves and then to their offspring. In this sense also, the story of hope is a gift that keeps giving.

Appendix A: The Young Children's Hope Scale—Story Form

Examiner's Instructions

Examiner Set.   The test should be presented to children as a game to arouse interest. Breaks should be given as needed. The examiner should give the child much praise for participating in the test, but not for giving specific types of answers.

Pretest Teaching Protocol.   During the pretest, the child's understanding of how to respond to the questions should be evaluated. The child being tested should say the name of the child most like him or her. This time should also be used for teaching children who are unclear of how to respond to the questions. Follow the Pretest Teaching Protocol if the child is unclear about how to respond to the questions. No scores are given for the pretest answers.

Test Items.   The child being tested should say the name of the child most like him or her. Circle the answer given by the child on the scoring sheet, then ask any questions specified on the test protocol. If the child clearly appears to be making a choice based on variables not related to the scenario (i.e., "He/she has my name," "I like his or her hair"), gently remind the child how to make a choice by saying, "Remember, listen to what is said about each child to know which child is most like you." If you suspect that a child has misinterpreted a scenario but has answered anyway, place a check in the column labeled "M?" on the scoring sheet. At the end of the entire test, go back to these scenarios and readminister each one. If the child understands the scenario when readministered, score as described above. If the child again misinterprets the scenario, place another check in the column labeled "M?" If more than three scenarios are misinterpreted, the entire scale is rendered invalid.

Scoring.   For each test item, add the weights of the circled answers. For the Waypower Subscale, add the scores for test items 1, 2, 6, 10, 11, 12, 15, 16, and 17. For the Willpower Subscale, add the scores for test items 3, 4, 5, 7, 8, 9, 13, 14, and 18. Add the scores from the Waypower and Willpower Subscales for the total score. The range of these scores will be between 0 and 18.

Pretest Teaching Protocols

Instructions. If the child does not respond to the first pretest question or answers "I don't know," proceed with the first phase of the teaching protocol for that particular question. If the child still does not respond appropriately, proceed with the second phase of the teaching protocol for that particular question. Even if the child never responds appropriately to the first pretest question, proceed to the second pretest question (P2). If necessary, follow the two phases of the teaching protocol with this question. Proceed with the third pretest question (P3) in the same manner. If the child does not appear to understand the test after the second phase of the teaching protocol with the third pretest question, discontinue the test.

Phase 1—Male Pretest Teaching Protocol. During this phase, direct the child's attention to the story about each child. Repeat and emphasize only the vital information of the question, including the scenario children's names. Then repeat the pretest question, "Which child is most like you?" ("WCIMLY?"). Below are the scripts for each probe.

(P1) "Listen to what is said about each child to know which is most like you. Rick is a boy. Lauren is a girl. WCIMLY?"

(P2) "Listen to what is said about each child to know which child is most like you. Scott has no brothers and sisters. Brent has (# brothers of child being tested) brothers and (# sisters of child being tested) sisters. WCIMLY?" Note: If child being tested has no brothers or sisters, Scott should have two brothers and three sisters.

(P3) "Listen to what is said about each child to know which child is most like you. For dessert, Mike wanted ice cream. John wanted an apple. WCIMLY?"

(P4) "Listen to what is said about each child to know which child is most like you. Frank thinks he is good at coloring. James does not think he is good at coloring. WCIMLY?"

Phase 2—Male Pretest Teaching Protocol. During this phase, the examiner should use him or herself as an example. Below are the scripts for each probe.

(P1) "Let me play. Rick is a boy. Lauren is a girl. I am a girl (boy). I am most like Lauren (Rick). Now you play. Rick is a boy. Lauren is a girl. WCIMLY?"

(P2) "Let me play. Scott has no brothers or sisters. Brent has (# brothers of child being tested) brothers and (# sisters of child being tested) sisters. If I have no brothers or sisters, I am most like Scott. Now you play. Scott has no brothers or sisters. Brent has (# of brothers of child being tested) brothers and (# sisters of child being tested) sisters. WCIMLY?"

(P3) "Let me play. For dessert, Mike wanted ice cream. John wanted an apple. For dessert, I would want an apple, so I am like John. Now you play. For dessert, Mike wanted ice cream. John wanted an apple. WCIMLY?"

(P4) "Let me play. Frank thinks he is good at coloring. James does not think he is good at coloring. I think I am good at coloring, so I am like Frank. Now you play. Frank thinks he is good at coloring. James does not think he is good at coloring. WCIMLY?"

Phase 1—Female Pretest Teaching Protocol. During this phase, direct the child's attention to the story about each child. Repeat and emphasize only the vital information of the question, including the scenario children's names. Then repeat the pretest question, "Which child is most like you?" (WCIMLY?"). Below are the scripts for each probe.

(P1) "Listen to what is said about each child to know which child is most like you. Lauren is a girl. Rick is a boy. WCIMLY?"

(P2) "Listen to what is said about each child to know which child is most like you. Sarah has no brothers and sisters. Karen has (# brothers of child being tested) brothers and (# sisters of child being tested) sisters. WCIMLY?" NOTE: If child being tested has no bothers or sisters, Sarah should have two brothers and three sisters.

(P3) "Listen to what is said about each child to know which child is most like you. For dessert, Mary wanted ice cream. Linda wanted an apple. WCIMLY?"

(P4) "Listen to what is said about each child to know which child is most like you. Danielle thinks she is good at coloring. Carrie does not think she is good at coloring. WCIMLY?"

Phase 2—Female Pretest Teaching Protocol. During this phase, the examiner should use him or herself as an example. Below are the scripts for each probe.

(P1) "Let me play. Lauren is a girl. Rick is a boy. I am a girl (boy). I am most like Lauren (Rick). Now you play. Lauren is a girl. Rick is a boy. WCIMLY?"

(P2) "Let me play. Sarah has no brothers or sisters. Karen has (# brothers of child being tested) brothers and (# sisters of child being tested) sisters. If I have no brothers or sisters, I am most like Sarah. Now you play. Sarah has no brothers or sisters. Karen has (# bothers of child being tested) brothers and (# sisters of child being tested) sisters. WCIMLY?"

(P3) "Let me play. For dessert, Mary wanted ice cream. Linda wanted an apple. For dessert, I would want an apple, so I am like Linda. Now you play. For dessert, Mary wanted ice cream. Linda wanted an apple. WCIMLY?"

(P4) "Let me play. Danielle thinks she is good at coloring. Carrie does not think she is good at coloring. I think I am good at coloring, so I am like Danielle. Now you play. Danielle thinks she is good at coloring. Carrie does not think she is good at coloring. WCIMLY?"

Male Test Items

Beginning Instructions Given to the Child. "I am going to tell you stories about two children. Listen carefully to what I tell you about each child. Then tell me which child is most like you."

1. Chuck and Larry have a problem. When they are at school, another child calls them names. Chuck and Larry want this child to stop calling them names. It is hard for Chuck to think of ways to stop the child from making fun of him. It is easy for Larry to think of ways to stop the child from making fun of him. WCIMLY?

2. Billy's parents are mad at him for not picking up his toys. David's parents are mad at him for not picking up his toys. Billy and David do not want their parents mad at them. It is easy for Billy to think of ways to get out of this mess. It is hard for David to think of ways to get out of this mess. WCIMLY?

3. Gary and Eddie are at the park. They want to play "tag" with the other children. Gary tries very hard to get the other children to let him play "tag." Eddie tries just a little to get the other children to let him play "tag." WCIMLY?

4. Chris wants his teacher to choose him to go first, before all the other children in class. Kevin also wants his teacher to choose him to go first. Chris tries a little to get the teacher to pick him to go first. Kevin tries very hard to get the teacher to pick him to go first. WCIMLY?

5. Doug and Michael are at home playing in the backyard. They want to build a special playhouse just for them. Doug works very hard to build the playhouse. Michael works a little to build the playhouse. WCIMLY?

6. Lee and Anthony are playing with a ball. The ball breaks a neighbor's window. They are in trouble. Lee and Anthony know the neighbor will be mad! Lee does not think there are lots of ways around this problem. Anthony thinks there are lots of ways around this problem. WCIMLY?

7. Russell and Tim have learned many new games. Russell thinks that knowing how to play these games will help him play other games a little better. Tim thinks that knowing how to play these games will help him play other games a whole lot better. WCIMLY?

8. George and Ray have learned to play nicely with others at school. George thinks that what he has learned will help him a whole lot next year in school. Ray thinks that what he has learned will help him just a little next year in school. WCIMLY?

9. Jason and Daryl have learned things from their parents. Jason thinks that what he has learned from his parents will help him a little when he is older. Daryl thinks that what he has learned from his parents will help him a whole lot when he is older. WCIMLY?

10. Bobby and Peter really want to play their favorite games with other children. It is easy for Bobby to think of ways to get other children to play his favorite games. It is hard for Peter to think of ways to get other children to play his favorite games. WCIMLY?

11. A principal gives prizes to some students. Mitch and Jack really want a prize from the principal. It is hard for Mitch to think of ways to get the principal to give him a prize. It is easy for Jack to think of ways to get the principal to give him a prize. WCIMLY?

12. Steve and Randy both have a pet at home. Steve and Randy really want their pets to love them. It is easy for Steve to think of ways to get his pet to love him. It is hard for Randy to think of ways to get his pet to love him. WCIMLY?

13. Paul and Mark always try to play nicely with their bothers and sisters. Paul does not think he has been able to play nicely with his brothers and sisters. Mark

TABLE A.1 Scoring Sheet for Male Test Items

Waypower	*Willpower*			*M?*	
_____		1. Chuck (0)	Larry (1)	_____	_____
_____		2. Billy (1)	David (0)	_____	_____
	_____	3. Gary (1)	Eddie (0)	_____	_____
	_____	4. Chris (0)	Kevin (1)	_____	_____
	_____	5. Doug (1)	Michael (0)	_____	_____
_____		6. Lee (0)	Anthony (1)	_____	_____
	_____	7. Russell (0)	Tim (1)	_____	_____
	_____	8. George (1)	Ray (0)	_____	_____
	_____	9. Jason (0)	Daryl (1)	_____	_____
_____		10. Bobby (1)	Peter (0)	_____	_____
_____		11. Mitch (0)	Jack (1)	_____	_____
_____		12. Steve (1)	Randy (0)	_____	_____
	_____	13. Paul (0)	Mark (1)	_____	_____
	_____	14. Timmy (1)	Robert (0)	_____	_____
_____		15. Dennis (0)	Joshua (1)	_____	_____
_____		16. Jim (1)	Ken (0)	_____	_____
_____		17. Phillip (0)	Cory (1)	_____	_____
	_____	18. Gordon (0)	Greg (1)	_____	_____

_____	+	_____	=	_____
Waypower Subscale Score		Willpower Subscale Score		Total Young Children's Hope Scale–Story Form Score

13. Paul and Mark always try to play nicely with their bothers and sisters. Paul does not think he has been able to play nicely with his brothers and sisters. Mark thinks he has been able to play nicely with his brothers and sisters. WCIMLY?

14. Timmy and Robert always try to do their work the best they can at school. Timmy thinks he has been able to do his schoolwork the best that he can. Robert does not think he has been able to do his schoolwork the best that he can. WCIMLY?

15. The neighborhood children are playing a game with a ball. The ball rolls down a big hill and falls into a hole. No one can play without the ball. Everyone wants to give up. Dennis knows he cannot figure out a way to get the ball. Joshua knows he can figure out a way to get the ball. WCIMLY?

16. Jim and Ken are at school. They are playing "hide and go seek" with the other children at recess. Two children start fighting. The playground rule is: If children fight, then everyone must go back to class early. No one wants to go back to class early. No matter what they do, no one can get the children to stop fighting. Jim knows he can figure out a way to stop the children from fighting. Ken knows he cannot figure out a way to stop the children from fighting. WCIMLY?

17. Phillip and his brothers and sisters, and Cory and his brothers and sisters, are trying to get their parents to take them to the store. No one can get their parents to take them. Everyone is about to quit trying to get their parents to take them to the store. Phillip knows he cannot figure out a way to get his parents to take them to the store. Cory knows he can figure out a way to get his parents to take them to the store. WCIMLY?

18. Gordon and Gregg want to have as many friends as they can. Gordon does not think he has as many friends as he can. Gregg thinks he has as many friends as he can. WCIMLY?

Female Test Items

Beginning Instructions Given to the Child. I am going to tell you stories about two children. Listen carefully to what I tell you about each child. Then tell me which child is most like you."

1. Rachel and Julie have a problem. When they are at school, another child calls them names. Rachel and Julie want this child to stop calling them names. It is hard for Rachel to think of ways to stop the child from making fun of her. It is easy for Julie to think of ways to stop the child from making fun of her. WCIMLY?

2. Crystal's parents are mad at her for not picking up her toys. Janice's parents are mad at her for not picking up her toys. Crystal and Janice do not want their parents mad at them. It is easy for Crystal to think of ways to get out of this mess. It is hard for Janice to think of ways to get out of this mess. WCIMLY?

3. Marilyn and Sharon are at the park. They want to play "tag" with the other children. Marilyn tries very hard to get the other children to let her play "tag." Sharon tries just a little to get the other children to let her play "tag." WCIMLY?

4. Christina wants her teacher to choose her to go first, before all the other children in class. Rhonda also wants her teacher to choose her to go first. Christina

tries a little to get the teacher to pick her to go first. Rhonda tries very hard to get the teacher to pick her to go first. WCIMLY?

5. Tammy and Nancy are at home playing in the backyard. They want to build a special playhouse just for them. Tammy works very hard to build the playhouse. Nancy works a little to build the playhouse. WCIMLY?

6. Theresa and Elizabeth are playing with a ball. The ball breaks a neighbor's window. They are in trouble. Theresa and Elizabeth know the neighbor will be mad! Theresa does not think there are lots of ways around this problem. Elizabeth thinks there are lots of ways around this problem. WCIMLY?

7. Marcia and Sandy have learned many new games. Marcia thinks that knowing how to play these games will help her play other games a little bit better. Sandy thinks that knowing how to play these games will help her play other games a whole lot better. WCIMLY?

8. Barbara and Natalie have learned to play nicely with others at school. Barbara thinks that what she has learned will help her a whole lot next year in school. Natalie thinks that what she has learned will help her just a little next year in school. WCIMLY?

9. Melinda and Emily have learned things from their parents. Melinda thinks that what she has learned from her parents will help her a little when she is older. Emily thinks that what she has learned from her parents will help her a whole lot when she is older. WCIMLY?

10. Pam and Brenda really want to play their favorite games with other children. It is easy for Pam to think of ways to get other children to play her favorite games. It is hard for Brenda to think of ways to get other children to play her favorite games. WCIMLY?

11. A principal gives prizes to some students. Renee and Vicky really want a prize from the principal. It is hard for Renee to think of ways to get the principal to give her a prize. It is easy for Vicky to think of ways to get the principal to give her a prize. WCIMLY?

12. Amanda and Cheri both have a pet at home. Amanda and Cheri really want their pets to love them. It is easy for Amanda to think of ways to get her pet to love her. It is hard for Cheri to think of ways to get her pet to love her. WCIMLY?

13. Donna and Jill always try to play nicely with their brothers and sisters. Donna does not think she has been able to play nicely with her brothers and sisters. Jill thinks she has been able to play nicely with her brothers and sisters. WCIMLY?

14. Valerie and Becky always try to do their work the best they can at school. Valerie thinks she has been able to do her schoolwork the best that she can. Becky does not think she has been able to do her schoolwork the best that she can. WCIMLY?

15. The neighborhood children are playing a game with a ball. The ball rolls down a big hill and falls into a hole. No one can play without the ball. Everyone wants to keep playing the game. No one can get the ball out of the hole. Everyone wants to give up. Denise knows she cannot figure out a way to get the ball. Tina knows she can figure out a way to get the ball. WCIMLY?

16. Ann and Marie are at school. They are playing "hide and go seek" with the other children at recess. Two children start fighting. The playground rule is: If children fight, then everyone has to go back to class early. No one wants to go back to

TABLE A.2 Scoring Sheet for Female Test Items

Waypower	_Willpower_			_M?_	
_____		1. Rachel (0)	Julie (1)	_____	_____
_____		2. Crystal (1)	Janice (0)	_____	_____
	_____	3. Marilyn (1)	Sharon (0)	_____	_____
	_____	4. Christina (0)	Rhonda (1)	_____	_____
	_____	5. Tammy (1)	Nancy (0)	_____	_____
_____		6. Theresa (0)	Elizabeth (1)	_____	_____
	_____	7. Marcia (0)	Sandy (1)	_____	_____
	_____	8. Barbara (1)	Natalie (0)	_____	_____
	_____	9. Melinda (0)	Emily (1)	_____	_____
_____		10. Pam (1)	Brenda (0)	_____	_____
_____		11. Renee (0)	Vicky (1)	_____	_____
_____		12. Amanda (1)	Cheri (0)	_____	_____
	_____	13. Donna (0)	Jill (1)	_____	_____
	_____	14. Valerie (1)	Becky (0)	_____	_____
_____		15. Denise (0)	Tina (1)	_____	_____
_____		16. Ann (1)	Marie (0)	_____	_____
_____		17. Diane (0)	Lori (1)	_____	_____
	_____	18. Jackie (0)	Carla (1)	_____	_____

_____ + _____ = _____

| Waypower
Subscale
Score | Willpower
Subscale
Score | | Total Young Children's Hope
Scale–Story Form Score |

class early. No matter what they do, no one can get the children to stop fighting. Everyone is about to quit trying. Ann knows she can figure out a way to stop the children from fighting. Marie knows she cannot figure out a way to stop the children from fighting. WCIMLY?

17. Diane and her brothers and sisters, and Lori and her brothers and sisters, are trying to get their parents to take them to the store. No one can get their parents to take them. Everyone is about to quit trying to get their parents to take them to the store. Diane knows she cannot figure out a way to get her parents to take them to the store. Lori knows she can figure out a way to get her parents to take them to the store. WCIMLY?

18. Jackie and Carla want to have as many friends as they can. Jackie does not think she has as many friends as she can. Carla thinks she has as many friends as she can. WCIMLY?

Appendix B:
Children's Books on
Hope-Related Issues

Abuse

A Family That Fights. Sharon Chesler Bernstein. Morton Grove, IL: Albert Whitman & Co., 1991. Henry, the oldest child, struggles with his father's abusiveness toward the whole family.

Don't Hurt Me, Mama. Muriel Stanek. Niles, IL: Albert Whitman & Co., 1983. Offers possible solutions and a positive conclusion for a young girl who is abused by her mother.

Adoption

Adoption Is For Always. Linda Walvoord Girard. Niles, IL: Albert Whitman & Co., 1985. Explores the confusion and upsetting emotions a little girl feels when she discovers that she is adopted.

My Real Family. Emily Arnold McCully. Orlando, FL: Bromndeer Press, 1994. After hearing that her family is adopting a sheep, a child bear thinks that she, too, is adopted. She runs away in order to find her "real parents" but returns home and realizes she has "real parents."

Tell Me Again About the Night I Was Born. Jamie Lee Curtis. New York: HarperCollins Publishers, 1996. A young girl has her parents retell the cherished family story about her birth and adoption.

Happy Adoption Day. John McCutcheon & Julie Paschkis. Boston: Little Brown, 1996. The love and joy of new parents watching their adopted child grow is described. An adoption day celebration is held each year.

How I Was Adopted. Joanna Cole. New York: Morrow Junior Books, 1995. The message is that adoption is just one way of making a family and that the love in an adoptive family is the same as in any family. Thus, family is shown to be about love and spirit, not blood ties or genetics.

Affection

The Original Warm Fuzzy Tale. Claude Steiner. Rolling Hills Estates, CA: Jalmar Press, 1977. Presents a story analogous to everyday life that encourages children to give as many "warm fuzzies" (love) as possible.

Alcohol/Drugs

I Wish Daddy Didn't Drink So Much. Judith Vigna. Niles, IL: Albert Whitman & Co., 1988. Describes how a little girl whose father drinks too much learns, along with her mom's help, to keep his drinking from ruining her life.

What's "Drunk" Mama? New York: Al-Anon Publications, 1977. Examines a young girl's feelings about her father's alcoholism and the negative effects it has on her family.

When Someone in the Family Drinks Too Much. Richard C. Langsen. New York: Dial Books for Young Readers, 1996. In simple terms, children are shown how to recognize alcoholism and its effects on the entire family. Ways to cope and where to get outside help also are addressed.

When a Family Is in Trouble. Marge Heegaard. Minneapolis: Woodland Press, 1993. In a workbook format, children are helped through the trauma of a parent's chemical dependency.

Anger

I Was So Mad. Mercer Mayer. Racine, WI: Western Publishing, 1983. Describes a boy "critter" who is mad because he keeps getting into trouble. Story teaches anger control and resolution.

That Makes Me Angry! Anthony Best. Racine, WI: Western Publishing, 1989. Shows how lack of communication can make people angry at each other. Bert and Ernie work out a communication problem without getting into a fight.

Arguing

Every Kid's Guide to Handling Family Arguments. Joy Berry. Chicago: Children's Press, 1987. Explores family fighting and teaches that arguing can be healthy, and that both good and bad can come out of it.

Every Kid's Guide to Handling Fights with Brothers or Sisters. Joy Berry. Chicago: Children's Press, 1987. Gives useful tips on how to handle brothers and sisters when they do things that upset a child.

Asthma (*see also* Physical Illness)

All About Asthma. William & Vivian Ostrow. Morton Grove, IL: Whitman & Co., 1989. The young narrator describes life with asthma, explaining its causes and symptoms and discussing ways to control it so as to lead a normal life.

Attachment (*see also* Love; Unconditional Love)

The Runaway Bunny. Margaret Wise Brown. New York: Harper Collins, 1982. Bunny learns that his mom loves him so much that she will follow him anywhere, even if he runs away.

I Love My Family. Wade Hudson. New York: Scholastic, 1993. A black family's annual reunion teaches the similarity of experiences among families of different races, including good family relations, love and respect for elders, and strong values.

Comparisons (*see also* Self-Acceptance)

Hard to Be Six. Arnold Adoff. New York: Lothrop, Lee & Shepard Books, 1991. A little boy compares himself to his sisters and wants to be older like them. His grandmother makes him realize it's good to be young and tells him, "Take time slow, make life count, pass love on."

Communication (*see also* Arguing)

Every Kid's Guide to Understanding Parents. Joy Berry. Chicago: Children's Press, 1987. Helps children identify with different kinds of parents and suggests steps for getting along with parents.

Yes, I Can Say No. Manuel J. Smith. New York: Arbor House, 1986. Gives strategies to help children respond assertively to peer pressure, compliments, criticism, and other forms of communication.

Confidence and Self-Esteem

100 Ways to Enhance Self-Concept in the Classroom. Jack Canfield & Harold C. Wells. Englewood Cliffs, NJ: Prentice-Hall, 1976. Contains exercises to help teachers improve the child's confidence and self-esteem in a nonjudgmental environment.

The Good Luck Pony. Elizabeth Koda-Callan. New York: Workman Publishing, 1993. A little girl finds the courage to ride when her mother gives her a tiny golden pony that radiates self-confidence.

Crying

I Am Not a Crybaby. Norma Simon. Niles, IL: Albert Whitman & Co., 1989. Gives reasons why people cry (e.g., a sad cry when one is hurt, or a happy cry at a wedding) and stresses that one is never too old to cry.

Death

Someday a Tree. Eve Bunting. New York: Clarion Books, 1993. A young girl, her parents, and their neighbors try to save an old oak tree that is poisoned by pollution. The girl finally discovers a solution that restores her hope.

When I Die, Will I Get Better? Joeri & Piet Breebaart. New York: Peter Bedrick Books, 1993. A six-year-old boy tries to come to terms with the death of his younger brother by creating a story about rabbit brothers that closely parallels his own experiences.

When Bad Things Happen to Good People. Harold S. Kushner. New York: Schocken Books, 1981. Written by a man dealing with the pain of a terminally ill child. Helps readers find the strength and hope to carry on.

Everett Anderson's Goodbye. Lucille Clifton. New York: Holt, Rinehart & Winston, 1983. Tells the stages of grief and how a boy passes through them after his father dies.

The Accident. Carol Carrick. New York: Seabury Press, 1976. Explores a young boy's feelings when his dog dies.

Gentle Willow: A Story for Children About Dying. Joyce C. Mills. New York: Magination Press, 1993. Amanda is upset that she is going to lose her friend Gentle Willow, but the Tree Wizards help her understand that her memories are gifts from her friend and that there are special ways of saying good-bye.

Coping with Death and Grief. Marge Heegaard. Minneapolis, MN: Woodland Press, 1990. This book's many stories touch upon young people's grief and the facts about death.

The Ugly Menorah. Marissa Moss. New York: Farrar Straus Giroux, 1996. A young girl struggles with her grandpa's death. She has a menorah for Hanukkah, but it is ugly and hard to look at. When grandma lights the candles, grandpa's presence is felt.

Help for the Hard Times: Getting Through Loss. Earl Hipp. Center City, MN: Hazelden, 1995. Answers questions of 11-to-17-year-old-children about loss. Offers a guide for handling crisis, emotions, and responsibilities.

When Grandpa Came to Stay. Judith Caseley. New York: Greenwillow Books, 1996. Because Benny's grandmother died, his grandfather comes for a visit—and stays. Benny doesn't understand much about death, but he and his grandfather talk about it and learn to cope.

When Someone Dies. Sharon Greelee. Atlanta: Peachtree Publishers, 1992. Suggestions are made for surviving the changes and remembering the good times when a loved one dies.

Determination

The Evergreen Wood: An Adaptation of the Pilgrim's Progress for Children. Alan & Linda Parry. Nashville, TN: Oliver Nelson, 1992. After a long and arduous journey, Christopher Mouse reaches the Evergreen Wood, where all the animals live in peace and safety.

Kids Can Succeed: 51 Tips for Real Life from One Kid to Another. Daryl Bernstein. Holbrook, MA: Bod Adams Inc., 1993. Tips for teens include goal setting, maintaining a positive outlook, and trying different approaches to solve a problem.

Horton Hatches the Egg. Dr. Seuss. New York: Random House, 1940. This is the classic story of an elephant who is loyal, dedicated, and determined to keep his word no matter what happens.

The Day the Dark Clouds Came. Phylliss Adams. Cleveland: Modern Press, 1986. A little robin uses hope, effort, and determination to overcome her fear of failure.

The Little Engine That Could. Watty Piper. New York: Platt & Munk, 1976. After a train filled with toys breaks down, several other trains refuse to help. Finally, a little blue engine comes along and delivers the toys to the children on the other side with determination and encouragement.

Left By Themselves. Charles Paul May. New York: Scholastic Book Services, 1982. Family members are rescued and their lives are saved, but only because of their strong determination and love for each other.

Diabetes (*see also* Physical Illness)

Even Little Kids Get Diabetes. Connie White Pirner. Morton Grove, IL: Whitman & Co., 1991. A two-year-old finds out that she has diabetes but learns that she is still a regular kid.

Shoot for the Hoop. Matt Christopher. New York: Little, Brown and Co., 1995. When Rusty is diagnosed with diabetes, his parents tell him to quit playing basketball. Rusty is determined to persuade his parents to let him play basketball, and he overcomes many obstacles so that he can.

Sarah and Puffle: A Story for Children About Diabetes. Linnea Mulder, R.N. New York: Magination Press, 1992. Upset by the restrictions imposed by her diabetes, Sarah dreams about a talking sheep who helps her accept her condition.

Disabilities (*see also* Learning Disabilities)

Little Tree: A True Story for Children with Serious Medical Problems. Joyce C. Mills, Ph.D. New York: Magination Press, 1992. Although she is saddened when a storm has taken some of her branches, Little Tree draws strength and happiness from the knowledge that she still has a strong trunk, deep roots, and a beautiful heart.

My Friend Leslie: The Story of a Handicapped Child. Maxine Rosenberg & George Ancona. New York: Lothrop, Lee & Shepard Books, 1983. A child with multiple handicaps is accepted in various school settings.

About Handicaps. Sara Bonnett Stein. New York: Walker & Co., 1974. A boy who is frightened of others' handicaps learns that people who are different can be good friends.

A Very Special Critter. Gina & Mercer Mayer. New York: Western Publishing, 1992. The first day at school for a little boy in a wheelchair is scary for him and the other children. Gives positive examples of relating to a child with a handicap and seeing similarities rather than differences.

Someone Special Just Like You. Tricia Brown. New York: Henry Holt and Co., 1984. Children with disabilities learn that all kids have the same wishes, joys, and desires, even though they may not see, hear, speak, or walk the same.

Howie Helps Himself. Joan Fassler. Morton Grove, IL: Albert Whitman & Co., 1975. Young Howie learns how to interact with others about his physical disability. The story also shows how anxiety toward people with handicaps can be reduced.

I Have a Sister: My Sister Is Deaf. Jeanne Whitehouse Peterson. New York: Harper Trophy, 1977. Sisters learn to handle their differences and to overlook handicaps so as to make their relationship stronger. Explains what it is like to be deaf to young readers.

Divorce and Stepfamilies

Living with a Single Parent. Maxine B. Rosenberg. New York: Bradbury Press, Macmillan Publishing Inc., 1992. This is a collection of firsthand stories by adolescents living with single parents.

When a Parent Marries Again: Children Can Deal with Family Change. Marge Heegaard. Minneapolis: Woodland Press, 1991. Grief surrounding the death of a parent and the emotions following remarriage are considered with the help of illustrations that the reader draws.

Helping Children of Divorce. Susan Arnsberg Diamond. New York: Schocken Books, 1985. Teachers, school officials, and divorced parents are helped to better understand and assist children whose parents are divorced.

Daddy Doesn't Live Here Anymore. Betty Boegehold. Racine, WI: Western Publishing, 1985. A little girl named Casey deals with the fact that her dad still loves her even though he is divorcing her mom.

Where Do I Belong? Buff Bradley. Reading, MA: Addison Wesley, 1992. This book helps children aged 8–12 deal with stepfamilies. Touches on divorce and living through it, being a stepchild, and so on.

Let's Talk About Stepfamilies. Angela Grunsell. New York: Gloucester Press, 1990. The author answers questions young people have when experiencing new additions to their home. Alleviates myths such as the "wicked stepmother."

Dinosaurs Divorce. Laurene Krasny Brown & Marc Brown. Canada: Little, Brown and Co., 1977. Dinosaurs get divorced and give rise to some tough situations to which young readers can relate. Positive ways of handling the difficulties of divorce are approached by using humor and lively examples.

Why Are We Getting a Divorce? Peter Mayle. New York: Harmony Books, 1988. The adjustment to living with one parent is explained along with how to overcome the loss and hurt that children of divorced parents experience.

When Mom and Dad Separate. Marge Heegaard. Minneapolis: Woodland Press, 1990. Through a workbook format, children are shown how to deal with their feelings about separation or divorce.

My Mother's House, My Father's House. C. B. Christiansen. New York: Macmillan Publishing Co., 1989. A young girl talks through the difficulties of living in two different houses after her parent's divorce.

Domestic Violence (*see also* Abuse)

Something Is Wrong at My House. Diane Davis. Seattle: Parenting Press, 1984. Children from violent and nonviolent homes are given permission to have feelings and to make decisions about how they wish to act upon those feelings.

Environment

Alejandro's Gift. Richard E. Albert. San Francisco: Chronicle Books, 1994. Teaching environmental awareness, the main character, Alejandro, explores different climates and environments. He finds hope in his adventure to the desert.
The Boy Who Didn't Believe in Spring. Lucille Clifton. New York: Dutton Children's Books, 1993. King Shabazz was a little boy who did not believe that springtime was coming. He did not see the blooming flowers, the chirping birds, or smell the fresh air. But one day he found a nest of unhatched bird's eggs, and then he believed that spring had arrived.

Epilepsy (*see also* Physical Illness)

Lee, the Rabbit with Epilepsy. Deborah Moss. Kensington, MD: Woodbine House, 1989. Lee is diagnosed with epilepsy, but medicine to control her seizures reduces her worries and she learns she can still lead a normal life.

Fear

Sometimes I'm Afraid. Jane Watson, Werner Switzer, Robert E. Hirschberg, & J. Cotter. New York: Crown Publishers, 1986. A young boy, afraid in many different situations, deals with his fear and gives reasons why he becomes afraid.
Scared Silly! Mark Brown. Canada: Little, Brown and Co., 1994. Spooky poems, riddles, jokes, and stories help young readers laugh at the things about which they are scared.
Hildilid's Night. Cheli Duran Ryan. New York: Alladin Paperbacks, 1996. Hildilid hates the night, but no matter how much she tosses and turns, the darkness does not go away. Finally, her fear lessens when she realizes that the sun rises the next morning.
What's Under My Bed? James Stevenson. New York: Puffin Books, 1983. Mary Ann and Louise spend the night at their grandparents' house, but they are afraid. Grandpa tells them he too used to be scared when he was their age, and this makes them feel better.

Friendship

Caleb's Friend. Eric Jon Nones. New York: Farrar, Straus & Giroux, 1993. When a storm threatens, Caleb and his friend learn that even if they cannot be together, they will never be truly apart.
Pinky and Rex Go to Camp. James Howe. New York: Avon Books, 1993. By sharing his fear of going to camp, Pinky finds support from his best friend and ends up having a great time.
Friends Forever: Six Stories Celebrating the Joys of Friendship. Debbie Butcher Wiersma & Veveca Gustafson. Racine, WI: Western Publishing, 1992. Stories about friendship are brought to life through various characters.

Little Mouse's Rescue. Ariane Chottin, adapted by Patricia Jensen. Pleasantville, NY: Reader's Digest Kids, 1990. A little mouse sneaks into a farm kitchen for a feast that is guarded by two cats. Her friends come to rescue her, and the power of friendship is revealed.

Goals

The Man Who Had No Dream. Adelaide Holl. New York: Random House, 1969. A rich, idle, and unhappy man finds a way to be useful and live a happy life.
Grover's 10 Terrific Ways to Help Our Wonderful World. Anna Ross. New York: Random House, 1992. Using the philosophy that the world takes care of us, and in return, we must take care of the world, Grover gives a list of things (e.g., plant a tree, do not waste, recycle) that children are capable of doing.
Oh, the Places You'll Go. Dr. Seuss. New York: Random House, 1990. The ups and downs that one might encounter in the future are shown. Encourages the reader to persevere and find the success that lies within.
Oh, the Thinks You Can Think. Dr. Seuss. New York: Random House, 1975. Colorful pictures and silly rhymes encourage use of imagination. Introduces the reader to creative ways of thinking.
Hector's New Sneakers. Amanda Vesey. New York: Penguin Books, 1993. Hector's parents cannot afford the sneakers he wants, and he learns that he can be happy without them. Explains children's feelings about fitting in and having the "right" things.
When I Grow Up. Mercer Mayer. New York: Western Publishing, 1991. A little girl dreams of the different things she might be when she grows up, such as a mountain climber, lion tamer, or a famous doctor. Exposes both boys and girls to nontraditional roles.

Health and Nutrition

What About Me? When Brothers and Sisters Get Sick. Allan Peterkin. New York: Magination Press, 1992. Laura experiences conflicting emotions when her brother becomes seriously ill. Includes suggestions for parents.
Every Kid's Guide to Nutrition and Health Care. Joy Berry. Chicago: Children's Press, 1987. Maintaining a healthy lifestyle by exercising, eating nutritional food, and adhering to bodily requirements are taught. Gives tips on hygiene and wearing appropriate clothing.

Hospitals

Going to the Hospital. Fred Rodgers. New York: Putnam's, 1988. Describes what happens during a stay in the hospital, including some of the common forms of medical treatment.

Individual Differences and Cooperation

Old Henry. Joan W. Blos. New York: William Morrow & Co., 1987. Shows how different kinds of people learn to get along.

The Ugly Duckling. Marianna Mayer. New York: MacMillan, 1987. An ugly duckling spends an unhappy year ostracized by the other animals before she grows into a beautiful swan.

The Rag Coat. Lauren Mills. Waltham, MA: Little Brown, 1991. Minna proudly wears her new coat made of clothing scraps to school, and the other children laugh at her until she tells them the stories behind the scraps.

The Mixed-Up Cameleon. Eric Carle. New York: Harper Collins, 1975. A chameleon goes to the zoo and wishes he could be like the other animals. When his wish is granted, he realizes he cannot be any good if he's like other animals.

We're Different, We're the Same. Bobbi Jane Kates. New York: Random House, 1992. Explores the physical and emotional similarities and differences among people and stresses that it is natural for people to be different.

Crow Boy. Taro Yashima. New York: Viking, 1983. A young boy is taunted by classmates because he seems strange and quiet. With a teacher's support, the boy opens up to his classmates and gains acceptance and respect.

If We Were All the Same. Fred Rodgers. New York: Random House, 1987. Lady Elaine visits the Purple Planet where everybody looks and lives the same. When these people visit Lady Elaine's world, they are impressed with how everything is different and decide to change their world to also have differences.

Learning Disabilities

Trouble with School: A Family Story About Learning Disabilities. Kathryn & Allison Boesel Dunn. Rockville, MD: Woodbine House Inc., 1993. A dual narrative between mother and daughter shows both perspectives about the struggles with the daughter's learning disability.

Sixth Grade Can Really Kill You. Barthe DeClements. Santa Barbara, CA: Viking Penguin, 1985. Helen, a child with a reading disability, struggles with her disability by acting up in school. This story has a promising conclusion.

Listening (*see also* Communication)

Oh, Bother! No One's Listening! Betty Birney. Racine, WI: Western Publishing, 1991. Winnie the Pooh and friends plan a party, but it doesn't turn out very well because no one listened when Rabbit read the list of what everyone was to bring. Christopher Robin explains how good listening skills can help.

Nobody's Perfect, Not Even My Mother. Norma Simon. Chicago: Albert Whitman & Co., 1981. Lets children know that it's okay not to be perfect. Suggests that no one is perfect and that everyone is good at something.

Love (*see also* Unconditional Love)

Guess How Much I Love You. Sam McBratney. Boston: Candlewick Press, 1994. A father rabbit shows everlasting love for his son.

Hope. Randy Houk. Fairfield, CT: The Benefactory, Inc., 1995. A caring family finds an injured pig and nurses it back to health at their family farm. Love and patience bring the pig back to good health.

Moving

My Friend William Moved Away. Martha Whitmore Hickman. Nashville, TN: Abingdon, 1979. Helps children understand that even though friends move away, there will be new friends.

The Lotus Seed. Sherry Garland. San Diego: Harcourt Brace Jovanovitch, 1993. A young Vietnamese girl saves a lotus seed and carries it with her everywhere, remembering a brave emperor and the homeland she has to flee.

Things You Need to Know Before You Move. Lisa Ann Marsoli. Morristown, NY: Silver Burdett, 1985. Prepares young people for the anticipated changes that come with a move.

Home of the Bayou. G. Brian Karas. New York: Simon & Schuster Books, 1996. A young cowboy learns how to deal with moving to a new place.

Obstacles

Into the Deep Forest with Henry David Thoreau. Jim Murphy. New York: Clarion Books, 1995. Thoreau and two companions struggle through the Maine wilderness. As they travel through hardships, details and beautiful sites of the untouched forests are described.

I Had Trouble in Getting to Solla Sollew. Dr. Seuss. New York: Random House, 1963. Troubles happen to the character on each page. The goal is to find someone who can teach how to overcome these obstacles.

Alexander and the Terrible, Horrible, No Good, Very Bad Day. Judith Viorst. New York: Aladdin Paperbacks, 1987. From having a bad hair day to eating lima beans, everything is going wrong for Alexander. His mother gives him hope for a better tomorrow.

Parent Travel

Traveling Again Dad? Michael Lorelli. Traverse City, MI: Publishers Design Service, 1996. Addresses how some families live with a parent who must be away from home because of work. Suggestions are made for dealing with this issue in a positive way.

Parental Relations

Understanding Parents. Joy Berry. Sebastopol, CA: Children's Press, 1987. Suggests that there are many different types of parents and that parents love their children and want what is best for them.

Something Is Wrong at My House. Diane Davis. Seattle: Parenting Press, 1984. Explores a boy's feelings about his parents' fighting and gives good solutions.

Physical Illness

When Someone Has a Very Serious Illness. Marge Heegaard. Minneapolis: Woodland Press, 1992. Using a workbook format, children are helped to deal with their feelings about serious illness.

Planning (*see also* Problem Solving)

Every Kid's Guide to Using Time Wisely. Joy Berry. Sebastopol, CA: Living Skills Press, 1987. Gives advice for managing time effectively.
The Kid's Guide to Social Action. Barbara Lewis. Minneapolis: Free Spirit Publishing, 1991. Encourages the use of surrounding resources to create petitions, surveys, and letters so as to make an impact on society. Contains stories that inspire and promote social awareness.

Prejudice and Race Issues

Yo! Yes? Chris Raschka. New York: Orchard Books, 1993. Two lonely characters, one black and one white, meet on the street and become friends.
Living in Two Worlds. George Ancona. New York: Lothrop, Lee & Shepard Books, 1986. Mixed-race children talk about themselves, including feelings and special challenges they face in belonging to two cultures.
Black Is Brown Is Tan. Arnold Adoff. San Francisco: Harper & Row, 1973. Two young boys are brought up by a white father and a black mother. They like it because the things around them are black or white—for example, white and black milk.
The Lily Cupboard. Shulamith Levey Oppenheim. New York: HarperCollins, 1992. A young Jewish girl during World War II learns that there are many heroes for her.
Abby. Jeannette Caines. New York: Harper & Row, 1973. The challenges of an adopted black girl living with white parents are described.

Problem Solving (*see also* Planning)

Every Kid's Guide to Decision Making and Problem Solving. Joy Berry. Chicago: Children's Press, 1987. Fosters an understanding of what a decision is and why people make decisions. Outlines decision-making steps.
Fall Out. Gudrun Pausewang. New York: Penguin Books, 1994. There is a leak at the nuclear power station near 14-year-old Janna's house. Janna is left alone to look after her little brother and must make difficult decisions about what to do.
The Story of Little Babaji. Helen Bannerman. New York: HarperCollins Publishers, 1996. An Indian boy has his new clothes stolen by wild tigers in the jungle. Babaji overcomes his fear of wild animals in order to get back his clothes.
Did I Ever Tell You How Lucky You Are? Dr. Seuss. New York: Random House, 1973. Puts problems in perspective by using humor. Shows that one can be happy with what one has.
The Book of Think. Marilyn Burns. Boston: Little, Brown &Co., 1976. Offers a variety of problem-solving strategies and approaches as well as practice exercises.
Every Kid's Guide to Responding to Danger. Joy Berry. Sebastopol, CA: Living Skills Press, 1987. Presents situations that could harm a child, as well as how to avoid or handle those dangerous situations.

Remarriage of Parent

When a Parent Marries Again. Marge Heegaard. Minneapolis: Woodland Press, 1993. In the context of a workbook, children are taught how to deal with their feelings about step-families.

School

Starting School. Janet & Allen Ahlberg. New York: Puffin Books, 1990. Preschoolers are shown that school is exciting and fun and a place where friendships can start.

Self-Acceptance (*see also* Comparisons)

The King's Equal. Katherine Paterson. New York: Harper Collins, 1992. In order to wear the crown of the kingdom, an arrogant young prince must find an equal in his bride. Instead, he finds someone far better than he.

I Wish I Were a Butterfly. James Howe. Orlando, FL: Harcourt, Brace, Jovanovich, 1987. A cricket who is unhappy with his appearance learns to accept himself. Encourages children to look at and accept what they have.

Least of All. Carol Purdy. New York: Aladdin Books, 1993. A little girl in a big farm family teaches herself how to read using the Bible and shares this knowledge with her brothers, parents, and grandmother during a long, cold Vermont winter.

I Hate Being Gifted. Patricia Hermes. New York: Minstrel Books, 1990. A teenaged girl is accepted into a gifted program, but she begins to lose her friends because they are jealous. She learns to deal with self-acceptance and peer pressure.

Separation and Independence

All By Myself. Mercer Mayer. New York: Western Publishing, 1983. A little boy "critter" finds that there are some things he can do by himself and that it's okay to ask for help with other things.

Shyness

How Come You're So Shy? Leone Castell Anderson. Racine, WI: Western Publishing, 1987. Two girls who are both shy learn to talk to each other and become friends.

Very Shy. Barbara Shook Hazen. New York: Human Sciences Press, 1982. Nancy asks her dad to help her get over her shyness and then follows his suggestions.

Sibling Relationships (*see also* Arguing)

Your Best Friend, Kate. Pat Brisson. New York: Aladdin Books, 1992. Kate's letters to her best friend show how much she loves her brother even though she fights with him.

Small Physical Size (*see also* Comparisons)

Little Puppy Saves the Day. Muriel Pepin, adapted by Patricia Jensen. Pleasantville, NY: Reader's Digest Kids Books, 1992. A little puppy is made fun of by the other farm animals because he is so small, but he proves his worth when he rescues a lost chick.

Staying Alone

All Alone After School. Muriel Stanek. Niles, IL: Albert Whitman & Co., 1985. A boy talks about the things he does after school while he is alone at home.

Suicide

When Living Hurts. Sol Gordon. New York: Union of American Hebrew Congregations, 1985. Explores suicide by showing how to deal with feelings such as anger, depression, and peer pressure. Also addresses questions about God and the purpose of life.

Traumatic Experiences

When Something Terrible Happens: Children Can Learn to Cope with Grief. Marge Heegaard. Minneapolis: Woodland Press, 1991. Helps process reactions to traumatic events with illustrations that the reader draws.

Good Answers to Tough Questions About Traumatic Experiences. Joy Berry. Chicago: Children's Press, 1990. Defines traumas that children may encounter and explains the steps to overcoming the related negative feelings. Shows how positive things can come out of negative experiences.

Every Kid's Guide to Coping with Childhood Traumas. Joy Berry. Chicago: Children's Press, 1988. Gives children specific terms to help in understanding their feelings related to various traumas. Also gives specific suggestions for dealing with their traumas.

When Something Terrible Happens. Marge Heegaard. Minneapolis: Woodland Press, 1992. In a workbook format, children are helped to deal with their feelings about traumatic events.

Travel

We're Taking an Airplane Trip. Dinah L. Moche. Racine, WI: Western Publishing Co., 1982. Elizabeth and her younger brother are flying alone for the first time. Anxious and excited, they have a wonderful experience.

Unconditional Love (*see also* Love)

Mama, Do You Love Me? Barbara M. Joose. San Francisco: Chronicle Books, 1991. A daughter questions her mother's love to see if it is conditional or unconditional. The story shows the special love that exists between a parent and child.

Working Moms

That Terrible Thing that Happened at Our House. Stan Bernstein. New York: Parent's Magazine Press, 1987. A young girl feels bad when her mother goes back to work, but the family learns to handle this new situation.

Notes

Chapter One

1. If you are interested in other works where we define hope, we recommend C. R. Snyder, *The Psychology of Hope: You Can Get There from Here* (New York: Free Press, 1994) as an overview. Writings that are more oriented toward a professional audience include the following: C. R. Snyder, L. M. Irving, and J. R. Anderson, "Hope and Health: Measuring the Will and the Ways," in C. R. Snyder and D. R. Forsyth (Eds.), *The Handbook of Social and Clinical Psychology: The Health Perspective* (Elmsford, NY: Pergamon Press, 1991); C. R. Snyder, C. Harris, J. R. Anderson, S. A. Holleran, L. M. Irving, S. T. Sigmon, L. Yoshinobu, J. Gibb, C. Langelle, and P. Harney, "The Will and the Ways: Development and Validation of an Individual Differences Measure of Hope," *Journal of Personality and Social Psychology* 60 (1991), 570–585; C. R. Snyder, "Hope for the Journey," in A. P. Turnball, J. M. Paterson, S. K. Behr, D. L. Murphy, J. G. Marquis, and M. J. Blue-Banning (Eds.), *Cognitive Coping, Families and Disability* (Baltimore: Brookes, 1993); and C. R. Snyder, "Conceptualizing, Measuring, and Nurturing Hope," *Journal of Counseling and Development* 73 (1995), 355–360. For a review of other recent perspectives on hope, read C. J. Farran, K. A. Herth, and J. M. Popovich, *Hope and Hopelessness: Critical Clinical Constructs* (Newbury Park, CA: Sage, 1995).

2. For further information about the importance of goals, we suggest L. A. Pervin (Ed.), *Goal Concepts in Personality and Social Psychology* (Hillsdale, NJ: Erlbaum, 1989), and E. A. Locke and G. P. Latham, *Goal Setting: A Motivational Technique That Works* (Englewood Cliffs, NJ: Prentice-Hall, 1984).

3. The process by which goals and their associated plans are categorized together is described by C. R. Berger, "Goals, Plans, and Mutual Understandings in Relationships," in S. Duck (Ed.), *Individual and Relationships, Volume 1* (Newbury Park, CA: Sage, 1993).

4. Two good recent reviews of the importance of agency in human action can be found in M. H. Kernis, *Efficacy, Agency, and Self-Esteem* (New York: Plenum, 1995), and M. E. Ford, *Motivating Humans* (Newbury Park, CA: Sage, 1992).

5. The survey data on the number of stories told per hour is taken from P. Miller and L. Sperry, "Early Talk About the Past: The Origins of Conversational Stories of Personal Experience," *Journal of Child Language* 15 (1988), 293–315.

6. For an examination of how children watch their mother's face longer than they do other faces, see R. L. Fantz, "Patterns of Vision in Newborn Infants," *Sci-*

ence 140 (1963), 296–297. For similar research, as well as information on how infants are capable of recognizing their mother's face, see M. E. Barrera and D. Maurer, "The Perception of Facial Expressions by the Three-Month-Old," *Child Development* 52 (1981), 203–206; and, M. E. Barrera and D. Maurer, "Discrimination of Strangers by the Three-Month-Old," *Child Development* 52 (1981), 558–563. In regard to infants' recognition of voices, see M. B. Stevenson, J. N. Ver Hoeve, M. A. Roach, and L. A. Leavitt, "The Beginning of Conversation: Early Patterns of Mother-Infant Vocal Responsiveness," *Infant Behavior and Development* 9 (1986), 423–440. For other resources on infants' perceptual capabilities, see C. R. Snyder, *The Psychology of Hope,* and M. Schulman, *The Passionate Mind* (New York: Free Press, 1991).

7. For an enjoyable and informative read about how children proceed from sensations to perception, as well as how they form linkages, we recommend M. Schulman, *The Passionate Mind.*

8. For an experimental example of how infants are capable of making connections, one study shows that two-month-old babies move their heads in a particular direction in order to make an overhead mobile move. In this regard, read J. S. Watson, "Cognitive-Perceptual Development in Infancy: Setting for the Seventies," *Merrill-Palmer Quarterly* 17 (1971), 139–152.

9. Some researchers have shown that pointing occurs as early as three months. For an example, see H. W. Stevenson and R. S. Newman, "Long-Term Prediction of Achievement and Attitudes in Mathematics and Reading," *Child Development* 57 (1986), 646–659. Others, such as M. Schulman, *The Passionate Mind,* suggest that pointing certainly can be in place by the age of 12 months.

10. For a description of the red nose experiment, see M. Lewis and J. Brooks, "Self-Knowledge and Emotional Development," in M. Lewis and L. A. Rosenblum (Eds.), *The Development of Affect* (New York: Plenum, 1978). Interestingly, this experiment evidently was patterned after an earlier one showing similar self-recognition achievements by young chimpanzees. For an excellent overview of the psychological birth process, we recommend L. Kaplan, *Oneness and Separateness* (New York: Simon & Schuster, 1978).

11. The utterance of capacities and volitions by toddlers is described by R. L. Corrigan, "Language Development as Related to Stage 6 Object Permanence Development," *Journal of Child Language* 5 (1978), 173–189. The quotations are taken from M. van der Meulen, *Self-References in Young Children: Content, Metadimensions, and Puzzlement* (Groningen, Netherlands: Stichting Kinderstudies, 1987), p. 30.

12. Psychological literature has a lengthy history of research showing how children get upset when they encounter barriers and do not have the capability to get around them. For the earliest example, see H. F. Wright, "The Effect of Barriers Upon Strength of Motivation," in R. G. Barker, J. S. Kounin, and H. F. Wright (Eds.), *Child Behavior and Development* (New York: McGraw-Hill, 1943), or R. Barker, T. Dembo, and K. Lewin, "Frustration and Regression: An Experiment with Young Children," *University of Iowa Studies in Child Welfare* 18 (1941), No. 1. For the reader who is interested in related literature on the concept of resiliency in children, see one or more of the following: E. L. Cowen and W. C. Work, "Resilient Children, Psychological Wellness, and Primary Prevention," *American Journal of*

Community Psychology 16 (1988), 591–607; N. Garmezy, "Resiliency and Vulnerability to Adverse Developmental Outcomes Associated with Poverty," *American Behavioral Scientist* 34 (1991), 416–430; and E. Werner and R. S. Smith, *Vulnerable But Invincible: A Study of Resilient Children* (New York: McGraw-Hill, 1982). The view that blockages can be seen as a source of renewed willpower and waypower is concisely described by W. Lynch in *Images of Hope* (Notre Dame, IN: University of Notre Dame Press, 1974), p. 61: "We learn to hold a goal in sight and seek a way. It is a time of endless motility and exploration. The collapse of the venture is meant to create movement, resourcefulness. Rigidity never wins the game. Each failure of hope becomes a source of energy. It is a time of imagination and freedom."

13. For an overview of the importance of attachment, we recommend a trilogy of books by J. Bowlby, including *Attachment and Loss, Volume 1* (New York: Basic Books, 1969); *Attachment and Loss, Volume 2: Separation* (New York: Basic Books, 1973); and *Attachment and Loss, Volume 3: Loss, Sadness, and Depression* (New York: Basic Books, 1980). In regard to the process by which a secure attachment results in an increase in goal-directed behavior, see I. Bretherton and E. Waters (Eds.), "Growing Points of Attachment Theory and Research," *Monographs for the Society for Research in Child Development* 50 (Serial No. 209, numbers 1–2, 1985), or M. Rutter, "Psychosocial Resilience and Protective Mechanisms," *American Journal of Orthopsychiatry* 57 (1987), 316–331.

14. For further information about the spurt in word power, see S. Carey, "The Child as Word Learner," in M. Halle, J. Bresman, and G. A. Miller (Eds.), *Linguistic Theory and Psychological Reality* (Cambridge, MA: MIT Press, 1978). For more on the increase in the preschooler's ability to put together strings of words, see R. Brown, *A First Language: The Early Stages* (Cambridge, MA: Harvard University Press, 1973). For more on the interactive properties of language, see E. Bates, I. Bretherton, and L. Snyder, *From First Words to Grammar* (Cambridge, England: Cambridge University Press, 1988).

15. A good overview of scripts can be obtained in R. C. Schank and R. P. Abelson, *Scripts, Plans, Goals, and Understanding* (Hillsdale, NJ: Erlbaum, 1977). For information on how scripts and the associated developing language skills improve narrative thinking of children, read J. A. Hudson, "The Emergence of Autobiographical Memory in Mother-Child Conversation," in R. Fivush and J. A. Hudson (Eds.), *Knowing and Remembering in Young Children* (New York: Cambridge University Press, 1990). The Hudson chapter, along with an article by K. Nelson, "The Psychological and Social Origins of Autobiographical Memory," *Psychological Science* 4 (1993), 7–14, provides information on how scripts help to form autobiographical memories that are recalled in adulthood.

16. For more information about how the preschooler learns to pay attention to the perspectives of others, see D. Frye and C. Moore (Eds.), *Children's Theories of Mind: Mental States and Social Understanding* (Hillsdale, NJ: Erlbaum, 1991), and T. K Ruffman and D. R. Olson, "Children's Ascriptions of Knowledge of Others," *Developmental Psychology* 25 (1989), 601–606.

17. This notion of reading to learn is an important part of the two following books: J. Chall, *Stages of Reading Development* (New York: McGraw-Hill, 1983), and J. Chall, V. A. Jacobs, and L. E. Baldwin, *The Reading Crisis: Why Poor Children Fall Behind* (Cambridge, MA: Harvard University Press, 1990).

18. The increase in memory and speed are discussed by R. Kail in *The Development of Memory in Children (3rd ed.)* (New York: Freeman, 1990), and in R. Kail, "Processing Time Declines Exponentially During Childhood and Adolescence," *Developmental Psychology* 27 (1991), 259–266.

19. For a discussion of how the child in the middle years improves his or her sense of what others are thinking, see D. Flapan, *Children's Understanding of Social Interaction* (New York: Teachers College Press, 1968). The increase in the social problem solving of the middle years is discussed by K. A. Dodge, "A Social Information Processing Model of Social Competence," in M. Perlmutter (Ed.), *Cognitive Perspectives on Children's Social and Behavioral Development: Minnesota Symposium on Child Psychology, Volume 18* (Hillsdale, NJ: Erlbaum, 1986). For further information on the recollections of high-hope adults about their friendships during the middle years, see C. R. Snyder, *The Psychology of Hope.*

20. For more on pairing, see D. C. Dunphy, "The Social Structure of Urban Adolescent Peer Groups," *Sociometry* 26 (1963), 230–246. The increase in sexuality in exclusive relationships is presented in J. H. Gagnon and W. Simon, *Sexual Conduct: The Social Sources of Human Sexuality* (Chicago: Aldine, 1973).

21. The inconsistency of behavior by children over the course of the adolescent years is described by S. Harter and A. Monsour, "Developmental Analysis of Conflict Caused by Opposing Attributes in the Adolescent Self-Portrait," *Developmental Psychology* 28 (1992), 251–260.

22. The fundamental premise of hope theory is that we human beings, from the youngest to oldest, are goal-directed creatures. We suggest that the journey metaphor that is part of the title of this book is a powerful one for the thoughts that are directed at the pursuit of goals during childhood and later. It is not just by chance that two of the most widely read psychology books over the previous two decades—R. S. Pirsig, *Zen and the Art of Motorcycle Maintenance* (New York: Morrow, 1974), and M. S. Peck, *The Road Less Traveled* (New York: Simon & Schuster, 1985)—are built upon journey metaphors. We are collectively on a passage from the past to the future.

Chapter Two

1. The role of personal narratives as valuable sources for understanding and helping people to cope better has been the focus of many recent writings aimed at professional audiences. Among these, we recommend the following: R. A. Neimeyer and M. J. Mahoney (Eds.), *Constructivism in Psychotherapy* (Washington, D.C.: American Psychological Association, 1995); C. Linde, *Life Stories: The Creation of Coherence* (New York: Oxford, 1993); R. Josselson and A. Lieblich (Eds.), *The Narrative Study of Lives* (Vols. 1, 2, and 3) (Newbury Park, CA: Sage, 1993, 1994, 1995); G. Howard, *A Tale of Two Stories: Excursions into a Narrative to Psychology* (Notre Dame, IN: Academic Publications, 1989); and S. Engel, *The Stories Children Tell: Making Sense of the Narratives of Childhood* (New York: Freeman, 1995).

2. For further discussion about the role of the internal and external audiences as well as how they are interrelated, read pp. 34–39 in C. R. Snyder et al., *Excuses: Masquerades in Search of Grace* (New York: Wiley-Interscience, 1983). For the

classic work on the process of presenting oneself to audiences, we recommend E. Goffman, *The Presentation of Self in Everyday Life* (Garden City: NY: Doubleday Anchor, 1959); moreover, the best recent overview of the impression management area is found in M. R. Leary, *Self-Presentation: Impression Management and Interpersonal Behavior* (Madison, WI: Brown & Benchmark, 1995).

3. The Marcel quote is taken from G. Marcel (translated by E. Crauford), *Homo Viator* (New York: Harper & Row, 1962), p. 53.

4. For insights about the personal narratives of teenagers dealing with the adversities and joys of inner-city existence, a superb source is T. Williams and W. Kornblum, *Uptown Kids: Struggle and Hope in the Projects* (New York: Grosset/Putnam, 1994).

5. For further information about the "Hope is a rope," as well as other hope-related metaphors, see J. R. Averill, G. Gatlin, and K. K. Chon, *Rules of Hope* (New York: Springer-Verlag, 1990). If you are interested in learning more about the use of metaphors in helping children to cope, see J. C. Mills, R. J. Crowley, and M. O. Ryan, *Therapeutic Metaphors for Children and the Child Within* (New York: Brunner/Mazel, 1986).

6. This story about God's love of tales is taken from Robert Murphy, as described in the fascinating volume by S. B. Kopp entitled *If You Meet the Buddha on the Road, Kill Him!* (New York: Bantam, 1972), pp. 20–21.

Chapter Three

1. The Young Children's Hope Scale–Story Form was developed, validated, and reported by Carla Dykeman Berkich in her 1995 doctoral dissertation to the Graduate School of the University of Kansas. The title of this dissertation was "Development and Validation of a Scale to Measure Hope in Preschool and Primary Age Children." The sample was comprised of 52 boys and 55 girls, with approximately similar numbers of children from kindergarten and the first, second, and third grades. This measure generally meets the psychometric standards related to internal stability, and the scores are somewhat consistent across a one-week retesting interval. On average, girls score higher (mean = 13.38) than boys (mean = 11.67). Scores on the Young Children's Hope Scale–Story Form appear to correlate modestly and positively with indices of overall competence and social acceptance (see S. Harter and R. Pike, "The Pictorial Scale for Perceived Competence and Social Acceptance for Young Children," *Child Development* 55 [1984], 1969–1982). Scores on the Young Children's Hope Scale–Story Form also positively predict school achievement for girls, but not for boys. Likewise, using a measure of internal-external locus of control (see S. Nowicki and M. P. Duke, "A Preschool and Primary Internal-External Control Scale," *Developmental Psychology* 10 [1974], 874–880), the Young Children's Hope Scale–Story Form correlated with a greater internal locus for girls, but not for boys.

2. The YCHS–Self-Report Form has been validated on a group of approximately 100 grade-school children. Scales scores produce substantial differences between differing children who take the test. See D. McDermott, C. R. Snyder, et al., "Development of the Young Children's Hope Scale—Self Report Form" (unpublished manuscript, 1996), University of Kansas, Lawrence.

3. For a detailed description of the development and validation of the Children's Hope Scale–Self-Report Form, see C. R. Snyder, B. Hoza, W. E. Pelham, M. Rapoff, L. Ware, B. Samuelson, M. Danovsky, L. Highberger, H. Rubinstein, and K. J.Stahl, "The Development and Validation of the Children's Hope Scale," *Journal of Pediatric Psychology* 22(3), (1997), 399–421. The Children's Hope Scale–Self-Report Form also is described in Chapter 3 of C. R. Snyder, *The Psychology of Hope: You Can Get There from Here* (New York: Free Press, 1994); see especially pp. 108–111. The Children's Hope Scale–Self-Report Form meets the psychometric standards for internal reliability, and in two samples retaking the scale after intervals of one week and one month, the scores remained stable. Higher hope as measured by the Children's Hope Scale–Self-Report Form relates negatively and significantly to other indices tapping hopelessness, depression, anxiety, and loneliness; moreover, scores relate positively to perceived competence and internal locus of control. Scores on the Children's Hope Scale–Self-Report Form do not correlate with intelligence, but they do relate positively with scholastic achievement. No gender differences have been found in scores for this instrument.

4. The Hope Scale is described for the professional audience in C. R. Snyder, C. Harris, et al., "The Will and the Ways: Development and Validation of an Individual Differences Measure of Hope," *Journal of Personality and Social Psychology* 60 (1991), 570–585; or, for an analysis of this scale that is written more for the layperson, see Chapter 2 of C. R. Snyder, *The Psychology of Hope*. The Hope Scale–Observer Form has been used by several different types of observers, and we have found that they are able to reliably rate hope in targeted adolescents.

5. The State Hope Scale is described (for the professional audience) in C. R. Snyder, S. Sympson, et al., "Development and Validation of the State Hope Scale," *Journal of Personality and Social Psychology* 70 (1996), 321–335; or see (for layperson audience) Chapter 2 of C. R. Snyder, *The Psychology of Hope*.

6. The Willpower and Waypower Subscales routinely produce correlations in the range of .50 to .70 with each other across many studies employing differing indices of hope in children. This suggests that there is considerable overlap in the two types of goal-directed thinking but that they are not synonymous.

7. Our research indicates that there are several reliable and valid measures of hope that can be used with children as well as with adults. For the reader who is interested in yet additional means of measuring hope, see C. J. Farran, K. A. Herth, and J. M. Popovich, *Hope and Hopelessness: Critical Clinical Constructs* (Newbury Park, CA: Sage, 1995).

8. In our research using various instruments for measuring hope in children who had faced, or were facing, major medical illnesses, the level of hope remained high. These children are remarkable for their high hope, but they are not unusual. As we note in Chapter 11 on the role of hope in children who have severe health problems, they are far from hopeless. It is probably safe to say that we adults have grossly underestimated the coping capabilities of children.

9. For a more in-depth discussion of the positive bias that is inherent in hope, see C. R. Snyder, B. Hoza, et al., "The Development and Validation of the Children's Hope Scale," *Journal of Pediatric Psychology* 22(3), (1997), 399–421. A particularly informative study is reported by M. D. Hinton-Nelson, M. C. Roberts, and C. R. Snyder, "Exposure to Violence and Early Adolescents' Perceptions of Hope and Vulnerability to Victimization," *American Journal of Orthopsychiatry* 66 (1996), 346–352.

10. For further information about the role of adaptive illusions, we recommend reading the following sources: C. R. Snyder, "Reality Negotiation: From Excuses to Hope and Beyond," *Journal of Social and Clinical Psychology* 8 (1989), 130–157; C. R. Snyder and R. L. Higgins, "Excuses: Their Effective Role in the Negotiation of Reality," *Psychological Bulletin* 104 (1988), 23–35; S. E. Taylor and J. D. Brown, "Illusion and Well-Being: A Social Psychological Perspective on Mental Health," *Psychological Bulletin* 103 (1988), 193–210; and S. E. Taylor and J. D. Brown, "Positive Illusions and Well-Being Revisited: Separating Fact from Fiction," *Psychological Bulletin* 116 (1994), 21–27. The best source written for laypeople is S. E. Taylor, *The Healthy Mind* (New York: Basic Books, 1988).

11. For additional discussion of how to find and nurture hope in children, read C. R. Snyder, "Hope for the Journey," in A. P. Turnball, J. M. Paterson, et al. (Eds.), *Cognitive Coping, Families and Disability* (Baltimore, MD: Brookes, 1993).

12. A full analysis of the seeming loss of hope followed by its reemergence can be found in C. R. Snyder, "To Hope, to Lose, and Hope Again," *Journal of Personal and Interpersonal Loss* 1(1996), 1–16.

Chapter Four

1. For more information on examining family stories and the messages they communicate through the generations, see Virginia Satir, *Peoplemaking* (Palo Alto, CA: Science and Behavior Books, 1972).

2. The stories we have presented in this book represent but a few of the high-hope stories available to interested readers. Robert Coles and Jane Hallowell Coles have brought together two volumes of stories about high-hope women from different walks of life and socioeconomic backgrounds; see their books *Women of Crisis: Lives of Struggle and Hope* (New York: Dell, 1978) and *Women of Crisis II: Lives of Work and Dreams* (New York: Dell, 1980).

3. John Byng-Hall in *Rewriting Family Scripts* (New York: Guilford, 1995) approaches family stories, legends, and scripts from a therapist's point of view, with change being the object. This book provides theory, technique and guided directions for detailed family script analysis and restructuring of messages toward higher hope.

4. The techniques mentioned in Chapters 4 and 8 specifically have their roots in cognitive therapy. Judith S. Beck has provided an excellent guide for a more thorough understanding of this model and how it is useful in a wide variety of situations; see her book *Cognitive Therapy: Basics and Beyond* (New York: Guilford Press, 1995).

5. Another excellent resource for restructuring techniques is D. D. Burns, *Feeling Good: The New Mood Therapy* (New York: Avon, 1980).

Chapter Five

1. The storm metaphor was originally developed in J. C. Mills and R. J. Crowley, *Therapeutic Metaphors for Children and the Child Within* (New York: Brunner/Mazel, 1986).

2. Three recommended references for building storytelling skills include C. Collins, *Tell Me a Story: Creating Bedtime Tales Your Children Will Dream On* (Boston: Houghton-Mifflin, 1992); N. Mellon, *Storytelling and the Art of Imagination* (Rockport, MA: Element, 1992); and R. Moore, *Awakening the Hidden Storyteller: How to Build a Storytelling Tradition in Your Family* (Boston: Shambhala, 1991). Therapeutic stories have been utilized in children's psychotherapy programs for the past 25 years. Richard Gardner is generally considered to be the first to conduct the formal technique of therapeutic storytelling; see R. A. Gardner, *Therapeutic Communication with Children: The Mutual Storytelling Technique* (New York: Jason Aronson, 1971). For additional background information about storytelling techniques, the interested reader might also want to consult R. Brooks, "Creative Characters: A Technique in Child Therapy," *Psychotherapy: Theory, Research, and Practice* 18 (1981), 131–139. Finally, over one dozen detailed therapeutic stories are available in J. C. Mills and R. J. Crowley, *Therapeutic Metaphors for Children and the Child Within.*

3. The techniques discussed in the remainder of this chapter (the five-step storytelling process, the story of Susie Q, and the turn-taking process) all were originally developed in a workshop manual for parents and therapists. For further information, see W. Cook, *The Handbook of Therapeutic Storytelling* (unpublished manuscript, 1994). For information about the manual, write William Cook, Ph.D., 2831 Fort Missoula Road, Suite 201, Missoula, MT 59804.

4. The turn-taking approach described in Chapter 5 was inspired by Richard Gardner's seminal work on therapeutic storytelling; see R. A. Gardner, *Therapeutic Communication with Children.*

Chapter Six

1. The full-length versions of the stories of Tori (the picky eater), Greta (the monster under the bed), Katie (the dream girl), and Frankie and Harry (the brothers) were originally written and compiled by W. Cook in *The Doctor Cook Storybook: Using Therapeutic Stories to Help Your Child with Psychological Difficulties* (unpublished manuscript, 1993). Write to William Cook for more information (see address in note 3 to Chapter 5).

2. For a related story theme, you may want to read the "Slow-Eater-Tiny-Bite-Taker Cure" in the B. McDonald classic *Mrs. Piggle-Wiggle* (New York: J. B. Lippincott Company, 1947).

3. Besides the "untold story of the monsters and the cupcake," you will find numerous other story ideas in J. C. Mills and R. J. Crowley, *Therapeutic Metaphors for Children and the Child Within* (New York: Brunner/Mazel, 1986).

4. The brothers' resolution to arrive at either shared goals or alternating goals is discussed in further detail in C. R. Snyder, *The Psychology of Hope: You Can Get There from Here* (New York: Free Press, 1994).

5. The complete story of Kateroo and Mariboo is contained in W. Cook, *The Handbook of Therapeutic Storytelling* (unpublished manuscript, 1994). Write to William Cook for more information (see address in note 3 to Chapter 5).

6. This summary vignette of Tojo's Rap Music Rules is taken from Chapter 1 of W. Cook, *The Doctor Cook Storybook for Schools: Teaching Tales to Help Pri-*

mary Grade Students with Social and Emotional Development (book manuscript in preparation, 1996).

7. For a full discussion of the important relationship between fears and hope, see C. R. Snyder, *The Psychology of Hope*. For a more recent empirical examination of this issue, see M. D. Hinton-Nelson, M. C. Roberts, and C. R. Snyder, "Exposure to Violence and Early Adolescents' Perceptions of Hope and Vulnerability to Victimization," *American Journal of Orthopsychiatry* 66 (1996), 346–352. For professional readers, this gradated story imagination of increasingly closer confrontation with the feared objects is consistent with the favorable outcomes that have come through a technique known as systematic desensitization, or stress inoculation. See, for latter example, D. Meichenbaum, *Stress Inoculation Training* (Elmsford, NY: Pergamon, 1985).

8. The story of the three P's was adapted from Chapter 3 of W. Cook, *The Doctor Cook Storybook for Schools*.

9. For other helpful approaches to enhance the problem-solving skills of children, we recommend K. H. and L. R. Krasnor, "Social-Cognitive and Social Behavioral Perspectives on Problem-Solving," in M. Perlmutter (Ed.), *Cognitive Perspectives on Children's Social and Behavioral Development: Minnesota Symposium on Child Psychology, Volume 18* (Hillsdale, NJ: Erlbaum, 1986), and G. Spivak and M. B. Shure, *Social Adjustment of Young Children: A Cognitive Approach to Solving Real Life Problems* (San Francisco: Jossey-Bass, 1974). For an excellent and easily understood series of books on increasing the problem-solving skills of children (from preschool through elementary), see M. B. Shure, *I Can Problem Solve: Volume 1 on Preschool, Volume 2 on Kindergarten & Primary Grades, Volume 3 on Intermediate Elementary Grades* (Champaign, IL: Research Press, 1992).

Chapter Seven

1. The summary story vignettes of this chapter (except for the stories of Ivy the Kitten, the fisherman and the teenage thief, and Trust Mountain) all were adapted from full-length versions originally written in W. Cook, *The Doctor Cook Storybook: Using Therapeutic Stories to Help Your Child with Psychological Difficulties* (unpublished manuscript, 1993). Write to William Cook (see address in note 3 to Chapter 5) for more information.

2. For a full description of how emotions offer important clues to the underlying unsuccessful or successful perception of goal pursuits, see C. R. Snyder, *The Psychology of Hope: You Can Get There from Here* (New York: Free Press, 1994).

3. The stages of grief are well described in H. S. Schiff, *Through Mourning: Finding Comfort and Hope When a Loved One Has Died* (New York, Penguin Books, 1986), and E. Kubler-Ross's seminal work *On Death and Dying* (New York, Macmillan Publishing Co., 1969).

4. The role of various types of trauma, loss, and abuse on children, as well as other means to treat them, are found in C. R. Snyder, *The Psychology of Hope*.

5. For an excellent, practical discussion of how to work effectively with attachment disordered children in foster care, we recommend R. Delaney, *Fostering Changes: Treating Attachment Disordered Foster Children* (Ft. Collins, CO: Walter J. Corbett, 1995).

6. Young adults who are high in hope report family structures where the rules were clear and the boundary infractions were enforced, and yet there was an overall context of respect, love, and appropriately doled-out autonomy (see C. R. Snyder, *The Psychology of Hope*).

7. The attainment of the child's desires in the context of rules and a concern for others is detailed further in C. R. Snyder, *The Psychology of Hope*.

8. For a good general parenting reference related to teaching responsibility through consequences, the interested reader may wish to consult F. Cline and J. Fay, *Parenting with Love and Logic* (Colorado Springs, CO: Navpress, 1990).

9. Self-control strategies for children with attention-deficit hyperactivity disorder have been utilized as basic treatment tools for nearly 20 years. These kinds of treatment strategies are discussed in P. C. Kendall and A. J. Finch, "Developing Nonimpulsive Behavior in Children: Cognitive-Behavioral Strategies for Self Control," in P. C. Kendall and S. D. Hollon (Eds.), *Cognitive-Behavioral Interventions: Theory, Research, and Procedures* (New York: Academic Press, 1979).

10. Additional information that provides more extensive character development for the "wise persons" consulted in the therapeutic stories of Chapters 5, 6, and 7 is contained in W. Cook, *The Secrets of Mount Jumbo* (book manuscript in preparation, 1996)

11. See M. White and D. Epston, *Narrative Means to Therapeutic Ends* (New York/London: Norton and Co., 1990) for additional descriptions of how to help children externalize a problem.

Chapter Eight

1. D. McDermott, D. Lind, B. Callahan, K. Gariglietti, K. Gingrich, and S. Hastings, *Hope Training in the Elementary Classroom* (unpublished manuscript, University of Kansas, Lawrence, 1996).

2. A great deal has been written about burnout in a wide variety of situations. Several of the especially relevant books and articles are C. Cherniss, *Professional Burnout in Human Service Organizations* (New York: Praeger, 1980); H. J. Freudenberger, "Burnout and Job Dissatisfaction: Impact on the Family," in T. C. Hanser (Ed.), *Perspectives on Work and the Family* (Rockville, MD: Aspen Systems Corp., 1984); and H. J. Freudenberger and G. North, *Women's Burnout* (Garden City, NJ: Penguin, 1985).

3. *A Clinician's Guide to Mind over Mood* and *Mind over Mood: A Cognitive Treatment Manual for Clients*, both by Christine A. Padesky (New York: Guilford, 1995), give further help to individuals interested in restructuring thinking in a high-hope direction. These books provide clear theoretical and applied concepts.

4. For more detail see D. McDermott, "Professional Burnout and Its Relation to Job Characteristics and Control," *Journal of Human Stress* 10, #2 (1984), 79–88.

Chapter Nine

1. Parents often feel at a loss as to how they can participate in their child's education. Frequently, the school and a teacher's work remain a mystery. M. S. Miller, *The School Book* (New York: St. Martin's Press, 1991) provides a comprehensive guide for parents who wish to act as partners with their children's teachers from

preschool through eighth grade. The book describes what goes on in the classroom and provides a list of questions to ask about the child's education and suggestions for ways parents can be involved.

2. Children need a disciplined classroom in which to develop hope. R. Duffy and L. Escobar, *Positive Discipline: A Teacher's A-Z Guide* (Rocklin, CA: Prima, 1996) provides many good suggestions for the elementary classroom.

3. As teachers help students set and achieve goals, it is important to attend to the affective side of student growth. A. Vernon, *Thinking, Feeling, Behaving: An Emotional Educational Curriculum for Grades 1 Through 6* (Champaign, IL.: Research Press, 1989) provides good suggestions for elementary teachers. Many students when failing at a goal do not know how to give themselves positive messages. D. Bloch with J. Merritt, *Positive Self Talk for Children* (New York: Bantam, 1993), is an excellent resource of ideas for both teachers and parents. The authors show how teachers and parents can instill more positive messages through the use of affirmations.

Chapter Ten

1. Risk and preventative factors are most frequently researched in terms of adolescent substance abuse, crime, and other dysfunctional behaviors. An excellent article for further reading is J. D. Hawkins, R. F. Catalano, and J. Y. Miller, "Risk and Protective Factors for Alcohol and Other Drug Problems in Adolescence and Early Adulthood," *Psychological Bulletin* 112 (1992), 64–105.

2. Ethnic minority young people are often among the most disenfranchised students in lower income areas. Crystal Kuykendall has written a helpful guide specifically addressing the needs of these students, entitled *From Rage to Hope: Strategies for Reclaiming Black and Hispanic Students* (Bloomington, IA: National Educational Service, 1992).

3. M. Lomask, *Great Lives: Invention and Technology* (New York: Simon & Schuster, 1991) provides a collection of high-hope stories that middle and high school students would find interesting. Similar to note 3 above, D. Faber and H. Faber, *Great Lives: Nature and the Environment* (New York: Scribner & Sons, 1981), provides good examples of high-hope individuals for the natural science classroom.

4. Not all counselors are trained to work with students who are from cultures different from their own. It is recommended that counselors and teachers who work in lower income schools, or schools where there is a heavy ethnic minority population, read current material to assist in understanding these populations. One such book is D. R. Atkinson, G. Morten, and D. Wing Sue, *Counseling American Minorities: A Cross-Cultural Perspective* (Madison, WI: Brown & Benchmark, 1993).

Chapter Eleven

1. Taken from E. Bombeck, *I Want to Grow Hair, I Want to Grow Hair, I Want to Go to Boise: Children Surviving Cancer* (New York: Harper & Row, 1989), p. 5.

2. From W. Ostrow and V. Ostrow, *All About Asthma* (Morton Grove, IL: Albert Whitman & Co., 1989), p. 8.

3. From "Jackie Joyner-Kersee: World Record Holder with a Winning Asthma Strategy," in *Air Currents* 3 (1996), p. 8.

4. For reviews of the benefits of humor, see H. M. Lefcourt and K. Davidson-Katz, "The Role of Humor and the Self," in C. R. Snyder and D. R. Forsyth (Eds.), *Handbook of Social and Clinical Psychology: The Health Perspective* (New York: Pergamon, 1991); R. A. Moody, *Laugh After Laugh: The Healing Power of Humor* (Jacksonvile, FL: Headwaters Press, 1978); and N. Cousins, *Anatomy of an Illness as Perceived by the Patient* (New York: Norton, 1979).

5. E. Bombeck, *I Want to Grow Hair,* p. 12.

6. E. Bombeck, *I Want to Grow Hair,* pp. 49-50.

7. *Bartlett's Familiar Quotations: Expanded Multimedia Edition* (New York: Time Warner, 1995).

8. *Bartlett's Familiar Quotations.*

9. Special thanks are given to Dr. Martye Barnard, associate professor, Department of Pediatrics, University of Kansas Medical Center; Mr. Huey Counts, sports editor for the *Independence Examiner;* and Danny's family for sharing his story.

Chapter Twelve

1. For an insightful discussion of the importance of listening to what children have to say about themselves, we recommend pp. 209–212 in S. Engel, *The Stories That Children Tell* (New York: Freeman, 1995).

2. By tying actions to a script, we are also allowing the child to solidify the underlying script. In turn, once the script is available, just practicing the sequence of events in one's mind can produce actual benefits in the subsequent performance in that particular arena. Thus, a story may provide means of mentally imaging that helps the child in goal-pursuit activities.

3. For a further discussion of the role of the family, and of factors associated with promoting hope among the primary care unit, see C. R. Snyder, "Children and the Price of Excellence: Hope for the Few or the Many?" in R. Friedman and J. Wright, *Advances in Understanding Children* (Washington, D.C.: American Psychological Association, in press).

4. This story was told in a university-wide address by United States Senator Nancy Kassebaum entitled "A Washington Update," April 13, 1996, at the University of Kansas.

5. For further concrete suggestions about how to foster hope in children, see chapter 5, "Nurturing Hope in Children," in C. R. Snyder, *The Psychology of Hope: You Can Get There from Here* (New York: Free Press, 1994).

6. An emerging body of psychological research suggests that the telling of one's story after a traumatic event or illness serves to alleviate distress. For an enjoyable read about this topic by the very scholar who has conducted the leading-edge research, we recommend J. W. Pennebaker, *Opening Up: The Healing Power of Confiding in Others* (New York: Morrow, 1990). Our interpretation is that the healing potential of such opening-up processes resides in their propensity to allow the "victim" to shed the passive stance and to move onto a more active, hopeful one. In other words, the retelling of traumas enable persons to no longer be tormented by

the specifics of negative events, and to learn from these events so as to proceed toward other, more favorable desired outcomes.

7. For the reader who is interested in more about the myth of Pandora, examine the edited volume by S. Kershaw (A. R. Maxwell-Hysop, translator), *A Concise Dictionary of Classical Mythology* (Oxford, England: Basil Blackwell, 1990). It should be noted that the general Greek tradition was to cast hope in a rather negative light. For support of this gloomy Greek view of hope, see J. R. Averill, G. Gatlin, and K. K. Chon, *Rules of Hope* (New York: Springer-Verlag, 1990). We are not alone, however, in concluding that the myth of Pandora leads to the conclusion that hope was to be the antidote for the other evils in the box. For a writer who concurs with our favorable prognosis of hope, see M. B. Smith, "Hope and Despair: Keys to the Socio-Psychodynamics of Youth," *American Journal of Orthopsychiatry* 53 (1983), 388–399.